MEN WHO WIN

MEN WHO WIN

WHO

PURSUING THE ULTIMATE PRIZE

STEVEN J. LAWSON

NAVPRESS

A MINISTRY OF THE NAVIGATORS
P.O. BOX 35001, COLORADO SPRINGS, COLORADO 80935

The Navigators is an international Christian
organization. Jesus Christ gave His followers
the Great Commission to go and make disciples
(Matthew 28:19). The aim of The Navigators is
to help fulfill that commission by multiplying
laborers for Christ in every nation.

NavPress is the publishing ministry of The Navigators. NavPress publications are tools to help
Christians grow. Although publications alone cannot make disciples or change lives, they can help
believers learn biblical discipleship, and apply
what they learn to their lives and ministries.

Cover photograph: © 1990 David Stoecklein/
The Stock Market

Some of the anecdotal illustrations in this
book are true to life and are included with the
permission of the persons involved. All other
illustrations are composites of real situations,
and any resemblance to people living or dead is
coincidental.

All Scripture in this publication is from the *New
American Standard Bible* (NASB), © The Lockman
Foundation 1960, 1962, 1963, 1968, 1971, 1972,
1973, 1975, 1977.

Printed in the United States of America

FOR A FREE CATALOG OF
NAVPRESS BOOKS & BIBLE STUDIES,
CALL TOLL FREE 1-800-366-7788 (USA)
or 1-416-499-4615 (CANADA)

CONTENTS

★

*This book is passionately dedicated
to my three sons,
ANDREW, JAMES, and JOHN
May you be "men who win" where it really counts:
with God.
You are my pride and joy.*

*"A wise son makes a father glad."
(Proverbs 10:1)*

FOREWORD

★

Nothing is more important than being a winner where it really counts. I have been a winner on the football field. But I know the most important thing is to be a winner with God. The Bible says, "Seek first the kingdom of God and His righteousness, and all these other things shall be added to you." So, we must be winners with God first and foremost.

As most of you know, I have competed and coached in athletics almost all of my life. It has occupied most of my adult life. But, far and away, the most important thing to me is my faith in God and my personal relationship with Jesus Christ.

Athletics has been a platform for my witness for Jesus Christ. It is through the vehicle of sports that I have sought to bring glory to God.

That is why I am excited to recommend to your reading this book by Steve Lawson. I first met Steve during his days at Dallas Theological Seminary, while I was coaching the Dallas Cowboys. Steve worked with the Cowboys by writing a Christian sports magazine called *Gospel Gridiron*.

During those days, I watched Steve begin a writing ministry of communicating the gospel of Jesus Christ through his interest in sports. I told Steve then that perhaps this was God's calling for his life. Perhaps he should use his writing as a means to spread the Christian faith. Now, some fifteen years later, I am thrilled to see this book, which combines Steve's love for Jesus Christ and his passion for athletics. But most of all, his commitment to Christ.

The Apostle Paul compares the Christian life to a race. Every Christian is called to run this race. It begins the moment we commit our lives to Him, and it will conclude at the moment of death. Everything in life between these two moments is the race that God has set before us.

We must run God's race to win. We must press on to win the heavenly crown.

The essentials for winning the Christian race are much the same as those required to be a champion on the football field: self-discipline, determination, concentration, perseverance, dedication, and the will to win.

I know, because I sought to instill these qualities into the men whom I coached for almost thirty years with the Dallas Cowboys. These men became world champions. I also know these virtues are necessary in the Christian life. These are the character qualities that lead to victory in God's race—the race of faith.

This book, *Men Who Win: Pursuing the Ultimate Prize*, contains the essential Christian message that can make any man a winner in whatever he does. I want to ask you to read this book and apply its truth to your life.

My prayer for everyone who reads this book is that you, too, will become a winner in the race of life. There is no higher call than the upward call of Christ to win Heaven's crown. May you truly be a winner as you run the race set before you.

Tom Landry
Former Head Football Coach
Dallas Cowboys

ACKNOWLEDGMENTS

★

Pete Dye is one of the world's foremost golf architects, known for his diabolical designs. PGA West. Sawgrass TPC. Crooked Stick. Dye was asked recently about one of his prized layouts, Harbour Town at Hilton Head. Officially, the name Jack Nicklaus appears as the coarchitect with Pete Dye.

"How much did Jack actually contribute?" asked the interviewer.

"Jack certainly helped," answered Dye. "But the course is the result of more than Jack's help. Six or seven people contributed significant input about its design—people whose names do not officially appear on the scorecards."

This book is much like that Pete Dye golf course.

Many people have made key contributions, people whose names do not officially appear on the scorecard. I feel compelled to mention them because they have had direct input into this book. Here they are.

Steve Webb, my editor at NavPress and personal friend, contributed a creative mind, theological balance, quick wit, and a sharp pencil. Steve, thanks for helping put the "spin on the ball"!

Bruce Nygren, editorial director, and Volney James, NavPress marketing director, both expressed confidence in this first-time author. Men, thank you for extending my ministry through yours.

The elders of The Bible Church, especially Dr. Carl Wenger, patiently counseled me to begin my writing ministry at this time. Men, thank you for setting me free to pursue God's will for my life.

Curtis Thomas, Todd Murray, and Jeff Kinley, my fellow pastors at The Bible Church, have been a wealth of creative genius, constant encouragement, and close support. Guys, you are all winners!

Roger Yancey, our church's school administrator, has made heroic contributions to this book. Roger was my "editor-in-residence" who brainstormed with me and edited my manuscript every Friday afternoon. Roger, you made a major-league contribution!

The Ladies' Prayer Group at The Bible Church have fervently prayed for the writing of this book. Ladies, your prayers have made the difference.

Sherry Humphres, my secretary, has put her life and schedule under my rigorous deadlines, typing and retyping (and retyping) the manuscript. Thank you!

Dr. Steve Farrar, author and conference speaker, first expressed confidence in me that I could write this book and personally walked me through the complex maze of the publishing world. Steve, you were right! Thanks.

If you were to peel back the layers of my heart, you would discover the ministry of my former pastor, Dr. Adrian Rogers, indelibly stamped upon my soul. Adrian, as you read this book, I hope you will find pleasure in hearing your voice echoing in these pages (2 Timothy 2:2).

Anne, my wife, has been my loving encourager as God's chosen *helpmate*. She, along with my three sons and daughter, Grace Anne, have prayed for me daily. Sweetheart, thank you for supporting me in God's call upon my life. You are God's precious gift, the bedrock of my ministry.

CHAPTER 1

OUT OF THE RAT RACE ... INTO THE RIGHT RACE

★

Nobody loves to win more than I do. Nobody.
I don't know when this drive to win first took hold of me. Maybe I was born with it. Maybe it's been instilled. Regardless, I love to win. No, make that, I *live* to win.

My competitive nature comes out in everything I do. No car has ever passed me on the highway, much less beaten me to a parking place at the mall. Not one. I love the challenge of beating a yellow light and making all the lights. I turn right on red, even when I want to go left, just to keep moving. Fast food can't be fast enough for me. It kills me for people to come in after me and then get their food before me.

My whole emotional disposition is controlled by winning—especially on the golf course. When I play well, I'm riding high. You can hear the laughing blocks away. But make a double bogey? That puts a damper on our family vacations (and don't try to cheer me up). I'm crying for days. Me—a preacher.

Recently, I coached my boys' Little League baseball team. Before the season began, I told the parents of our players my priorities for the team. First, to have fun; second, to build character; third, to develop athletic skills; and, fourth, to win. Sounds good, doesn't it?

I lied.

Winning has never been fourth on my list. How could I possibly have fun without winning?

WINNING IS EVERYTHING

Let me show you the dark side of my moon. I'm a pastor and recently had a wedding rehearsal to perform on Friday evening at six o'clock. The only problem was I had a ball game at five and the ball field is twenty-five minutes away. I told my minister of music to start the rehearsal without me; I'd be there as soon as possible. I reassured him and the couple that the rehearsal was more important than winning a ball game (trying to convince myself).

As the game began, I briefed my assistant coach that I would have to slip out before the end of the game. He could manage the last two innings and give the postgame talk. I explained that the rehearsal was more important than winning this game (still trying to convince myself).

With two innings to go, we were ahead 10-3. As I was preparing to leave the game, confident of victory, the other team scored three runs. Maybe I'd better hang tight.

We didn't score in our half of the last inning. Hmmm. The other team led off the bottom of the last inning with a home run. Now it's 10-7. Forget the wedding rehearsal. This is getting serious!

With two outs, we were clinging to a three-run lead. Then the roof caved in. We committed four consecutive errors, "unpardonable sins," and we lost the game by one run.

I was devastated. The team was crying. I huddled them around me and tried to say something mature.

"It doesn't feel good to lose, does it?" I told them. "Losing hurts. It stings. It bites. Winning is a lot more fun, isn't it? Winning feels good." You would have thought I was dressing down the New York Yankees after losing the World Series.

I glanced at my watch. It was 6:30. The wedding rehearsal! I was already late and still twenty-five minutes from the church. I hopped in my car and frantically made a mad dash to the church.

As I walked into the sanctuary, the rehearsal was already in progress. Everyone was so happy, chipper, and full of smiles. The precious couple was about to experience the happiest day of their life, and I came in moping, as solemn as a funeral procession.

Can you believe it? I'm a minister, pouting in my own sanctuary, in the very pulpit area where I have just preached that our circumstances should never control our joy. But that was before we lost.

Nobody loves to win more than I do. Nobody.

None of us likes to lose. We all love to win. We have a drive to get ahead. There's a fire burning within us to excel. Perhaps your drive is not as intense as mine. Whatever your calling in life—your work, your family, your church—you have a passion to win. Personally, I agree with Vince Lombardi: "Winning isn't everything. It's the *only* thing." I only wish Solomon had said it first.

Winning on the Right Track

This book is all about winning. Not in Little League baseball, but in the big leagues with God. Not in temporal or trivial things, but in the eternal things. It's about winning in the right things—God's things, spiritual things, the truly important things. It's all about being a champion in life!

I want to destroy a deadly misconception. I want to annihilate the false thinking that being a Christian means you have to suddenly become a loser. To roll over and play dead. No way! In fact, you cannot truly become a winner until you first become a Christian. Then God wants to rechannel your competitive drive to excel in the right direction for His Kingdom, His glory. He wants you to run the race to *win* (1 Corinthians 9:24). That's what this book is all about.

Thank God, when we become Christians, we don't have to check our drive to win at the front door of the church. We don't have to stop competing. We just get on the right track and run a new race, with all the passion and energy of our soul. We simply redirect our competitive drive to run His race. So while we don't suppress our will to win, we must let Christ rule it—and use it for His glory.

As Christians, we still live to win, but we compete listening to the voice of a new Coach, who calls from the finish line, rather than shouting from the starting blocks. Our feet still make dust as we run with all our might, but it's a new track we run, a narrow path that leads to life. Our hearts still pound as we sprint toward the finish line, hoping to break the tape and claim first prize, but this race is for an eternal crown.

Men, my hope is that this book challenges you to become a winner where it really counts—in your relationship with God and His direction for your life. I want to get inside your skin and allow God to infuse you with a holy passion to win in the Christian life. I want to ignite in you a fire to live victoriously. I want to help you mark your course, set your pace, and point you to the finish line. I want to help you design a game plan to "run in such a way that you may win" (1 Corinthians 9:24).

Which Race Will You Run?

All men are running—either the rat race, or the right race. So we must be careful in which race we run. The race we choose will determine the course of our life today, and it will determine our eternal destiny tomorrow.

Jesus identifies these two races. He says, "Enter by the narrow gate; for the gate is wide, and the way is broad that leads to destruction, and many are those who enter by it. For the gate is small, and the way is narrow that leads to life, and few are those who find it" (Matthew 7:13-14). Two races, two crowds, two starting points, two tracks, two finish lines.

What does this have to do with winning? Everything. To be a winner, we must run and win the right race. To win the wrong race is to lose the right one. We can only win if we run and win the right one—God's race.

Let's begin by examining the wrong race . . . the rat race.

IN LANE NUMBER ONE . . . THE RAT RACE

Jesus describes the rat race this way: "The gate is wide, and the way is broad that leads to destruction, and many are they that enter by it." A wide gate, a broad way, a destructive end, and many travelers. Men, that *is* the rat race.

When Jesus spoke these words two thousand years ago, He was standing on a grassy hill overlooking the Sea of Galilee. His band of ignominious followers (people like you and me) and the curious multitude surrounded Him. As Jesus concluded His most heart-searching sermon—the Sermon on the Mount—He spoke of a broad path and a narrow path that all men were traveling. In His day, roads were paths of dirt, worn down by constant traffic, accommodating travelers on foot or donkey. If our Lord were speaking these words to our generation today, He would probably describe the rat race as a different type of thoroughfare. Quite possibly this broad path would be a busy, concrete-paved superhighway—maybe a major artery through the heart of a metropolitan city. Here's the updated version of the broad path.

Bumper-to-Bumper Rat Race
It's Friday afternoon, straight up five-o'clock, rush-hour traffic. Cars are stacked up bumper to bumper on LBJ Freeway in Dallas, Texas. All eight lanes are clogged. The traffic is creeping along at a snail's pace. Do you know what is the world's largest parking lot? LBJ at rush hour.

Impatiently drivers jockey back and forth from one lane to the next, seeking any advantage. One car darts in front of you. You jam on your brakes. It seems all you do is ride your brakes. Red brake lights have been staring you down ever since you left the office. Suddenly, the cars in your lane come to a complete standstill. There's a wreck ahead. In your lane.

You try to switch to the next lane, but there's no break. "Please, somebody let me over?" Fat chance. You just sit tight with your blinker going.

The sun is baking down. It is blinding you as it reflects off the gold-glassed office towers.

As you approach Central Expressway, the traffic really clogs up. "Where do all these people live?" you mutter. Good grief, it's still another forty minutes before you even get home.

It has been one long day at the office. You spent a month there this afternoon. A stack of unfinished papers are left on your desk. And a pile of unreturned phone calls. The whole mess will be staring you in the face on Monday morning. And so will the weekly office meeting, bright and early, and you still haven't met quota.

Billboards along the expressway entice you, "Come Fly With Us." To Bermuda. To Hawaii. You agree, "That's what I need—a vacation. Get out of town. A break from the rat race." But right now, you can't even get out of your lane. Another billboard boasts, "We're Ready When You Are." Ready? "I'm *past* ready! Put a fork in me; I'm done."

This is the rat race. The fast lane. But today, it couldn't be any slower. You are one of a million rats in search of the elusive cheese. When Jesus talked about the broad path, He probably had something like LBJ Freeway in mind.

What Does the Race Look Like?
Let's talk about the rat race. What's it all about? Who's on it? Where is it headed? Jesus says it is wide-open, crowded, deadly, and easily accessed.

First, the rat race is *wide-open*.

Jesus says it is a "broad path." That means an expansive thorough-fare, a spacious freeway, an immense superhighway. Because it is broad, it is not confining or limiting. You can do your own thing. Anything goes. You can live by any values, any priorities, any morality. At any price.

The broad path. It is inclusive, permissive, and attractive. A man can set his own agenda and run his own life. He can be his own boss, make his own decisions, call his own shots. It all revolves around *self*. Not God, but self.

It is self-fulfilling, self-centered, self-serving. A man can "do his own thing." There is constant movement ahead. A feeling of accomplishment, achievement, and advancement. There are few rules. Few boundaries. Tolerance of anything. There are plenty of lanes to try. He can live however he pleases. Just go with the flow.

Like a dead fish floating downstream.

This is the rat race, the broad path. *It is the wide-open pursuit of this world to the exclusion of God.* In a nutshell, this broad path always leads to living for self. For self-fulfillment, self-comfort, self-preservation. For money, knowledge, popularity, respect, prestige, position, or possessions. It is living to make a living rather than living to make a life. It is the mindless, futile pursuit of this world.

The Lingo of the Rat Race

Recently, in a bookstore, the lingo of the rat race struck me. It's all about "me," "my," and "mine." The unholy trinity. "What's in it for *me*?" "It's *my* life!" "Those are *mine*." The world's smooth-talking evangelists spew out a success-driven "gospel" for people with a craving to get ahead. They preach things like "The Superachiever's Secret," "The Success Formula," "Take Charge Now," "Peak Productivity," "Wealth Unlimited," "Numero Uno," "Getting the Most," "Getting Set for Life," "How to Play the Tax Game and Win." The advertisements read, "Nice Guys Finish Rich," "Success Achievement," and "The Neuropsychology of Achievement." (I'm not making this stuff up!)

That is precisely the message of the rat race. One headline reads, "If the corporate ladder's wrung you out, give us a call." In other words, it gives you everything except what you want—peace and fulfillment. Another corporate climber put it this way: "I spent all my life climbing the corporate ladder only to get to the top and discover it was leaning against the wrong wall." Talk about futility.

Does that sound like winning? No way. The rat race is a treadmill.

We run but never arrive. We reach but never obtain. We strive but never succeed. Sure, we may get ahead, but ahead of what? Ahead of others? Ahead of last month's performance? Ahead in position, prestige, and possessions? Is this truly winning?

Other rat racers are literally running for their lives. They're running to stay just ahead of the creditors. Running from paycheck to paycheck. Running to make ends meet. Never getting ahead in what really counts, like satisfaction, joy, peace—*the issues of the heart*. The broad path leads, not to fulfillment, but to futility.

It's a Jam-Packed Rat Race

Not only does Jesus tell us the rat race is wide-open, but it is also crowded.

Jesus commented that "many" are on this path. It's jam-packed, full of travelers. The rat pack. Most everyone is on it. If you don't think so, just look around. Most of the people with whom we rub shoulders are on it. Most of our peers are on it. Most of our neighbors are on it. Most of our families are on it. Most everyone. Maybe even us!

Who are these rat racers? Anyone who is under the influence of the world system. Anyone who lives just to get ahead and pushes God to the back shelf. Or to no shelf at all. There are two breeds of rat racers. One breed is those who have never initially committed their life to Christ. These are men, many of whom are good, hardworking people, who are so caught up in the push of life that they absolutely have no time for God. They live their lives independent of God. They may tip their hat to God and go to church occasionally. We call them CEOs. That stands for "Christmas and Easter Only." But their heart is not in it. Jesus calls these rats "lost." They need to be found by the Good Shepherd and brought into God's flock. They live with little thought or care for eternity, Heaven, or Christ. They live only for the here and now. For what they can see, touch, and deposit. There is another breed of rat racers. A hybrid breed. Half spiritual, half worldly. These are Christians who have committed their lives to Christ, but have strayed off track . . . back to the rat race. They are being squeezed back into the world's mold. (It's amazing how quickly a sheep can start looking and acting like a rat.)

Because we Christians are in the minority, the majority message of the world can powerfully seduce us back to a secular lifestyle. This second breed tries to live in two worlds at the same time—with one foot in Heaven, and one foot in the world. And they are miserable in both worlds. They are miserable when they sit in church—and they are miserable when they punch in at work. No longer strangers and aliens in the world, they have returned to friendship status with the broad path.

Wide-open, crowded.

A Path That Seems Easy

Third, Jesus tells us the rat race is *deadly*.

He emphatically warns where this race is headed. He says it leads to "destruction." The word *destruction* has a chilling ring of sobriety about it, doesn't it? Destruction means the ruin and loss of everything that is valuable. It is the complete loss of well-being. It is the loss of happiness, peace, and contentment. It is the loss of meaningful relationships, significance, and the true purpose for living.

On the outside, rat racers look like they have it all together. Their smiling faces and attractive appearances look successful. But inwardly, they begin to realize that their lives have little purpose, a creeping feeling of destruction. Outwardly, their houses are beautiful and their lawns are neatly manicured. But inwardly, their homes are being slowly but surely destroyed. Their path is strewn with bankrupt marriages, failed dreams, hollow lives, alienated sons and daughters, and embittered relationships. Destroyed. Devastated. Empty.

Ultimately, the rat race empties into hell and a Christless eternity. Solomon put it this way, "There is a way which seems right to a man, but its end is the way of death" (Proverbs 14:12).

This is the rat race. Attractive, appealing, and crowded with travelers. It's easy to choose the broad path. You just go with the crowd.

No matter how you keep score, winning the rat race is losing. It is scoring a touchdown in the *wrong* end zone. It doesn't score for you—it scores for the opposition. It leads to your own destruction. The rat race is deadly to the soul.

Wide-open, crowded, deadly.

Fourth, the rat race is *easily accessible*. Jesus concludes that the entrance onto the rat race is a "broad gate." In other words, it is very easy to get onto the rat race. Very easy. It has a wide entrance ramp. Anyone can slip on. Even stumble on. No one is ever turned away. Whosoever will may come. Whether lured on, sucked on, or pushed on, it is always easy access.

We Christians must be constantly on guard, watching over our hearts for the subtle temptation to reenter the rat race. It looks enticing and promises much, but it destroys all that is valuable. It ruins the very life we live.

Gentlemen, this is the rat race—wide-open, crowded, deadly, easily accessible. No wonder Jesus warns us against it.

IN LANE NUMBER TWO . . . THE RIGHT RACE

Let's talk now about a totally different race. A different starting line. A different lane. A different crowd. A different finish line. This race is the right race. It is God's race for our lives.

Jesus calls this track "the narrow path." He says, "Enter by the narrow gate. . . . For the gate is small, and the way is narrow that leads to life, and few are those who find it" (Matthew 7:13-14).

Recently, I went to Israel for a month of study. During my stay, I went to the Sea of Galilee and stood exactly where Jesus stood when He first spoke these words on a grassy hill. Only a lonely tree stands in the field overlooking the sea. As I began the long walk back to the tour bus, I unexpectedly stumbled onto a worn, dusty footpath. Where it was headed, I cannot tell you. Who would be walking there, I cannot say. All I know is that it was a narrow path—just wide enough for a person to slither through. Barely. Only one person at a time could walk this path.

As I stopped, my instructor pointed to the path and said, "Steve, now there's a picture for you to take. The narrow path. Just like the one Jesus made reference to when He said, 'The way is narrow that leads to life.'" Certainly, such a path vividly communicated to the hearers of Jesus' day. But how many of us today walk to work by a narrow path? Through a grassy field? How would Jesus describe the narrow path today?

Now, Here's a Narrow Path!

Perhaps this way. Let me take you from the crowded expressways of Dallas to the lonely back roads of Carolina. Here is what I see. My wife's parents live in the Smoky Mountains of North Carolina part of the year. My father-in-law wants to be as far away from the hustle and bustle of the city as possible, so he bought a mountain (everybody ought to have their own mountain, right?) and lives up on top during the summer months. To travel to his mountain, we take a four-lane interstate from Arkansas, to a two-lane highway, to a side road, to a single-lane dirt road, to a squirrel trail. Trust me, this place is remote!

As we approach the base of this mountain, we see an iron gate hanging between two stone pillars. The brass sign reads "Private Drive." Behind the gate is the road leading to the top. The *only* road, I might add, to the top—an old logging trail that has been graded and paved.

So we begin the steep climb up this narrow path. Our kids instinctively roll down the windows and hang out the sides. The scenery out the windows is breathtaking (remember, I went to school in west Texas!). Lofty pines, towering birches, the greenest grass you've ever seen. You can hear the mountain brook flowing alongside the road. Massive mountains dwarf us on every side. My children crane their necks and strain their eyes, hoping to be the first to catch a glimpse of the house on top. (And they always claim they can see it before they actually can.)

Everyone is enjoying the scenery. Everyone except me. My eyes are glued to the road. This road is tight. Barely a single lane. There is no guardrail. No curb. No shoulder. One wrong turn and we are back at the bottom. In a heartbeat.

Needless to say, no one else is on this private road. There is no traffic, no approaching car, no one jumping into our lane. It's just you and the Smokies. You don't take this road to get to the store, nor to catch another road. It only leads to one place. To the top. There is only one reason to be on this road—to get to the top.

As the road spirals upward, weaving and winding through the massive trees, the air grows cooler. Each turn is sharp, traversing back hard. We pass through a bank of floating clouds to see the cows grazing on the mountainside, past the foreman's cabin above the road, past the red barn, past the rows of planted Christmas trees. Now we are back into a dense forest. One final turn and, finally, we are at the top. Now, that's what I call a front driveway!

The view from the top is unforgettable. It looks like we are on top of the world. Across the valley is the main ridge of the Great Smoky Mountains, painted in muted shades of purple and blue, with Mount Pisgah looming across the horizon. Clouds dot the valley below. A look in every direction reveals protruding tree-covered mountain peaks. There is the family house, the tennis courts, and a guest cabin on the very top peak. Best of all, even in the dead of summer, it is cool. The drive up is fun, but the view from on top is downright spectacular.

This lonely mountain road stands in stark contrast to the clogged LBJ Freeway in Dallas, Texas. Or the freeway you may travel—in Los Angeles, or New York, or Chicago, or Denver, or wherever. This road is narrow, tight, secluded, lonely, hard to find, and leads to an unforgettable experience. Just like the Christian life. Let's pursue that.

What Does the Narrow Path Look Like?

First, the narrow path is *tight*.

This road, Jesus says, is "narrow," meaning very tight, confining, and constricting. It is a one-lane road. Its travelers are hemmed in by carefully defined boundaries. The perimeter is nonnegotiable. Stepping over the edge leads to certain danger. It is a narrow ledge on a precipice. It confines, not in a stifling way, but in a protective sense. This road is tight, giving its travelers singleness of direction and purpose. And it alone takes you where you want to go—to the top.

Jesus Christ teaches that this narrow path is, in fact, the Christian life—a life lived in humble submission to Him. It is seeking first the spiritual Kingdom of God and His righteousness, while trusting God to provide the earthly and physical things of life. Because it is narrow, there is no room for side issues. There is only room on this path for a man to walk with Christ, to follow Him closely, and to enjoy an intimate, personal relationship with Him. There can be no other gods.

Jesus said, "If any one wishes to come after Me, let him deny himself, and take up his cross, and follow Me" (Matthew 16:24). That is a very narrow path. It mandates our exclusive loyalty and total allegiance to Him. On another occasion Christ said, "If anyone comes to Me, and does not hate his own father and mother and wife and children and brothers and sisters, yes, and even his own life, he cannot be My disciple" (Luke 14:26). No other first loves can be tolerated. He must be number one.

Second, the narrow path is *almost empty*.

Jesus says that, because it is narrow, "few" travel it. This road is no LBJ Freeway. It is the road less traveled.

Jesus calls the Church His "little flock," meaning His "micro" flock (Luke 12:32). Most men we know are not on this path. The great number of people we went to school with are not on this narrow path. Most of the people we sat next to on the airplane last week are not on this path. Few shall find it.

Few.

To run the right race requires breaking from the rat pack to run God's race. Sure, there are others running God's race, but they are few and far between. It is a lonely race. Many times we will run alone. We find our strength, not in numbers, but in the Lord.

Third, Jesus says the narrow path *leads to Heaven*.

Let's hear Jesus' words again: "The gate is small, and the way is narrow that leads to life, and few are those who find it" (Matthew 7:14). He is talking about our eternal destiny.

There are only two destinies that await us beyond the grave. Heaven and hell. All people will spend eternity in one of the two. No exceptions. Jesus is saying that only one road leads home to God. To eternal blessing. To an eternal dwelling with God.

What is life? The very opposite of death. Death is separation from the source of life. A severance from God. By contrast, life is vital union with God, who is life. A personal relationship with God.

When Jesus says this narrow path leads to life, He means it leads to Heaven. To eternity with God. Forever.

Fourth, the narrow path is *secluded*.

Jesus cautions, "Enter by the narrow gate . . . the gate is small . . . and few are those who find it." This road is hard to find and requires earnest searching with all our heart. It is off the beaten path, away from the noisy throng. This narrow path is hard to find because it requires the Holy Spirit's guidance to discover it (1 Corinthians 2:14-16). It is hard to enter because it is narrow, requiring heart-searching repentance and complete faith. No one stumbles upon it. Nor does anyone stumble through it.

This narrow gate is Jesus Christ Himself. He is the door for the sheep: "I am the door; if anyone enters through Me, he shall be saved, and shall go in and out, and find pasture" (John 10:9). He invites us to come to Himself. Entering this gate requires a simple step of faith in Christ. It involves the commitment of our life to Christ, entrusting our life to Him. No amount of good works are required to enter. Or will be accepted. It means coming to Christ and receiving Him as our personal Lord and Savior. And once we enter the narrow gate, we then follow Christ daily every step of the race. Committing our life to Christ is not an isolated event in our past, but a continuing experience every day.

Men Who Win

We need to be very clear at this point. The world says winning is getting ahead in the rat race. The world's philosophy of winning is, "He who dies with the most toys wins the game." But God says winning is running a *different* race, by a *different* set of rules, to win a *different* prize. Winning the rat race is *not* winning. Only winning the *right* race is winning.

The world says winning is living before you die. Jesus says winning is dying before you live. Dying to self, dying to the pursuit of this world. In dying, we find life.

Men who win trust Christ; men who lose trust themselves. Men who win love Christ; men who lose love this world. Men who win follow Christ; men who lose follow the rat race. Men who win seek Christ's approval; men who lose seek man's applause.

Winning is coming to know God in a personal relationship through Jesus Christ. It is committing our life to Christ and choosing to live not for self, but for Him. Winning is following Christ in willing obedience, seeking to do His will in all of life. It is competing for Him and running the race He has set before us. Winning is serving Christ and giving our life away to help others in this same pursuit. It is leading others into the race and encouraging them along the way. Winning is running faithful to the end, persevering to the finish line, overcoming life's obstacles, and winning Christ's incorruptible crown. That is what winning is!

If a man wins God's race, it doesn't matter where else he loses. If a man loses God's race, it matters not where else he may win.

WHICH RACE ARE YOU RUNNING?

I have just described two totally different races. We are all running one of those two races. Either the rat race down the broad path, or the right race down the narrow path. Which race are you running?

There is the rat race—run on the crowded expressway of life; and there is the right race—run on a narrow single-lane back road of life. One is a crowded road; the other a road less traveled. One leads to destruction; the other to life. One is self-focused; the other God-focused. One is easy to enter; the other is hard to find, much less enter. One is marked by the constant push of this world; the other by the rest, peace, and tranquility that Christ alone offers.

Which race are you running?

Are you in the rat race? I will assume that you are a genuine Christian if you are reading this book. But, if you are not, I will be showing you how to enter the right race through faith in Jesus Christ. More about that later.

Some of you have entered the right race. But you may feel yourself drifting back into the old rat race. Don't be disheartened. This book is especially for you. That is a temptation with which we all struggle. Still. Our focus can be too easily shifted from the Lord on to this world. The Apostle John warns us, "Do not love the world, nor the things in the world" (1 John 2:15). The rat race is a fatal attraction that we must all resist.

My Own Struggle

I must confess something to you here. To this day, the enticement of the rat race is still a powerful temptation in my life. I must be aware that I can still be sucked back into the old rat race. It can still entice and hypnotize my heart. My struggle with the lure and the glitz of the world continues. Even after entering the right race, I still must fight the seductive temptation of the rat race.

Years ago, I made the decision to go to seminary and enter the ministry. That was a major decision to leave my career in finance and banking to pursue God's call upon my life in a new direction.

In order to pay the bills while at Dallas Seminary, I wrote and marketed my own sports magazines. I wrote a publication called *Gospel Gridiron* in which I covered the Dallas Cowboys with a distinctively Christian agenda. I weekly interviewed either Tom Landry, Mike Ditka, Dan Reeves, Roger Staubach, or the other Cowboys who had a Christian faith, wrote Bible studies, and had a section called "Pigskin Prophet" in which I predicted the scores of the upcoming games. Not only was it a fun enterprise, but something subtle quietly began to occur.

Writing this magazine began to eat up an increasingly larger chunk of my time. It drained my energy. Then my spiritual vitality. My heart became so focused upon the business that my heart for God began to grow callous and cold. The publication soon became successful and paid my freight to school.

I then expanded into baseball publishing. After approaching the Texas Rangers with an idea, I soon found myself creating and writing their official newsletter, which I named *Pennant Fever*. Almost overnight, it became very successful. Not only was *Pennant Fever* sold in the Rangers' stadium, but many convenience stores began selling it, too. The momentum began to snowball. Then a bank in Fort Worth wanted to buy my publication's logo for its bumper stickers. All this had major-league benefits for me. Soon the Rangers offered to me the rights to their annual yearbook, a nice glossy book. Then an NBA team, the Dallas Mavericks, saw my publication and approached me to write and publish a similar magazine for their fans. Before I knew it, I had a year-round, full-time business in place to steamroll ahead.

But wait a minute! I thought. *What am I doing?* The tail was now wagging the dog. I was suffering from pennant fever. School was on the back shelf, and this business was front and center in my heart. A choice between memorizing Greek verb tenses or interviewing Reggie Jackson was too seductive for my particular calling from God. I was blinded by the stadium lights. Without realizing it, I was being tempted into a rat race that had little to do with God's calling on my life. It fed my ego and competitive drive. But now I would have to make a choice one way or the other. Seminary or sportswriting? In reality, my choice was between God's will or my own.

Can you believe it? Here I was in seminary, giving my life to serve the Lord, and I was about to bail out! I was being stampeded by the rat race.

I must tell you, only through God's Word and His indwelling Spirit convicting my heart was I enabled to dodge the bullet and stay in the right race.

Please don't misunderstand. You don't have to go to seminary to do God's will. But you do have to pursue God's agenda for your life, not your own.

Let me be clear. It can happen to all of us, even to believers. The world can reach out and grab our hearts as it dangles its cheap trinkets before us. It appeals to our competitive nature to get ahead and to push to the top. The rat race almost ate my lunch. And it can happen to you.

If you are living under the constant threat of the rat race, reading this book may help you remain firm in your conviction to run the right race. I wish I could tell you that the struggle is over and that I no longer am tempted by the rat race. But I cannot. I still fight it.

Some of you, after entering the right race, have slowed down. Perhaps you are weary or tired. Maybe you have tripped and fallen into sin. Possibly, your schedule has become so full that your focus is divided between God and the rat race. It could be that excess baggage you have picked up along the way is slowing you down. Your energy is drained, impeding your speed. If so, I want to help you remove those needless encumbrances so that you can be liberated to run God's race and win.

We all go through times when our spiritual progress and growth are slowed down. It is critical that we learn how to work through our dry seasons without losing the race. Wherever you are, it is important that you be alert and not miss the opportunity before you to win God's race. Wake up to the race before you.

WAKE UP . . . AND GO FOR BROKE!

The year was 1968. It was my senior year in high school, and we had a pretty good football team. Despite the fact that I was the quarterback.

We were undefeated and ready to play our arch rivals, who were also undefeated, in the biggest game of the year. The stage was set for a schoolboy showdown, certainly one of the most important events in our young lives.

It was Friday afternoon. We went into our gym, a big domed coliseum, to get dressed. The routine was to put on our uniforms and go into the coliseum and "get our game face on." We'd lay flat on our backs and think about the game. We'd just stare at the ceiling and visualize executing the plays and how we were going to beat our opponent.

There were about sixty of us in the pitch dark gym. It was so still, you could hear a pin drop. Suddenly, it was time to go to the stadium. Our coach came in and softly said, "All right, men, let's get on the bus and go to the game."

My heart was pounding! I grabbed my helmet and shoes. We tip-toed out in our stocking feet, got on the bus, and headed to the stadium. The scene was electric. The whole community had packed the stadium.

We blew our rivals out of the water! The score was 35-0 at halftime. We didn't even punt. Five possessions, five touchdowns. The final score was 41-6. What a blowout!

After the game, everyone was elated! The student body, the parents, the band, the faculty—everybody was excited! As we came off the field and loaded the bus for the jubilant ride home, our fans were cheering and pounding us on the head!

It seemed like everyone was at the gym when our bus pulled up. We got off and had to fight through the crowd again. Everybody was slapping us on the back, cheering. Everybody was singing the school fight song; the band was playing.

The locker room was complete bedlam. Everybody was boxing, jostling each other, and popping one other with towels.

I slipped into the coliseum to be alone and began peeling off my jersey and pads. I replayed the whole game in my mind, savoring every play. I was replaying the first play, the second play, and so on.

As I was peeling off my jersey, I looked across the coliseum and saw the figure of a body lying at midcourt. The red exit sign—the only light in the gym—was shining over the silhouette of this motionless body.

I had thought I was the only person in that pitch dark coliseum. I walked over and looked down at the figure and saw that it was a person. He had his full football uniform on—number 29. I didn't know if he was dead or alive.

I nudged him with my foot, gently. As soon as I did, BOOM! He shot up, put his helmet on, and said, "Let's get on the bus and go to the game!"

I said, "The game's over." (The funny thing is, we didn't even miss ol' number 29.)

I said, "It was the biggest game of our lives! We won, 41-6! You missed the whole thing." My friend had apparently stayed up late the night before and when he laid down, he went to sleep. For good.

Men, wake up and get in the game. Don't miss out on the greatest opportunity of your life: to win the race that God has set before you. Don't buy into the world's seductive message of position, prestige, and possessions. Don't go to sleep on the broad path that leads to destruction. Stay on the narrow path that leads to life. Get out of the rat race . . . and into the right race.

Nobody wants *you* to win more than God does. Nobody.

CHAPTER 2

HEAVEN'S HEISMAN

✭

The Master's green jacket. The Olympic gold medal. The Lombardi Trophy. A World Series ring. The Wimbledon cup. An NBA championship.

These are all coveted prizes from the world of sports. Hyped by the media. Coveted by athletes. The dream of young boys everywhere. Highly prestigious, cherished, and esteemed, these emblems of success mark out our champions for fame and immortality.

But there is one trophy that stands alone. One trophy that towers head and shoulders above the rest. One trophy that overshadows the pack. The winner of this award vaults to the pinnacle of athletic stardom. It is the Heisman Trophy.

The Heisman is awarded each year by the Downtown Athletic Club of New York City to the most outstanding collegiate football player in America. No small recognition. The list of past Heisman winners reads like a who's who of gridiron greats. Recent winners include Roger Staubach, O. J. Simpson, Tony Dorsett, Earl Campbell, Herchel Walker, and some guy who knows a lot named Vincent "Bo" Jackson. (Could we assemble a backfield with these guys, or what?) Winners in past years include hall of famers like "Doc" Blanchard, Glenn Davis, Doak Walker, Paul Hornung, and Billy Cannon.

These are larger-than-life legends who dominated the game. Gridiron greats who packed stadiums. Saturday-afternoon heroes who redefined the standard of excellence. Shooting stars who rose above the competition.

First awarded in 1935, the Heisman Trophy has become the most widely recognizable icon in sports. It depicts a muscular football player driving for yardage, sidestepping and straight-arming his way to a touchdown. Cast in bronze, the statue is unimposing in size—a little more than a foot long and high, mounted on a seventeen-and-one-half-by-five-and-one-half-inch base, and set on a three-foot marble pedestal. Yet, it is gigantic in significance, symbolic of the highest level of achievement. It is the most coveted award in American sports.

The mystical aura of the Heisman is further intensified by the announcement of the winner live on television. The five finalists are all flown to New York to attend the presentation at the Downtown Athletic Club. There, on a Saturday in December, the winner is dramatically announced and presented the Heisman before the watching eyes of the nation.

Imagine their emotions building as these finalists gaze at the richly paneled, lavishly decorated trophy room. Portraits of past winners line the walls. The tension builds inside as each finalist contemplates the highly publicized accomplishments of the other all-Americans vying for the same coveted prize.

Dramatically, the winner is announced. As he steps to the podium, he fights back tears. His voice quivers. He humbly thanks his parents, who gave him the emotional support needed to excel. He thanks his coaches and teammates. He then holds up the trophy triumphantly for all to see. The quest for the Heisman is now complete. It has once again marked out the best America has to offer.

The esteem of winning such a prestigious trophy is nothing new. In fact, there was just such a highly coveted award in the world of sports two thousand years ago. It became the passion of the Roman Empire. This ancient award became synonymous with the most popular figures of the day and was bestowed on the winners of the Olympic and Isthmian athletic games. The victor's crown was a wreath of pine leaves. The Heisman Trophy of the first century.

THE HEISMAN OF ANCIENT DAYS

Let's turn back the sports calendar. Come with me to the year AD 53. We are traveling with the Apostle Paul from the city of Corinth, the most splendid city of ancient Greece, across the natural land bridge that joins southern Greece with the mainland, to the famous Isthmian Games.

It is here on the shores of the Mediterranean Sea that the Isthmian Games, second in importance only to the Olympic Games, were held. These athletic games were a major event, held every two years.

As we arrive at the Isthmian stadium, several sights attract our attention. We are immediately impressed with the massive throngs that are gathering from all corners of the Roman Empire. Thousands have descended upon Isthmus to witness the spectacle.

We are impressed with the huge sports coliseum. Its massive marble blocks are imposing. Its perfectly symmetrical rows are striking. The emperor's velvet box is filled with the political dignitaries of the day. These games were the place for the rich and famous to be seen.

We are impressed with the beautifully manicured track and field nestled in the center of the stadium. On the track, we see assembled the finest physical specimens of the known world. These athletes are the most popular figures of their day. The subjects of poets. Chiseled in marble. Painted on canvas. Cicero complained they were afforded more fame than a conquering general. The statues of past champions line the entrance leading to the stadium. It is the dream of every young boy to become one of these athletic gods.

The Race
The main feature was the five-event pentathlon, which consisted of the long jump, the javelin and discus throws, wrestling, and the footrace. Far and away the most popular event was the footrace. This race was called the *dromos*, a race of one lap around the 600-yard track (a third longer than our present 440-yard tracks). Later, the long-distance marathon race was added, called the *agon*.

Down on the field, we focus upon a single athlete—a distance runner. He has trained and worked out for ten months under severe discipline and strict diet. The last month he has spent in Corinth, working out under the personal supervision of an official. The runner now jogs to the far end of the track and dips his hands in a bucket of blood, swearing that he has submitted to ten months of rigorous training and agreeing to compete according to the rules.

He comes to the starting line and positions himself in the starting block. Every muscle is taut; every nerve is tense. His mind is singularly focused. He is riveted on one thing: winning.

Across the infield is the finish line. There, a ladderlike pedestal is strategically positioned, and on it hangs the most coveted prize in all the Roman Empire—the victor's crown! This crown will be awarded to the winner of the footrace. It is for this crown that these athletes have rigorously trained for months and years. It is for this crown that they have punished their bodies to masochistic limits. Only one runner will win this crown. So nothing will be held back.

Inside the stadium, we feel the electricity in the air. The atmosphere is crackling with excitement.

In the center of the stadium is a solitary site that leaves an indelible mark on every Christian. Just to the side of the track, near the finish line, is a wooden platform. This platform is raised, rectangular, and mounted by a series of steps. Upon the platform rests a seat.

The *Bema*—the Judge's Seat

Upon that seat sits the umpire, the presiding judge of the games. This seat is called, in the Greek language, the *bema*. It is to this *bema* that every athlete must report after he runs his race.

The runners take their mark. Rome's fastest explode out of the starting blocks like anxious thoroughbreds out of the gate. The race looks dead even as the runners head down the backstretch. As they come around the final turn, they sprint for the tape. A mere hundred yards lay between them and glory. Two runners push to the finish, neck and neck. The finish is too close to call. The crowd is silent in suspense.

Every eye strains and focuses upon the *bema*, awaiting the judge's decision. Which runner will be awarded the winner's wreath? The umpire's call will be final.

As the athletes approach the judge's stand, we feel the sting of regret as the umpire disqualifies a runner because he violated the rules. We feel remorse as the judge passes over the other runners who lost and withholds from them the cherished prize.

But we are going to thrill to a vivid spectacle. The judge of the games takes the wreath of leaves and calls out the winner's name. The champion steps forward and stands before the *bema*. The judge crowns the head of the new victorious champion. The stadium roars! The crowd spontaneously begins chanting his name. The applause is deafening. This one moment of glory makes all the months and years of training worthwhile. As the new champion circles the track in a customary victory lap, he proudly displays the cherished victor's crown for all to see.

The Judgment Seat of Christ

It is against this background that the Apostle Paul writes to these Corinthians, "We must all appear before the judgment-seat of Christ, that each one may be recompensed for his deeds in the body, according to what he has done, whether good or bad" (2 Corinthians 5:10).

Every Corinthian knew precisely the context of Paul's statement. The Isthmian Games, held just outside of Corinth, were intimately familiar to those early believers. Just as an athlete would appear before the judge's seat following his race, so every Christian will one day appear before the judgment seat of Jesus Christ to be judged and, possibly, rewarded. This scene, a very vivid picture in the minds of the early Christians, became a constant focus of the Christian life. Likewise, it must grip our hearts and compel our lives. We must run the race to win!

Paul writes, "Do you not know that those who run in a race all run, but only one receives the prize? Run in such a way that you may win. . . . They then do it to receive a perishable wreath, but we an imperishable" (1 Corinthians 9:24-25). Every believer must run to win an imperishable crown. Heaven's Heisman. Paul must have been an avid observer of sports. His frequent athletic allusions in Scripture show he probably was a keen sports enthusiast, as he dips into the world of sports to communicate key truths about the Christian life.

In this chapter I want to consider several factors concerning the judgment seat of Christ. *Who* will appear before the judgment seat of Christ? *Why* will we appear? *How* will our performance be assessed?

THE PEOPLE ASSEMBLED

First, *who* will appear before the judgment seat of Christ? The Bible teaches that every Christian will be summoned to appear before this judgment seat. Every Christian. If you have trusted Jesus Christ to be your Savior and Lord, you will stand there. Paul writes, "For we must all appear before the judgment-seat of Christ, that each one may be recompensed" (2 Corinthians 5:10). The language—"all," "each one"—is all-inclusive. Not just some believers, but every Christian. We will all stand before the judgment seat of Christ.

Can you even imagine what a day that will be? Standing before the *bema*. Face to face with Heaven's Judge, Jesus Christ. We will behold His nail-scarred hands and His nail-pierced side. We will look upon His majestic face. We will gaze upon His dazzling, unveiled glory. We will see Him just as He is, King of kings and Lord of lords (1 John 3:2). We will not see the suffering servant of the Lord (Philippians 2:6-7). Nor the humble carpenter from Nazareth. We shall see Him as the unrivaled King of Heaven and earth. Sovereign and awesome. Holy and righteous. The Judge of all creation.

It is before this glorified Christ, enthroned as Lord over all, that we will stand. It will be an awesome spectacle in that day. The Apostle John, in his description of the glorified Christ (Revelation 1:9-20), gives us a fore-gleam of what our experience will be like. The aged apostle was given a celestial vision and was privileged to see Christ standing supremely in the midst of the churches, clothed as a king in a regal robe that flowed to His feet and girded as a priest with a priestly golden girdle across His breast.

In this vision, Christ's head and hair were white like the fairest wool and virgin snow, revealing the unstained purity of His holy character. His piercing eyes were like a flame of fire, penetrating deeply into the unseen hearts and lives of men. Nothing escapes His all-seeing eyes. His strong feet were like burnished bronze, glowing in a red-hot furnace, depicting the ironclad strength of His judgments. His decrees cannot be annulled or appealed. There is no higher court to appeal to.

When this Judge speaks, His voice is like the sound of many waters, drowning out all other appeals and arguments. His verdicts alone are heard. In His right hand He holds seven stars, portraying His protective care over His spiritual leaders who speak God's Word. Out of His mouth comes a sharp, two-edged sword, envisioning the sovereign authority and truthfulness with which this Judge speaks. All His judgments are right and true. And His face is dazzling like the sun shining in its glory, revealing the composite majesty of His divine person.

When John saw this Christ presiding over Heaven's court, he fell at His feet like a dead man, struck in awe and terror.

Men, it is before this very same Christ that you and I will one day stand at the end of life's race. We will be equally awestruck by His majesty as He reviews our life.

This appearance before Heaven's Judge will occur at the end of time. At the end of the race. Not during the race, but after the race. Our prize awaits each of us at the finish line. At the consummation of this age. After the Second Coming of Christ. In the book of Revelation, Jesus says, "Behold, I am coming quickly, and My reward is with Me, to render to every man according to what he has done"

(22:12). Clearly, our Lord coincides His judgment and the giving of His rewards with the time of His return.

THE PURPOSE ASSIGNED

Second, *why* will we appear there? What is the purpose of the judgment seat of Christ?

First, I should say that the purpose is not to see if we shall be admitted to Heaven. The issue of our salvation is already settled. The moment we personally trusted Jesus Christ as our Savior and Lord, we received eternal life. Forever. We were just as assured of Heaven then as though we had already been there ten thousand years.

Let me say it one more time. This eternal reward to be won is not our salvation. We could never earn salvation by our good works. Salvation is the gift of God, freely given, neither earned nor deserved. Christ won salvation for us through His death on the cross, and He offers eternal life as a prepaid free gift. Only our faith in Christ may receive it.

So, what is the judgment seat of Christ all about, then? The purpose of the *bema* is for Christ to review our Christian life and determine how our life counted for His Kingdom. According to our faithful stewardship of all that He entrusted to us, He will reward our lives. The issue is not salvation. The issue is the reward of the saved.

The Bible says when we must appear before Christ, it will be more than a bodily appearance. The word *appear* carries the idea of being made manifest, to be stripped of every outward facade, to be carefully examined and openly revealed. There will be no secrets in Heaven.

The author of Hebrews tells us, "There is no creature hidden from His sight, but all things are open and laid bare to the eyes of Him with whom we have to do" (Hebrews 4:13). We will be fully known by Him in that day. This brings both comfort and conviction. All our life will be played back before us. In that day, "The Lord . . . will both bring to light the things hidden in the darkness and disclose the motives of men's hearts; and then each man's praise will come to him from God" (1 Corinthians 4:5).

This is how Paul states the purpose: "that each one may be recompensed for his deeds in the body, according to what he has done, whether good or bad" (2 Corinthians 5:10). Following our review, Christ will reward the good deeds we did in our body. The word *recompense* means to receive your due, to receive the payment justly coming to you.

While standing before His judgment seat, we will receive from Christ His eternal reward for our spiritual service and faithful sacrifice. We will receive an incorruptible crown. Heaven's Heisman.

In that Final Day, Jesus will distinguish between our good and bad works. Our good works are all that we do to glorify Christ in the power of the Holy Spirit according to God's Word. They are the things that will count for eternity, the gold, silver, and precious stones. These good works will be officially recognized and gloriously rewarded by Christ.

What About Our Sins?

Our bad works are all that we do that is useless. Worthless. Of no eternal value. Not necessarily evil or sinful. Just worthless. It is the trivia we do in the energy of our flesh. All that we do without any bearing on eternity. Wood, hay, and straw. These useless works will bring no reward.

Maybe you are wondering if our personal sins will be revealed in that day. If that were the case, I would be in major-league trouble. Don't worry. As Christ sorts through our good and bad deeds, He will not manifest any of our sin. Why? Because Jesus already dealt with our sin two thousand years ago on the cross and it will never come up again. Never.

Think of it this way. When I was in high school, I played quarterback for a team that ran the triple-option offense. After the season, my football coach was asked to speak at the annual NCAA Coach's Convention on how to effectively run the triple option.

To best communicate, our coach spliced together a highlight film of our best option plays. You should have seen this film! In all humility . . . we looked awesome. It showed none of our bad plays, only our good plays. Any team could look great with only their good plays shown. The fact is, we looked better than we really were.

But over the years, something tragic occurred. Our highlight film has been lost! Gone! All our good plays are lost forever. (Now we are only legends in our own minds.)

I have all of our game films. Guess what it is like now to watch those reels? Horrible. All my fumbles, incompletions, and misdirections—every one of those clunkers—are permanently recorded. They still haunt me. All of my touchdowns, big plays, and completions are gone. (All right, so it was a short highlight film.)

Why couldn't it have been just the opposite? All of my bad plays gone, the game film erased, and only my good plays remaining? At the judgment seat of Christ, it will be exactly that way. All of our sinful deeds will be erased from God's film. Only the good will remain. God has been recording on heavenly film, if you will, our entire life. All our works, our thoughts, our attitudes—He has it all on tape. When we stand at the judgment seat of Christ, our life will be replayed and reviewed by Christ. But fortunately, God has edited out our bad plays and has spliced together only the good ones. What a highlight film that will be!

In that day, I will give an account of myself to Christ as a servant to his master. He will determine how faithful I have been with what He has entrusted to me. Have I invested it in His kingdom?

Men, this day of accountability is coming. How we live life today counts forever. It does matter how we run life's race. He will be there at the finish line. So, we must run faithfully today if we are to be rewarded in that Final Day.

THE PERFORMANCE ASSESSED

Third, *how* will Christ assess our performance? How will He determine if we won the race or not? First, let me tell you that God does not see as you and I see. We look on the outward appearance, but God looks on the heart. God sees the race and identifies His winners differently than the natural eye sees. It will take another world to show who the true winners are.

Jesus said, "Many who are first will be last; and the last, first" (Matthew 19:30; see also 20:16). Many who seem to be losers by this world's estimation will be winners in that day. And many winners down here will be losers up there.

Things will seem so different then. The last will be first and the first, last. Losers will be winners and winners will be losers. Those who are losers in the world's eyes will be winners in Heaven. And earth's winners will be Heaven's losers.

In the ancient Greek games, only one runner could win the prize. But in God's race—and this is really great news—we can all be winners. We are competing against the course, not one another. Thus, we can all win.

So, we must ask ourselves, "What will be the divine criteria of His final judgment? What will be the standard of His test?" I want to suggest five questions that we must ask ourselves which will help lead us to victory on that Final Day.

Am I Running the Right Race?

First, I must ask myself, "Am I running the right race?" There are many tracks open before us. We must run the right race if we are to have any chance of winning, the race that is divinely laid out before us. The crown awaits those who get on track—the right track—and run in the right direction.

God has a plan for each of our lives. This plan is called His will. Success in life is, very simply, doing the will of God, no more and no less. Each of us has a purpose here. That purpose is found in doing His will. This plan includes what I am to do, how I am to serve Christ, where I am to live, who I am to marry, where I am to attend school. God has everything about my life, both big and small, all planned out. Winning is finding and doing God's will. Or entering and running God's race.

Am I running the right race? Am I fulfilling my purpose for being here? Am I running on the right track in the right direction?

The 1929 Rose Bowl will forever be etched in gridiron history because it became the showcase for football's most unforgettable play. California was playing Georgia Tech and the Golden Bears were leading 7-6 in the first half. Georgia Tech had the ball deep in their own territory with their backs against their own goal line.

Then it happened. A Tech runner fumbled the ball and a California defender, Roy Riegels, recovered the loose pigskin.

Suddenly, the unthinkable occurred. As Riegels attempted to advance the ball, he got turned around. Somehow in the mad confusion of his teammates blocking Georgia Tech defenders, he lost his sense of direction. Roy took off for the end zone and ran what would be the race of his life. Before him lay eighty yards of infamy. Riegels was running the wrong way!

The crowd shouted in horror. Which only made him run faster. The twenty . . . the thirty . . . the forty . . . the fifty! Only fifty yards separated Riegels from the end zone and immortality. By this time, Riegels' teammates took off in hot pursuit. Benny Lum, a speedy California halfback, was closing in on Roy. "Roy, Roy, stop!" he yelled.

But Roy only ran faster, thinking his teammates were actually cheering him on.

Just as Roy reached the goal line, Lum tackled his own beleaguered teammate from behind. Roy Riegels had run the wrong way and almost scored a touchdown. In the wrong end zone.

Can you imagine his shock to discover his mistaken identity? He was sincere. But he was sincerely wrong.

At the judgment seat, Christ will review our direction. He will ask, "Did you run in the right direction?" "Did you score in the right end zone?" "Was there clarity of spiritual purpose and eternal direction about your life?"

Don't be shocked on that Final Day. Run the right race.

Am I Running According to the Rules?

Second, I must evaluate, "Am I running according to the rules?" Every athlete must compete according to the established rules of the game. Breaking the rules will bring a penalty, or disqualification. Paul writes, "And also if any one competes as an athlete, he does not win the prize unless he competes according to the rules" (2 Timothy 2:5).

Just as an athlete must adhere to the rules, so I must make the Word of God my standard in all things. Victory will be my final reward as I live my life according to God's Word. His Word tells me how to play the game, how to run the race. No unfair start ahead of others. No pushing another runner. No leaving the track. No shortcuts through the infield. No drugs or steroids. These are the governing rules. If I violate these rules, it will always bring painful consequences in the end. Even possible disqualification.

It is possible for a runner to actually cross the finish line first, be cheered by the spectators as the winner, and yet when he comes before the judge's stand, be disqualified. And the crown given to someone else. Why? Because he did not compete according to the rules.

Men, it is critically important that we, too, run according to the rules—God's Word. We must obey His Word in every area of our life—our business life, our home life, our personal life, our ministry, our relationships, our values. All must be governed by the Word.

Our obedience today will bring victory tomorrow at the *bema*.

This potential danger of disqualification is what Paul meant when he wrote, "I buffet my body and make it my slave, lest possibly, after I have preached to others, I myself should be disqualified" (1 Corinthians 9:27).

Am I Helping Others Win?

Third, I must consider, "Am I helping others win?" The Bible says there is a reward for those who help other runners in the race. Let me explain.

Jesus Christ says, "He who receives you receives Me, and he who receives Me receives Him who sent Me" (Matthew 10:40). To "receive" means to bring into one's care. When you and I receive another Christian into our care—whether it be through financial, material, emotional, or spiritual help—we are actually receiving (or serving) Jesus Christ. And when we serve Christ, we are serving God the Father. An inseparable identity exists between God the Father, God the Son, and His people. A Holy Triangle. When we receive One, we actually receive all Three.

Jesus further explains, "He who receives a prophet in the name of a prophet shall receive a prophet's reward; and he who receives a righteous man in the name of a righteous man shall receive a righteous man's reward" (Matthew 10:41). A prophet is one who proclaims God's Word. A righteous man lives God's Word. A prophet will receive one reward, and a righteous man another. Both are worthy of receiving a reward, yet they do not receive the same reward.

Now, here is the encouraging part. In fact, downright exciting! When I "receive" a preacher or a godly saint, I share in his reward. When he wins, I win. Why? Because I helped him win. The one who helps participates in the reward of the one who wins.

But what about helping those who are less high-profile? Don't we need to serve common, ordinary folks? People like you and me? Absolutely!

Jesus continues, "And whoever in the name of a disciple gives to one of these little ones even a cup of cold water to drink, truly I say to you he shall not lose his reward" (Matthew 10:42).

Who are these "little ones" whom we are to serve? Perhaps they are the least in God's Kingdom. Perhaps new believers. Perhaps those who serve unnoticed. Regardless, Jesus says that when we serve one of these "little ones," it will not go unnoticed by God. Nor unrewarded.

Any service—whatsoever—done for any of God's people—whosoever—is service done to Jesus Christ Himself. Whether it be helping a preacher, a "behind-the-scenes" worker, or a brand-new Christian. Even something as seemingly insignificant as giving a cup of cold water to a thirsty disciple will be rewarded by God. Count on it.

Men, sometimes our ministry goes unnoticed by others. But it never goes unnoticed by the One who keeps Heaven's accounts. God will one day reward us for helping others in the race, whether they be teachers, prophets, or widows. God will reward it.

Is there something you can do to help another runner today?

Then do it!

Am I Still Running?

Fourth, I must ask myself, "Am I still running?" Running the right race matters little if I do not finish my race. I must actually push to the finish if I am to receive the crown.

The great theologian Yogi Berra once said, "It ain't over 'til it's over." Amen. It matters little to have the lead at the beginning. We must finish well. Victory is won at the finish line, not the starting blocks. That's where it counts.

Paul writes about the end of his race: "For I am already being poured out as a drink offering and the time of my departure has come. I have fought the good fight, I have finished the course, I have kept the faith; in the future there is laid up for me the crown of righteousness, which the Lord, the righteous Judge, will award to me on that day; and not only to me, but also to all who have loved His appearing" (2 Timothy 4:6-8).

Here's a sprinter who explodes out of the starting blocks. No one has ever started this fast. He is well ahead of the field. He is running the race of his life, lapping the field. Then suddenly, something strange occurs. He pulls up and stops running. Just completely stops running. He then walks up into the grandstands and sits down to watch with everyone else. And stays there. In a short while, everyone he had passed earlier passes him. Guess who wins the crown? Not the one who started well. But the one who finished well.

So keep running.

In the 1972 Summer Olympic games, America's hope for the gold medal in the 1500-meter run was a runner named Jim Ryun. Jim had run in the 1968 games, but was beaten by a better man. For four years, Ryun rigorously trained to bounce back and bring home the gold. He spent countless hours on the track, early mornings and late nights. He had sacrificed it all for this one chance at victory.

There, at the starting line, he stood next to the finest athletes from all over the world. The gun sounded and the race began.

But something tragic happened with a little more than a lap to go. Jim stepped in the path of another runner and they both fell to the infield track. The rest of the pack left them far behind. All hopes of victory were gone.

Bruised and in pain, Jim got up with no chance of winning the gold. He nevertheless finished the race—alone. Dead last. No prize. No glory. No medal.

But in defeat, Jim Ryun showed himself to be a champion. By

finishing the race, he revealed the true character of his heart.

I can just see the *bema*. The Lord is passing out His rewards. And it just may be that a believer who stumbled and fell early in life's race, but who got up and finished running the race—without quitting—will be the gold winner in that Final Day. I don't know. But I do know that many of the last will be first.

Don't you find encouragement in that truth? It may seem that others are way ahead of you. It may appear that they are doing so much more for Christ. Don't get discouraged and quit. Just be faithful. Hang in there. Finish the race like Jim Ryun did. Many of the last will be first. There just may be Heaven's Heisman awaiting you.

Am I Running with the Right Motives?

Fifth, I must ask, "Why am I running? Is it with the right motives?" Am I running for the approval of men? Or for the applause of Heaven? What is the driving motivation of my heart? At the *bema*, the Judge will bring to light our motives for running.

Paul wrote, "Therefore do not go on passing judgment before the time, but wait until the Lord comes who will both bring to light the things hidden in the darkness and disclose the motives of men's hearts; and then each man's praise will come to him from God" (1 Corinthians 4:5). If we run for the glory of God, we will receive a reward from God. But if we compete for self-glory, we forfeit what reward would have been ours.

The Pharisees stand as exhibit A of people who expended much energy in running (the wrong race) with wrong motives. They ran to receive the applause of this world. The result? No reward.

Jesus strikes a nerve within us all when He says, "Beware of practicing your righteousness before men to be noticed by them; otherwise you have no reward with your Father who is in heaven" (Matthew 6:1). If we run God's race simply to steal the spotlight, God will withhold His reward. But if we sacrifice this world's applause during the race, God's praise will await us at the end.

The Oscar-winning movie *Chariots of Fire* is based on the quest of Harold Abrahams and Eric Liddell to win gold medals in the 1924 Olympics, something they both accomplished.

There is an obvious difference between Abrahams and Liddell in the movie. Abrahams runs for himself, while Liddell runs for the glory of God. Two classic scenes in the movie contrast these two motives for running.

In the first scene, Eric's sister, Jennie, mistakes her brother's love of running for rebellion against God. She pressures him to return to the mission field in China, where they both were born and their parents lived. Jennie is upset because Eric missed a mission meeting, so he decides to have a talk with her. They walk to a grassy spot overlooking the Scottish Highlands.

Clutching her arms, Eric tries to explain his calling to run: "Jennie, Jennie. You've got to understand. I believe God made me for a purpose—for China. But He also made me fast!—and when I run, I feel His pleasure!"

The second scene in the movie occurs one hour before the final race of the Olympics. While his professional coach and trainer give him a rubdown, Harold Abrahams laments, "I'm twenty-four and I've never known contentment. I'm forever in pursuit, and I don't even know what it is I'm chasing."

Both men were awarded a gold medal, but only one won his medal for God.

At the judgment seat, the Lord will disclose the motives of our hearts. If we ran for the glory of God, then our prize will come from Him.

I don't know about you, but that thought lights my fire. Men, let us run for the Master until we cross the finish line and collapse in His arms.

THE PRIZE AWARDED

In ancient athletic games, a fragile, leafy crown was awarded the winner. This garland—called the victor's crown—was a collection of pine leaves, wild olive leaves, parsley, celery leaves, or ivy. In the Isthmian Games, the prize was a pine wreath. With this crown came instant fame, high acclaim, and the life of a hero. Winners were immortalized, much as they are today. These wreaths were taken home with great pride. But in a few days they would soon wither and discolor.

Making a striking comparison, Paul contrasted these earthly crowns with the imperishable crowns of Christ—Heaven's Heisman. What can be said about God's eternal crown?

Heaven's crown is, first, called "the unfading crown of glory" (1 Peter 5:4). It is a glorious crown that will never lose its beauty or value. Ancient athletes were awarded floral crowns. But they quickly faded away. Believe me, I know. I have a box full of old trophies, varsity letters, and newspaper clippings in my parents' attic. They are all tarnished, moth-eaten, and faded! Their glory is past and forgotten (except in my mother's estimation).

But our heavenly crown of glory will be unfading, lasting forever. It will be incorruptible, timeless, valuable forever. This crown, often called the shepherd's crown, will be given in recognition of selfless labor for Christ and His Kingdom.

Second, it is called "the crown of righteousness" (2 Timothy 4:8), for those who have competed righteously, in conformity to God's Word. This crown belongs to those who competed according to God's rules. Paul states, "And also if any one competes as an athlete, he does not win the prize unless he competes according to the rules" (2 Timothy 2:5). This verse teaches that just as an athlete must play according to the rules, so a believer must adhere to the requirements of God's Word if he is to win God's reward.

Third, it is called "the crown of life" (James 1:12), one bringing the highest joy and gladness. A man's time on earth may be full of trials and sorrow. He will walk through the valley of the shadow of death. Perhaps he may even be called upon to die a martyr's death. But in Heaven there awaits him a crown of life, full of joy and happiness. This crown is promised to those who love the Lord.

Fourth, it is called an imperishable wreath (1 Corinthians 9:25), in stark contrast to the perishable fame that the world offers. Its value will not diminish with time.

When we stand before Christ, we will long to hear Him say to us, "Well done, good and faithful servant." The Master's approbation, His approval, is all that will matter. Then Christ will take an incorruptible crown, shining in all its resilient glory, the emblem of God's approval for a race well run, and place it upon our head.

Our hearts will pound with excitement. Tears of joy will flood our eyes. An overwhelming feeling of unworthiness will grip our hearts. We will prostrate ourselves before His throne, awed by this spectacle of Heaven's King and His reward.

After our Lord reviews and judges our life, He will justly determine our eternal reward. Perhaps he will signal one of the angels to bring the crown. He will gracefully place it upon our bowed head.

A sense of our personal unworthiness will immediately grip our hearts. In an act of worship and overflowing adoration (Revelation 4:10), we will then feel compelled to cast our crown back at His feet. We will return the crown to Him, signifying that it was all done from Him, through Him, and to Him (Romans 11:36). He alone called us into the race. He alone empowered us to run the race. He alone was the motivation to serve.

THE GIVER OF THE CROWN

What will make this crown so special? The simple fact that it will come from Jesus Christ. That's all. Just because it will come from Him. It would be meaningful in that Final Day just to receive a tin cup. Because it will come from His hand. The glory is found primarily in the giver of the crown, not in the crown itself.

One of the happiest days of my family's life was when my younger brother, Mark, graduated from the University of Tennessee Medical School. It was an especially meaningful time because my father was a professor on that same faculty. My brother had always wanted to grow up and be a doctor like my dad. (I still faint when I see blood, so medicine was never an option for me.)

My family gathered for Mark's graduation with great pride and anticipation. The graduation service was very impressive, with all the pomp and circumstance of a high academic ceremony. After the commencement address, the graduating class lined up in single file at the front of the stage on which were seated the president of the medical school and the entire faculty. One by one, each of the graduating seniors walked across the platform to receive his or her diploma from the president.

As the moment came for my brother to walk across the platform, our chests were swelling with pride. Buttons were popping. My mother dispatched my sister, with camera in hand, to the foot of the platform for a close-up picture.

As Mark stepped onto the first step of the platform, something strange occurred. Something very unusual. My father, outfitted in his finest academic regalia—a black robe with multicolored doctoral stripes, topped off with doctoral mortarboard—was seated in the faculty section immediately behind the president. He rose to his feet just as Mark prepared to mount the stage. Every eye in the coliseum was riveted on the lonely figure of my dad sliding down his row to the aisle. I thought, *Dad, what in the world are you doing? Wherever you are going, now is the* wrong *time!*

Dad came walking down the aisle and turned left to approach the very center of the platform where the president was standing. Good grief! How embarrassing! Every eye was focused on my dad parading around.

Dad walked right up to the president. My brother proceeded across the stage. Dad took my brother's diploma from the president's hand and, as Mark approached, to our total surprise and absolute amazement, personally handed my brother his doctoral diploma. And shook his hand. My sister's camera flashed.

Unknown to all of us, there was a tradition at the medical school that a faculty member with a child graduating could personally bestow the diploma.

How meaningful to Mark! Not just to receive his diploma. But to receive it from his very own role model, our father.

If I could amplify the emotion and significance of this graduation scene a million times a million, it would fail to capture the full magnitude of that Final Day when we will walk across the stage of eternity. The presiding Judge, the Lord Jesus Christ, is going to be standing there. Our heart will leap out of our chest with excitement when our Savior takes a gold crown, as we come before His throne, and places this incorruptible crown upon our head. And we will hear Him say, "Well done, My faithful servant. You ran the race well and you won."

That day will make all the toil and hard work of running the race become absolutely meaningless. Memories of all the pain, all the sacrifice, all the self-discipline will evaporate. It will all be worth it when Jesus Christ Himself places that crown upon your head. Heaven's Heisman.

What is winning? It is winning God's approval on that Final Day. It is winning Heaven's Heisman.

CHAPTER 3

THE THRILL OF VICTORY (AND THE AGONY OF THE FEET)

✮

O kay, it's time I come clean with you. We're into this book too far to masquerade any longer. I've got to get this off my chest. Confession time.

I don't run.

That's right. I don't even jog. And here I am writing a book about running a race. I dislike almost everything about running. I don't like the pain, the gasping for air, the bursting lungs, the throbbing knees, the sore ankles, the numb arms. I don't like any of it.

Why would anyone jog? Really? Have you ever seen a happy jogger? No, and you never will, either. Runners are always taking their pulse. To make sure they're still alive, I guess.

If God loves me and has a wonderful plan for my life, it cannot include running. No way.

Golf is my favorite sport. With a riding cart. Golf has got to be God's favorite sport, too. Which sport do you think He would bless? One known for Heartbreak Hill or one known for the Amen Corner?

In the early years of my ministry, a young man named Tom Jones joined my church. Tom had been the starting quarterback for the University of Arkansas Razorbacks for the three previous years. He was a great athlete from a very athletic family. Maybe you remember his brother, Bert Jones, the number one pick of the 1974 NFL draft, an all-pro quarterback for the Baltimore Colts.

Tom suggested we start running together several evenings a week. Fresh out of college, Tom was still in impeccable shape. My wife had encouraged Tom to help get me in better shape for preaching (although, trust me, no one has ever accused me of being short-winded in the pulpit). In a moment of insanity, I agreed. Two days later, we met at the local junior high track for our first "workout."

I knew I was in trouble when Tom showed up with a stopwatch. A stopwatch! "I want to check our times for each lap," he said stoically. Good grief! All I wanted was to get my heart rhythm up, and he was turning this into an Olympic tryout.

"Let's run about twelve laps (three miles) and see how we do," Tom said as if a Cotton Bowl bid were still at stake. "No problem," I lied, too prideful to admit I would never make it.

We started jogging with Tom setting the pace. A very fast pace. A pace I might use to run one lap—if I could keep it up. Tom was jogging; I was sprinting.

"One minute, forty-five seconds," he said, as we finished the first lap. All I could think was, "Only eleven laps to go. Lord, we'll never make it."

By the third lap I it felt like I would die. I could barely hold my head up. My mouth was drier than sun-bleached sand. Perspiration was pouring out of my skin. Red and yellow sunspots were blurring my vision. My lips were becoming chapped. My mind was playing games with me: "Quit, you fool. He's ten years younger than you." To which I answered myself, "You're not going to let some kid in your church beat you, are you?"

I looked over at Tom and noticed he had barely broken a sweat. We made eye contact and he smiled at me. Smiled? Good grief, he's enjoying this!

By the fourth lap, I was planning who would speak at my funeral. I was praying for the Second Coming, or any divine intervention. Eight more laps. How can I get out of this?

Finally, I had a breakthrough. "Tom, you look a little tired," I blurted out. "Why don't we stop and fellowship for a while?"

Tom nodded and slowed to a stop. I crashed and burned. Have you ever seen a grown man do a spread eagle on a cinder track? Face down, I mumbled, "Tom, why don't we have some prayer together while I'm down here on my knees."

That was eight years ago, and I'm proud to tell you I have not jogged since. Today, I won't even jog my memory. My nose won't even run.

Why not? Because all my friend Tom could tell me was that if I jogged today, it would add five, maybe ten, years to the end of my life. In other words, my only reward for jogging was a long time off. Jogging wouldn't help me until I was sixty-five years old. The benefit was too far away. Too distant. Too removed.

Now, if Tom had sold me on the present payoff to jogging, I might have taken it up, despite the pain. If he had told me it would help me to sleep better *tonight*, I might have bought into it. Or, if he had told me I would feel better *today* and have more stamina to preach *this Sunday*, I would have gone for it.

The same principle holds true for the spiritual life. Knowing there is a future reward in Heaven is not always enough motivation to keep me running. Not when everything inside me is screaming, "Quit! Drop out of the race!"

You and I must know there is a present-day payoff. Right now. In the here and now. In other words, there's something in it for me *now*.

In the last chapter, I told you about Heaven's Heisman—the future reward awaiting us at the end of the race. This chapter will focus on the present reward. Sure, we know that the heavenly reward is important. But I also want you to know what running God's race will do for your life today. This year. This month. This week. This very day.

GIVING UP ONE KINGDOM TO GAIN ANOTHER

Jesus Himself said there is a present payoff. Listen to the words of the Master: "Truly I say to you, there is no one who has left house or wife or brothers or parents or children, for the sake of the kingdom of God, who shall not receive many times as much *at this time* and in the age to come, eternal life" (Luke 18:29-30, emphasis added).

Did you hear that? "At *this time*!" Right now. Today. In this life. On this earth. Immediately. Plain and simple.

We must ask ourselves, "In what way do I 'receive many times as much at this time'?"

As I unpack these words of Jesus and show you their meaning, I want to first put out a disclaimer. I am not—I repeat, not—espousing a "name it and claim it" Christianity. A health, wealth, and prosperity gospel. You know, "My God shall supply all your *greeds* according to

His riches in glory" (2 Televangelists 4:7).

No way. If "name it and claim it" were the game, Jesus failed to practice what He preached. The Son of Man had no place to lay His head. He possessed only the coat on His back to wear. There was no second home in Egypt. No yacht on the Nile.

So what is Jesus saying?

You will notice a cause and effect. A condition and result. First, we must leave house, wife, brothers, parents, and children. All for the Kingdom of God. Second, we will receive many times as much in this lifetime, and eternal life in the age to come. We must leave behind our kingdom to receive His Kingdom.

Mark's record says, "He shall receive a *hundred times as much* now in the *present age*, houses and brothers and sisters and mothers and children and farms along with persecutions" (Mark 10:30, emphasis added). A hundredfold! Jesus is saying we shall receive hundreds of houses and brothers and sisters and mothers and children and wives. Hundreds of wives. (Think about it!)

What does this mean? Let's take a closer look. In order to understand these passages' meaning, we must look at the context. These verses immediately follow the account of the rich young ruler. Here is how the story begins.

"A certain ruler questioned Him, saying, . . . 'What shall I do to inherit eternal life?' " (Luke 18:18). Don't you wish people were busting your door down, asking that question? He was asking, "What must I do to be saved?"

Who was this man? He was young, rich, and powerful (Matthew 19:20,22). This guy was a walking success story. Honest. Devout. Wealthy. Prominent. Highly respected. Influential. He had everything going for him.

Except God.

Notice how Jesus, the master Evangelist, responded to this man. He used ways that don't quite fit our methodology. No points and a prayer. He just used the Word of God to unmask this upstart's need for a deep transformation of heart. To expose his self-righteousness.

"You know the commandments," Jesus said, listing numbers five through nine. "Do not commit adultery, do not murder, do not steal, do not bear false witness, honor your father and mother" (Luke 18:20).

In other words, Jesus is saying, "Just be perfect."

"All these I have kept from my youth," was the reply. In other words, "No problem here. Why do you ask? Next question, please."

Jesus saw through the outer facade into his heart. To the greed. To the materialism. To the worldliness. To the self-centeredness. What Jesus saw was a bankrupt heart. Empty and void.

With the skill of a deft surgeon, Jesus cuts to the real issue of this man's heart: "One thing you still lack; sell all that you possess, and distribute it to the poor, and you shall have treasure in heaven; and come, follow Me."

No, Jesus was not saying he must buy his way to Heaven. This man's problem was that money and power had become his master. His god. His life pursuit. Jesus was saying, "You must change ships in midstream and follow a new Master. I must become your new Number One. Reassign your life and all your possessions under My authority."

Or it's no deal.

This rich yuppie first looked at his money. Then at Christ. Back to his money. Then back to Christ. Which would it be? It was a moment of decision. Who would be his God? Money or the Master?

The decision was cast. And money and power won.

This young exec turned on his heels and vanished, leaving sad and grieved. His face fell, dejected. Why? Because he could not have it both ways. His money was too much to give up.

Jesus watched him as he faded into the horizon and turned to His disciples saying, "How hard it is for those who are wealthy to enter the kingdom of God!" (Luke 18:24).

Yes, it is hard for the rich to be saved. Hard because they have more "things" to forsake. Hard because they have to stand in line like everyone else and receive a free gift. Hard because they are more tied to this world. Hard because it is hard to forfeit power and control.

How hard?

"For it is easier for a camel to go through the eye of a needle, than for a rich man to enter the kingdom of God," Jesus said.

Now, that is hard. Hard, as in impossible. Camels don't fit through sewing needles. Unless it is in the movie *Honey, I Shrunk the Camel.*

It is impossible for anyone to be saved who wants to keep control of his life and money. Impossible. I-M-P-O-S-S-I-B-L-E!

The disciples took a big gulp and swallowed hard. "Then who can be saved?" they asked.

Jesus explained, "The things impossible with men are possible with God." In other words, only God can save. Man cannot buy his way. Nor earn his way. Nor decide his own terms to follow Christ. Only a gracious work of God in our hearts can pry loose the iron-clad grip of the world to follow Christ.

You can hear the wheels turning inside Peter's head.

Peter said, "Behold, we have left our own homes, and followed You." Interpreted, "Lord, we *have* already done what this yuppie refused to do. We *have* transferred the ownership of all our life and all that we possess to You. We *have* sold out to You. We *have* taken that step of faith to follow You."

Listen to Peter's words once more: "Behold, we have left our own homes, and followed You." What else do you hear? Reading between the lines, I believe Peter is asking, "Lord, what's in it for us?" Or, "Read us the benefit clause of the contract one more time."

Benefits? Jesus responded, "Truly I say to you, there is no one who has left house or wife or brothers or parents or children, for the sake of the kingdom of God, who shall not receive many times as much at this time and in the age to come, eternal life."

This is the benefit clause for following Christ. The payoff for running God's race. There is a benefit at this time, and in the age to come. One present; one future. Houses and family now; eternal life later.

So, what do we gain now?

Presently, we "shall receive a hundred times as much now in the present age, houses and brothers and sisters and mothers and children and farms" (Mark 10:30). Hundreds of houses. Hundreds of wives, brothers, parents, and children.

Here is how it works. When I entered God's Kingdom, I left behind my old life—a life without Christ. I surrendered the control of my life. I reassigned all my life and possessions to Christ. Impeaching self, I enthroned Christ in my heart. I chose greater loyalty to Him than to any earthly relationship, whether with my wife or children, my brothers or parents.

In giving up, I gain far more. I enter God's family and gain a new network of brothers and sisters in Christ. Millions of them around the globe. I also gain welcome in hundreds, even millions, of homes where I now have a common bond and kindred spirit in Christ.

I gain hundreds, even millions, of new spiritual brothers and sisters. I gain their support, encouragement, and strength. As I have needs—whether spiritual, material, emotional, or financial—my new spiritual family rallies to meet my needs. And vice versa. As I see needs in other Christians' lives, I give to help them. All that I possess is theirs because I have already transferred the ownership of all I have to God.

Then, as He makes me aware of others' needs, He prompts my heart to share with them. I give because my possessions no longer belong to me. Neither does my life belong to me. It all belongs to the Kingdom. Lock, stock, and barrel. And it all belongs to those who are in the Kingdom.

Do not write off our Lord's words. This is not communism. The state does not own my possessions. This is Christianity where I, not the government, hold my possessions; but I hold them for God, who owns them all.

Permit me an illustration. Jerry, an old friend of mine, recently swung through Dallas on a business trip and, while there, stayed with me. One day during his visit, he introduced me to some of his friends—Christian businessmen in the Dallas community. Later that evening, Jerry began to recount the generosity of these men in supporting him through some tough times.

Jerry had worked for a Christian ministry in Dallas in which he was to raise his own financial support for salary. As is often the case under such arrangements, Jerry got behind in his salary support. Very far behind. And he had a wife and precious children to feed. And he had a bank that liked to be paid.

Crunch city! Jerry was hurting.

One day Jerry's predicament came to the attention of a Christian man who had become very successful in the restaurant business. This brother told Jerry, "God has blessed me greatly. I believe I should share it with you. I want to financially support you for *x* amount. And, by the way, here are ten other names of businessmen who I believe will support you, too." And they did!

This network of godly businessmen met Jerry's needs. They financially covered his salary so that Jerry could carry out his ministry. But it was so much more than the financial support. Deep friendships were formed. Mutual encouragement was given. Prayer support was established. They gave out of their abundance to help Jerry.

I believe my friend experienced these verses. Jerry and his wife, Becky, left behind a prominent career and comfortable family backgrounds to serve Christ. Yes, they sacrificed a lot to run God's race. Literally, they left house and family to follow Christ.

But didn't God meet their needs? Sure He did. And God did so in the here and now. Not with "pie-in-the-sky" stuff. But with real, tangible help to meet real, tangible needs.

Men, this is precisely what Jesus is saying. If we will leave it all, we will gain it all. If we will give it all up to follow Christ, there is a new network of support into which we enter.

We can receive hundreds of houses. Hundreds of wives, brothers, parents, and children. Today. All by entering into the network of God's Kingdom.

AN ETERNAL BENEFIT

There is also an eternal benefit. It begins right now and continues throughout the ages to come. Yes, an eternal benefit that starts today.

Jesus added to our benefit clause these words, "And in the ages to come, eternal life."

Eternal life? What is it? This refers not to a length of years, but to a quality of life. It is the dimension of the supernatural, the eternal, come to abide in our life. It is not adding years to our life, but life to our years.

This eternal life begins the moment we receive Jesus Christ, as Jesus Himself promised us: "He who hears My word, and believes Him who sent Me, has eternal life, and does not come unto judgment, but has passed out of death into life" (John 5:24). That is present tense, my friend! He who believes *has* eternal life. Right now.

I used to think eternal life began the moment I got to Heaven. If I could just hold out faithful to the end and make it to Heaven, I could slam the door shut behind me. Whew! Safe at last. Now, eternal life will begin.

But that is not what the Bible teaches. Eternal life does not begin once I enter Heaven. It begins now. Today. It began the moment I received Christ into my life. At my conversion eternity invaded my earthly life.

And it continues forever. Throughout the ages to come. Uninterrupted. Never to be forfeited.

Jesus says, "My sheep hear My voice, and I know them, and they follow Me; and I give eternal life to them; and they shall never perish, and no one shall snatch them out of My hand. My Father, who has given them to Me, is greater than all; and no one is able to snatch them out of the Father's hand" (John 10:27-29).

My friend, that is eternal life *forever*! What is settled for eternity can never be undone in time. It is signed, sealed, and delivered.

It begins in this lifetime and continues throughout the ages. We are always safe in the Father's hand. Always secure in the Shepherd's fold.

Specifically, I want to note several key aspects of this eternal life into which we have entered.

First, eternal life means knowing Christ. Now and forever.

Knowing Christ is nothing less than eternal life. Jesus prayed, "And this is eternal life, that they may know Thee the only true God, and Jesus Christ whom Thou hast sent" (John 17:3). Eternal life is a new dimension of living. A new quality of life. A supernatural life. It is the life of God in the soul of man.

It is not just getting man out of hell and into Heaven. It is also getting God out of Heaven and into man.

The moment we enter God's race, we are introduced to a personal knowledge of Christ. And that is only the beginning. We grow to know Christ more intimately each step of the race. While finite man can never completely know an infinite God, we can grow to know Him better. The Apostle Peter writes, "Grow in the grace and knowledge of our Lord and Savior Jesus Christ" (2 Peter 3:18).

It has been my privilege to meet some special, even famous, people. I have personally met Billy Graham and shaken his hand on the platform after he preached to fifty thousand people. I have met Tom Landry in his Cowboy office and interviewed him several times. What a thrill! And I will never forget watching a Cowboy game film with Roger Staubach. I was in awe.

I have met several governors, the world's richest man, and President Reagan's secretary of energy. I have met five Heisman Trophy winners, not to mention hall of famers like Yogi Berra, Reggie Jackson, and Brooks Robinson. I have met golfing greats like Jack Nicklaus and Arnold Palmer.

But let me be frank. Sure, it is something special to meet a famous athlete or politician. But that is nothing compared with knowing Jesus Christ. The greatest privilege in all the world is to know God and His Son, Jesus Christ. This is eternal life (John 17:3). We were made in God's image with the capacity to know Him. Our hearts were made to know Christ. Knowing Christ is the fulfillment of our deepest longing.

Men, some of you are trying to fill that void with other relationships. But none will satisfy like knowing Christ. A round world will not fit in a triangular heart. Augustine said, "Our hearts are restless until they find their rest in God."

Let's clarify what exactly it means to know Christ. The Greek word for *know* (*ginosko*) means experiential knowledge, or what I have come to know by firsthand experience. Knowing Christ means to personally experience a relationship with Him. Internally, intimately, continually. Just like I know another person, I know Jesus Christ. Only much deeper.

Wait a minute. Time out!

I can hear some of you saying, "Hey, Jesus Christ lived two thousand years ago across the ocean in a distant land. He's a part of ancient history. How can I possibly know Him *today*?"

Although Christ was crucified, He rose from the grave. He is alive! We cannot know a dead man. We can only know someone who is alive. Because Jesus Christ is alive today, we can know Him. Personally, deeply, closely. When we receive Christ into our hearts, He comes to live within us (Colossians 1:27). He establishes His royal residence within. His Holy Spirit indwelling gives us the knowledge of Christ.

Knowing Christ is much the same as knowing another person. What are the marks of a close relationship with another person? Intimacy. Communication. Transparency. Self-disclosure. Mutual support. Commitment. Concern for the other person's feelings. All this and more characterizes my relationship with Jesus Christ.

What a world of difference there is between knowing *about* Christ and knowing Christ. It is the difference between mere intellectual assent and experiential knowledge, between knowing with the head and knowing with the heart, between empty religion and eternal life. Knowing Christ is so much more than merely knowing some facts about an important historical figure. To know Christ means to have a personal relationship with Him. Within my heart.

Let me explain. I used to know *about* Augusta National and the Masters Golf Tournament. I had read several books about the Masters. I had talked to others who had played Augusta. I had memorized all the holes. I knew all about its rich history. I was a walking encyclopedia on the Masters. But I had never attended. I only knew about it from a distance.

But then came that glorious day when I traveled to Augusta, Georgia, and was privileged to attend the Masters myself (Amen!). I walked the lush fairways. I climbed the steep Georgian hills. I smelled the blooming azaleas. I felt the crowd's excitement. I met the tour players. I tasted the mystique of the Masters. I experienced it firsthand. What a difference. I had only known about Augusta National with a factual head knowledge. Now it is a personal, firsthand experience.

Multiply that privilege a trillion times a trillion times a trillion. And we only begin to scratch the surface of the privilege of what it means to personally know Jesus Christ in our heart.

How much better to know the Master than the Masters!

Men, God wants us to know Him, first and foremost. He does not want a performance, He wants a relationship. Christ is more interested in us knowing Him than in our performance in the race. Especially if our running is empty and void of a growing intimacy with Christ.

Second, eternal life means God's forgiveness. Now and forever.

Jesus says, "For God so loved the world, that He gave His only begotten Son, that whoever believes in Him should not perish, but have eternal life. For God did not send the Son into the world to judge the world; but that the world should be saved through Him" (John 3:16-17).

Eternal life is a right standing with God. The guilt and burden of our sin is removed. Forgiven. Washed away. Removed. All our sins—past, present, and future—are taken away, and we receive the perfect righteousness of Jesus Christ.

The Apostle Paul writes, "Not having a righteousness of my own derived from the Law, but that which is through faith in Christ, the righteousness which comes from God on the basis of faith" (Philippians 3:9).

The righteousness of God. Just what does that mean? It means, despite being guilty, receiving a right standing before the Holy Judge of the universe. Receiving an acquittal in Heaven's court. Being declared righteous. We are given a perfect standing before God.

If we look through a piece of red glass, everything is red; if we look through a piece of blue glass, everything is blue; if we look through a piece of yellow glass, everything is yellow; and so on. When we believe in Jesus Christ as our Savior, God looks at us through the Lord Jesus Christ. He sees us in all the white holiness of His Son. Our sins are charged to the account of Christ, and His righteousness is charged to our account.

Clearly, this righteousness is not from ourselves. It comes from God. It is not something that we can drum up. We cannot pull ourselves up to Heaven by our bootstraps and gain a right standing before God. Not any more than we can flap our wings and fly to Heaven.

A right standing before God must come from God. It is a free gift that He alone gives to undeserving people like you and me. And this gift is received by faith: "For by grace you have been saved through faith; and that not of yourselves, it is the gift of God; not as a result of works, that no one should boast" (Ephesians 2:8-9).

Jesus Christ alone, by His death on the cross, provides this gift.

Because of His death, the perfect life He lived (remember, He is the only one who has ever lived without sin) is charged to our account in Heaven. Next to our name, God records "the perfect righteousness of Jesus Christ." Once guilty and condemned, we now receive God's righteousness and forgiveness. We are unconditionally accepted. Once forgiven by Christ, God will never bring our sins back up again.

If I gave you a deposit slip for my account and you deposited your money with my deposit slip, it would be posted to my account. I have not earned it. Nor worked for it. It is simply deposited to my account. That is the way salvation occurs for us. When I believe, the righteousness of Christ is deposited into my account in Heaven. I have not earned it, nor worked for it. But it is legally mine. A right standing before God.

A man was telling his close friend about an argument he recently had with his wife. "Oh, I hate it," he said. "Every time we have an argument, she gets historical."

The friend replied, "You mean hysterical."

"No, I mean historical," he insisted. "Every time we argue, she drags up everything from my past and holds it against me."

Aren't you glad God never gets "historical" with us? Once forgiven, He never dredges up our past sins as evidence against us in His courtroom. Indeed, this is unconditional acceptance.

Let me apply this. What does Christ's righteousness have to do with me running God's race? Plenty. It means that I run God's race *not* in order to become right before God. *Not* to gain His acceptance. *Not* to enter His Kingdom. Instead, I run because I am *already* forgiven and accepted by God. Because I have received Christ's righteousness as a free gift, I run out of love—not out of guilt. That, my friend, is a world of difference.

Think of what powerful motivation that is to run to win. I run without the fear of His condemnation at the finish line. Paul writes, "Therefore having been justified by faith, we have peace with God through our Lord Jesus Christ" (Romans 5:1).

If I was running a race and knew there was a strong probability that I would be assassinated at the finish line, how fast do you think I would run? Believe me, not too fast. I would slow down to a snail's pace. I would prolong being shot as long as possible. In fact, I would stop running completely. Anything to avoid being shot. I would absolutely dread the finish line every day of my life. I would even reverse my field and run the other way—anything to avoid the finish line.

But just the opposite is true in God's race. When I run God's race, I receive Christ's perfect righteousness—a right standing before God. Therefore, God awaits me at the finish line with open arms of love and acceptance. He calls me with an encouraging voice. That acceptance impels me each day to run for the glory of God. I run not with a morbid self-preoccupation of how God will receive me, but knowing He already accepts me in Christ. He loves me unconditionally. I am forgiven.

Hallelujah, what a Savior!

Third, eternal life means God's supernatural grace within me. Now and forever. God's grace enables me to live the Christian life. His power strengthens me to run God's race. To pursue the ultimate prize.

Paul says, "I can do all things through Him who strengthens me" (Philippians 4:13).

God's power indwells us in the person of the Holy Spirit, received at the moment of our conversion. Our problem is that we so often fail to tap into His power. But it is always there. We are often like the man who was pushing his car up a hill only to discover he merely needed to turn the key and ignite the powerful engine. How much more efficient to turn on the power and enjoy the ride.

Running is a very demanding sport. Just like life. It drains every ounce of energy a man possesses. Whether we are running God's race or the rat race, it saps all our energy and power. We become drained mentally, emotionally, and physically. That's just the nature of running. It's full of hard knocks and disappointments. Mountains to climb. Obstacles to overcome. The winds of adversity to endure. The scorching sun of trials to zap us.

At times we grow weary. We want to pull over and rest. To sit down and collapse on the bench. To catch our breath. But the race of life keeps moving. We cannot stop. There are no yellow caution flags to stop this race, no pit stops, no halftime rests in the locker room.

Just the daily grind.

We need the power of God to run life's race. What we need, God provides. In our weakness, God's power is perfected. The very same resurrection power of God that raised Jesus Christ from the dead two thousand years ago now raises us to live the Christian life. It now energizes us to run life's race. We are raised to walk a new life in Christ. A resurrection life. An abundant life. A powerful life. An eternal life.

Too often, we are like the man who went into a hardware store one Saturday morning to buy a saw. Seeing an easy mark, the salesman showed him a fancy chain saw. He commented that it was their best seller with the latest in technology, and guaranteed it to cut ten cords of firewood a day.

The inexperienced customer was impressed with the sales hype and bought the chain saw on the spot.

Later that day, this same man returned to the store, chain saw in hand, looking somewhat haggard, exhausted, and exasperated. "Something is wrong with this saw," he moaned. "I worked as hard as I could and only managed to cut three cords of wood. I could do four cords with my old-fashioned saw."

Looking confused, the salesman said, "Here, let me try it on some wood we keep out back." They went to the woodpile, the salesman pulled the cord, and as the motor went "Vvvrooommm," the customer leaped back and exclaimed, "What's that noise?"

Men, we can be much like this exasperated customer, attempting to live the Christian life in our own strength. But we have God's power within us to do the impossible. We have power to resist temptation. Power to love the unlovely. Power to rejoice in trials. Power to overcome the world. Power to resist the Devil. Power to witness for Christ. Power to break old habits. Power to live the Christian life. Power to run God's race.

I recently flew from Charlotte, North Carolina, to Little Rock, Arkansas, via Atlanta, where I was to preach early the next morning. It seems everything is routed through Atlanta. (At the Second Coming, we will be routed through Atlanta.)

Unfortunately, my flight was very late leaving Charlotte, which caused us to circle Atlanta for the longest time. When we finally landed in Atlanta, it was exactly one minute *after* my flight to Little Rock was to leave.

I made a mad dash through the terminal, down the escalator, to the underground tram and got there just in time to miss the departing tram. Great! I had no time to wait for the next one. My only hope was to run to the next terminal, hundreds of yards away. So I took off.

As I ran, dodging unsuspecting travelers, I noticed a moving sidewalk before me. It went all the way to the next terminal. I leaped onto this "skywalker." It began moving me to the next terminal, but still not fast enough. So, I did the only thing a desperate man would do. I began running on the moving sidewalk.

You can't believe how fast I was going on this contraption. I was flying! Passing everybody. Even the tram! I was at the next terminal in no time. I then bounded up the escalator to my terminal and sprinted down to my flight's gate—just as they were closing the plane's door.

I made it! The smiling stewardess said, "I guess you were just supposed to make this flight." (Interestingly, I was flying back to Little Rock to preach on God's providence.)

The moving sidewalk made the difference. It enabled me to run faster and longer than I ever could have in my own strength. The combination of my running and the skywalker moving me forward propelled me like I had been shot out of a cannon. I ran, but with a great power enabling me.

That's it, my friend. That is precisely how the resurrection power of Christ works in my life—and your life. God has a race for us to run, and we are responsible to run it. We must make the effort to put one foot in front of the other. As we do, the power of God energizes us and propels us forward. We are divinely enabled to run faster, longer, and straighter than we ever dreamed.

As we run by faith—yielding our life to Christ—He releases His resurrection power in us. He supernaturally propels us forward to run the race in His power.

Make no mistake about it, I run. I am not passive, but aggressively active. But I run in the resurrection power He provides.

Indeed, this is supernatural power!

Men, do you see the present payoff for running God's race? Do you want this present payoff? You can have it! Now and forever. There is a network of relationships—the family of God—all pulling with you to help meet your needs. Hundreds of houses and family members all for your good. And eternal life is yours. Now and forever. Knowing Christ. The pardon of Christ. The power of Christ.

Not only forever. But now.

Go for it!

RUN FOR YOUR LIFE!

I began this chapter by telling you about Tom Jones, a great quarterback for the Arkansas Razorbacks. I want to conclude by telling you about another great Razorback—Don Horton—who was involved in a play that will forever be etched in Arkansas football history.

The year was 1957. Arkansas and Texas A&M were clashing in the biggest game of the year. The Aggies came to Arkansas undefeated and on a fast tract to a coveted national championship. Coached by the legendary Paul "Bear" Bryant, the Aggies boasted the 1957 Heisman

Trophy winner and future NFL great John David Crow, as well as other noted players like Gene Stallings and Jack Pardee.

Late in the game, Texas A&M was clinging to a 7-6 lead. The Aggies were driving the length of the field for a second touchdown, which would have sealed the victory and paved the way to the national title. And they were keeping the ball on the ground, thus eating up precious time on the clock. Arkansas was out of timeouts, and time was running out. On all counts, the Razorback cause seemed hopeless.

As A&M was but just a few yards away from the game-clinching touchdown, they lined up with a receiver split wide to the left hash mark. He was covered by a lonely Razorback defender, Don Horton.

Then the unthinkable occurred.

Roddy Osborne, the Aggie quarterback, threw a pass into the left flat. Don Horton, the Arkansas defensive back, gambled all the way and stepped in front of the Aggie receiver. Guessing right, Horton intercepted the pass on the dead run. He was now running full speed with the ball heading for the Razorback end zone!

Before him lay ninety yards of green grass, fame, and glory. A national upset. His name surely would be recorded in Arkansas history for as long as football is played in the Ozarks.

Horton, a high school track star with big-time, blazing speed, set off on the run of his life.

As Horton sprinted down the east sideline, the Arkansas student body was on their feet. Cheering. Hollering. Delirious. The Aggies' national championship crown was about to be denied them.

Suddenly—out of nowhere—came a streaking blur. It was Roddy Osborne, the Aggie quarterback who had thrown the interception. Pursuing all the way across the field, he came running like a madman.

Incredibly, Osborne was narrowing the gap. Osborne, blessed with only average speed (he'd probably consider that a compliment), somehow overtook the lightning-fast Horton at the Aggie eighteen yard line, making the game-saving tackle. Even though Osborne had to run farther, he overtook the faster Horton. No one on the field had possessed the speed to catch Don Horton that day. Yet the slow-footed Osborne ran him down.

Arkansas could not score from the eighteen and Texas A&M hung on to preserve the victory, 7-6, and finish the season number one.

After the game, the reporters huddled around Bear Bryant in the Aggie locker room and asked, "How could Roddy Osborne possibly catch Don Horton?"

As only the Bear could answer, he growled, "Horton was only running for the game-winning touchdown. Osborne was running for his life."

My friend, we, too, are running for our lives—motivated not so much by fear—but out of gratitude for such undeserved benefits of God's grace.

We run with a higher calling—a heavenly call—and yet with earthly benefits we can experience today. Right now. In this life. On this earth. Today.

CHAPTER 4

PUMP UP AND AIR OUT!

★

S o you want to run a marathon?

Great! But I need to break some news to you first. This is deeply profound, so you'd better read this sitting down. Ready? No one just wakes up one morning and, on a whim, suddenly decides, "I think I'll run a marathon today." You might as well say, "I think I'll swim the Pacific Ocean today."

Can you imagine anything so ridiculous? If you tried to run a marathon without getting into shape, you would never make it. You would run as far as you could (in my case, about a mile and a half!) and lay down and die.

Do you realize how long a marathon is? Twenty-six-plus miles! My summer vacations aren't that long. You get frequent-flyer miles at that distance. Twenty-six miles? You pass through three time zones. See America! Run a marathon.

Any race that long requires months of rigorous training. Perhaps years. No one would dare to run a marathon without first getting in shape. It is just too demanding. Too long.

Yet this is precisely how many people are living their Christian lives. Running God's race without ever training. Never getting into shape. And dying in the process.

As Christians, we learn from the marathon runner. A runner must be committed to rigorous training to succeed. He must train countless hours if he is to win. Let's turn the sports calendar back again. To the first century.

An Ancient Training Ritual

In the ancient Olympic and Isthmian games, an athlete would begin training ten months before the race. A long-distance runner would submit to rigorous discipline. He would undergo disciplined eating and sleeping habits, an exercise program, and his daily running routine. His goal was clear, his purpose sure: to hone his body into the best possible shape to run. To win.

Then, one month before the games, this athlete would move to Corinth, ten miles from where the Isthmian Games were held. There he would submit to training under the watchful eye of a personal coach. This training meant early rising and long days spent in lifting weights, rigorous exercise, and pushing himself to the limit. All this to prepare for the games and to run the famous marathon.

Any success experienced was due, in largest measure, to the intensity of his preparation. Nowhere is training more important than in the marathon.

So it is in the Christian life.

Men, if we are to run God's race—a lifelong marathon—we must submit to serious training. We must run to win the longest race of our lives, and winning requires discipline.

It was that great theologian (and international diplomat) Bobby Knight who once said, "The will to win is not nearly as important as the will to prepare to win." Amen. We must prepare to win through training, discipline, and hard work.

We entered God's race the day we were converted to Christ. And we will run this race until the day we die. But there is a sense in which we must constantly submit to rigorous spiritual training while we run. If we are to run victoriously, we must discipline ourselves in training.

This chapter is all about training for Heaven's crown. It focuses on the spiritual discipline necessary to prepare to win God's race.

The key passage that epitomizes this spiritual program is 1 Timothy 4:7-11. The Apostle Paul writes, "Discipline yourself for the purpose of godliness; for bodily discipline is only of little profit, but godliness is profitable for all things, since it holds promise for the present life and also for the life to come" (verses 7-8).

Paul is saying, "Get your heart in shape. Strengthen your commitment to Christ. Develop your spiritual muscles. Build up your faith. Get your mind in shape." That involves four key basics: (1) a strong commitment, (2) a special diet, (3) a strenuous workout, and (4) a sure hope.

A STRONG COMMITMENT

First, as a runner, I must be strongly committed to a training program. Training is not easy. Discipline is hard work. If I do not make a solid commitment, I will start the process only to soon falter, fail, and fall by the wayside.

Have you ever decided, "I'm going to start jogging to get in shape?" You probably have at some time.

First, you buy the newest model of jogging shoes. Awesome! They have more gadgets and features than your VCR. And are twice as expensive! Then you buy a running suit. You look great! You are now ready to begin a lifetime of jogging.

You see others jogging. They make it look so effortless. No problem. You think, *I can do it, too. Why didn't I start earlier?*

You map out a course through the neighborhood. It will probably become famous one day after you make it big. Your first track. The price of real estate along your route is sure to go up once *Runners World* finds out where you run.

You are ready to launch your new jogging career. A piece of cake. Two miles, at a slow pace. Everyone at the office knows all about it. You are now an official jogger.

Your first workout is scheduled for early tomorrow morning. Before sunrise. It is your maiden voyage. You go to bed rehearsing your acceptance speech for "newcomer of the year." But in the still quiet of the early morning hours—Buzzzzzzz!—the alarm goes off, sending you through the ceiling. You subconsciously slap the alarm off. It is a lightning-quick chop that would make a karate black belt green with envy. You think, *It is so cold. I'm going to stay under the warm covers. Just a few more minutes.* Before you know it, you have dozed back to sleep. No jogging this morning.

You reschedule your jaunt for tomorrow morning. No problem. Space shuttles are often rescheduled for a later blast-off. But as you are watching the evening news, you hear there is a 10 percent chance of morning showers. *Hmmm, I better not chance it tomorrow*, you think. *I can't afford to get my new shoes wet.*

Day after day, your creativity approaches the genius level as you design new excuses not to run. Finally, after a few isolated runs to the mailbox and back, your aspirations to jog are dead. Your jogging career is history. Ancient history.

What was the problem? Your grand illusions had no commitment. Pure and simple.

It is one thing to feel warm fuzzies about getting in shape. But it is something totally different to discipline yourself morning after morning to run. Training happens only with a strong commitment.

Don't Be a Spiritual Couch Potato

Commitment is a lost word today. What is commitment? For too many of us, commitment is a task we are absolutely, positively, unequivocally going to do—until something easier or better comes along. But real commitment is making a solid agreement to do something in the future—no matter what. Regardless. Sink or swim. It is being firmly obligated to a task or person.

Too many Christians are spiritual "couch potatoes." Fat, flabby, and fleshy. For these gospel blimps, commitment to spiritual discipline means nothing. They have passing moments of great intentions, but zero commitment to get in shape.

They are content to be season-ticket holders at church, but never seem to get out of the starting blocks. They are professional spectators, but amateur runners.

Serious training begins with counting the cost. Jesus says, "For which one of you, when he wants to build a tower, does not first sit down and calculate the cost, to see if he has enough to complete it? Otherwise, when he has laid a foundation and is not able to finish, all who observe it begin to ridicule him, saying, 'This man began to build and was not able to finish'" (Luke 14:28-30).

Men, it will cost to be God's champion. The price is never marked down. Godliness is never on sale. No "cash-and-carry" deals. It always requires paying the full price of hard work and strenuous exercise. Plus tax.

The Cost of Commitment

What will it cost us? Spiritually, it will cost us time, hard work, and self-denial.

First, it will require a commitment of our time to work out in the Word of God. It will require our time in prayer. Prayer and Bible study must be fixed priorities in our scheduling. Nonnegotiable. It will require bringing our schedule into submission to our spiritual goals.

Time has been called a seamstress specializing in alterations. Let me warn you. Don't cut out Bible study and prayer. Not if you want to win.

Are you willing to pay this price?

Second, it requires hard work. It will require studying God's Word. Study demands our intense concentration in the Scriptures. It takes mental energy to remain focused and memorize Scripture.

Are you willing to pay this price?

Third, it requires self-denial. It will require saying no to the world and yes to God. It will require resisting the Devil and obeying God. It means I must decrease and He must increase.

Are you willing to pay this price?

If the answer is yes, then purpose in your heart to take this first step out of the starting block. Drive the stake down. By God's grace say, "I will pay the price to get into the Word. No matter what the cost."

Just do it!

Men, remember paying the price has eternal dividends. Working out in God's Word and prayer is like making a deposit in the bank. You are investing in your future. And one day there will be a spiritual payoff. With compound interest. You will be crowned a champion for Christ.

What most characterizes a true champion is his heart. His will to win. His resolve to train. His determination to pay the price. The difference lies in the heart.

A man once went to his high school reunion, accompanied by his twenty-year-old son. He could hardly wait to find his old football coach and show off his muscular son, who was now playing college ball.

After introducing his son, the beaming father asked the coach, "Who is the bigger man?"

The coach looked at the aging man, now bald and bulging. Then at his growing, bulky son. Clearly, the son was now bigger, taller, and stronger.

But the coach suddenly grabbed the father's chest, clutching his shirt right over his heart. He said, "This is how I still measure a man. By his heart."

Men, this is how God measures a man. By his heart. A long-distance race goes not to the swiftest of foot, but to the strongest of heart.

In 1 Samuel 16:7, the Lord tells us plainly, "Do not look at his appearance or at the height of his stature . . . man looks at the outward appearance, but the LORD looks at the heart."

The first step toward winning the crown of life is making a heart commitment to pay the price in rigorous training.

A SPECIAL DIET

Second, Paul refers to the importance of nourishment in the Word. He says we are to be "constantly nourished on the words of the faith and of the sound doctrine" (1 Timothy 4:6). As a proper, balanced diet is critical to a marathon runner, so it is to the Christian.

I am the last person in the world to talk about this. I eat from the three basic food groups—McDonald's, Wendy's, and Burger King. I have a personality clash with vegetables. They don't like me, and the feeling is mutual. But a champion runner must rise above such "oddities" and maintain a special diet for energy and health.

Strenuous workouts can burn an extra 1500 calories a day. Without a high-energy diet, fatigue will take over and prevent him from reaching his goal. But the fatigue factor can be avoided through a strict diet.

Just as carbohydrates provide fuel for the body, so the Word of God provides high-energy food for the Christian. Spiritual fatigue can be avoided through nourishment from the living and abiding Word.

Nourished is the key word here. Nourishment means that we are feeding on the right food—God's Word—and digesting it into our spiritual system. It means drawing the needed nutrients and energy supply from God's Word to run God's race with endurance.

We must be constantly nourished on God's Word. Not a sporadic meal here and there. But constantly feeding on the Scriptures. Daily.

Irregular eating habits will kill a runner's energy level. Skipping meals can leave him drained and fatigued. This same thing will happen with our spiritual stamina if we do not maintain consistent, regular feeding on God's Word. Daily.

We should set aside time every day to read and devour God's Word. At least fifteen minutes each day is needed. Probably more. We must constantly feast on God's Word to have the daily energy needed to run God's race.

The Apostle Peter writes, "Like newborn babes, long for the pure milk of the word, that by it you may grow in respect to salvation" (1 Peter 2:2). God's Word, like nutritious milk, contains what is needed to produce spiritual growth and maintain our health. So, crave it. Long for it.

Jesus says, "Man shall not live on bread alone, but on every word that proceeds out of the mouth of God" (Matthew 4:4). God's Word, like bread, is the basic staple of a Christian's diet. It is our true daily bread. So, devour it.

Paul refers to God's truth as "milk" and "solid food" (1 Corinthians 3:2). Like meat and solid food, Scripture is necessary for spiritual growth and development. So, feast on it.

David testified, "How sweet are Thy words to my taste! Yes, sweeter than honey to my mouth!" (Psalm 119:103). God's Word, like honey, is sweet, satisfying, and provides lasting energy. So savor it.

Jeremiah wrote, "Thy words were found and I ate them, and Thy words became for me a joy and the delight of my heart" (Jeremiah 15:16). We must feed our minds and nourish our hearts on Scripture. So, enjoy it.

Men, the Bible remains the "breakfast of champions." We must eat at God's training table and be nourished by His Word. Daily.

Five Daily Nutrients

Let me suggest five strategic steps for consistent spiritual nourishment in the Scriptures. Remember! These require commitment! Discipline!

Master the Word

The first step is to *master God's Word*. We must read and study God's Word to strategically grasp its truth. Paul says, "Be diligent to present yourself approved to God as a workman who does not need to be ashamed, handling accurately the word of truth" (2 Timothy 2:15).

This requires having a game plan to read the Bible. The "lucky dip" method of randomly opening the Bible and reading a passage here and there will never work. I heard about a man who read his Bible using the "lucky dip" method. He randomly opened it and read, "Judas went out and hung himself." Hmmm. He then opened it again. He read, "Go and do likewise." More confused, he plopped his Bible open one more time and read, "What you do, do quickly." The "lucky dip" method can get you into a lot of trouble.

Instead, read through an entire book in the Bible, rather than bits and pieces here and there. Or perhaps daily read a few chapters of an Old Testament book and then chapters of a New Testament book. Follow this pattern until you have finished both books. Or, read the same book in the Bible through several times consecutively. Each reading will reveal new and hidden truths.

As you read God's Word, give attention to the context, key words (especially those that are repeated, significant, and theological), and historical setting. These will shed more light on the verses you are reading.

You will want to pay special attention to the following: Who is speaking? To whom is he speaking? What is the historical setting? What was the intended application for that day? What does it mean to me today?

Ask God, as the psalmist does, to open your spiritual eyes to His truth: "Open my eyes that I may behold wonderful things from They law" (Psalm 119:18). Ask Him to plant His message in your heart, like precious seed in the soil, so that it will germinate, sprout, and bear fruit. Ask the Holy Spirit to enlighten your mind and direct your life accordingly.

Magnify the Word

The second step is to *magnify God's Word*. Recognize its authority. When the Bible speaks, God speaks. Give it a place of preeminence in your life. Obey its commands. Follow its examples. Apply its principles. Claim its promises. Heed its warnings.

Follow Paul's advice to the believers at Colosse: "Let the word of Christ richly dwell within you" (Colossians 3:16). Allow Scripture to settle down and be at home in your hearts. Make it the absolute authority of your life. Permit it to set deep roots into your heart. And it will bear precious fruit in your life.

Obey it. Live it. Follow it.

Memorize the Word

The third step is to *memorize God's Word*. We must regularly deposit God's Word in our heart by memorizing it. The psalmist testified, "Thy word I have treasured in my heart, that I may not sin against Thee" (Psalm 119:11). To treasure His Word means to hide it, like a valuable buried treasure, in your heart.

Memorizing God's Word allows the Holy Spirit to better reprove, correct, and train us to win the race. Hide it in your heart, and your heart will never be the same.

Our Lord Jesus Christ memorized much of God's Word. Probably all of it. But most importantly, He used it. He was able to use it because it was hidden in His heart. He carried it with Him wherever He went. In the wilderness, our Lord was tempted three times by Satan, and each time He resisted by quoting God's Word. He said, "It is written. . . . It is written. . . . It is written" (Matthew 4:4,7,10).

If Jesus Christ, the perfect Son of God, memorized God's Word, we certainly need to do likewise. We need to memorize God's Word if we are to run victoriously.

Meditate on the Word

The fourth step is to *meditate on God's Word.* Meditation suggests digesting the meal you have eaten. The word *meditate* pictures a cow chewing its cud throughout the day. Over and over. Sucking out every drop of tasty juice and healthy nutrients. We, too, must chew on God's Word over and over until we understand it better, appreciate it more fully, and grasp its meaning for our lives.

As the psalmist declares, "Thy servant meditates on Thy statutes. . . . Make me understand the way of Thy precepts, so I will meditate on Thy wonders" (Psalm 119:23,27).

Minister the Word

The fifth step is to *minister God's Word.* God has committed to all believers the message of reconciliation (2 Corinthians 5:19). As ministers of reconciliation, we must use God's Word to minister to others in the name of Christ. When we counsel others, we must use the wisdom of God's Word. When we encourage others, it is the comfort of God's Word we share. And when we confront others, we use the authority of God's Word to challenge their lives.

The more we minister God's Word, the more it becomes a part of us. All believers are to be ministers for Christ, ministering His Word (Ephesians 4:12). Whether from a church pulpit, a business office, a school classroom, or wherever, we are all to be about the business of sharing and teaching God's Word.

These five steps are all necessary for a healthy spiritual life. There must be not only a constant intake, but also an outflow, of God's Word from us into the world.

Our lives will be either like a stagnant swamp or a mighty river. A stagnant swamp has an inflow but no outflow. The water just sits there. Going nowhere. Soon the stagnant water begins to stink. This swamp pictures a Christian life with much inflow of God's Word, but with no outflow into the lives of others. The Word just sits there, self-contained. Lifeless. Stinking.

Conversely, a mighty river is characterized by constant movement and flow. The water is not stagnant, but always moving. As soon as it flows into a given area, it flows right on. This pictures a believer's life where the Scriptures are constantly flowing in and through a willing heart, touching and impacting others. This healthy dynamic is the final stage of a spiritual diet.

STRENUOUS WORKOUT

The third step in training is rigorous exercise. Strenuous workout. Paul says, "On the other hand, discipline yourself for the purpose of godliness; for bodily discipline is only of little profit, but godliness is profitable for all things, since it holds promise for the present life and also for the life to come" (1 Timothy 4:7-8).

The word *discipline* means exercise, training, working out. It actually means to work out in a gym. It comes from the same word from which we have derived the English word *gymnasium*, which literally means to be naked. Discipline originally meant stripping down for the purpose of working out. Young athletes worked out in the nude for freedom of movement, and the gymnasium was the place where they trained. So, discipline came to mean the strenuous training in a gymnasium, which helped the athlete get in shape.

Every successful athlete must train and work out. No exceptions. He must exercise, lift weights, do stretching exercises, situps, pushups, and pullups. All to get into shape and keep his muscles toned.

"Discipline yourself," Paul says. This is something I myself must do. It is my personal responsibility. No one else can discipline me. As an act of my will, I must choose to engage the training process.

This discipline is "for the purpose of godliness." Spiritual discipline produces godliness, or devotion to God. Godliness is the virtue of heartfelt reverence and piety toward God. It is loving God and becoming like God.

Sure, bodily discipline is profitable. It strengthens the body and builds character. But it is "only of little profit" because it only develops the body (not the spirit) for now (not for eternity). But spiritual discipline is profitable for all things. For body, soul, and spirit. For time and eternity. Paul says, "It holds promise for the present life and also for the life to come" (verse 8). Spiritual training is far more important because it impacts all of my life. Forever.

The Power Hour
When I think of discipline, I think of our football team's off-season conditioning drills at Texas Tech. Our winter workouts (January,

February, and March) prepared us for the fall football season (September, October, and November). The victories of the football season were often won months earlier in the winter training program. Any advantage we could achieve through conditioning our bodies would often mean the difference between victory and defeat.

Our daily workout program was divided into four fifteen-minute periods. We called it the "Power Hour," a demanding training program designed to develop and train every aspect of the athlete.

First, there was the *weight-lifting room*. This was designed to build our bodily strength. To make us strong. Specially designed weight machines could accommodate three or four athletes, each working on a separate exercise.

The athletes advanced through the weight room, pumping the weights as many times as they could. We moved from one machine to the next, like a long train winding through a valley.

This was all designed to build up our muscles. Every exercise had specific muscles it was designed to bulk up and strengthen. No muscle was overlooked or left dormant.

Like a weight machine, the Word of God functions to build up our faith and strengthen our commitment to Christ. Paul affirmed, "The word of His grace . . . is able to build you up" (Acts 20:32). He said that the Word preached and taught is profitable for "the building up of the body of Christ" into a growing knowledge of Christ and Christlikeness (Ephesians 4:12-13). Only the Word of God can do this.

Building Spiritual Agility

Second, there was the *agility room*. This was designed to develop body control, coordination, agility, and quickness. In a fast and furious fifteen minutes, athletes would run in place, roll sideways, and somersault backward and forward, all to the response of a coach's signal.

We were able to do things with our body that we never dreamed possible.

Similarly, we must discipline ourselves to be immediately responsive to the leadership of the Holy Spirit. And to the direction of God's Word. We must quickly respond with our entire being—heart, eyes, body, mind, feet—to God's direction for our lives.

We must respond with our hearts: "You shall love the Lord your God with all your heart, and with all your soul, and with all your mind" (Matthew 22:37).

We must respond with our eyes, "fixing our eyes on Jesus, the author and perfecter of faith" (Hebrews 12:2).

We must respond with our body: "Present your bodies a living and holy sacrifice" (Romans 12:1).

We must respond with our minds: "Set you mind on the things above, not on the things that are on earth" (Colossians 3:2).

We must respond with our feet: "How beautiful are the feet of those who bring glad tidings of good things!" (Romans 10:15).

Building Spiritual Quickness

The third workout station was the *wind sprints*. These were run on the football field itself and were designed to develop our speed and quickness.

We would line up and run fifty-yard wind sprints at a coach's signal. We would have about thirty seconds to catch our breath. Then another coach would signal us to sprint back to the first coach. This would be repeated quickly for the entire fifteen-minute period. (I still break out in a sweat just thinking about this.)

Speed is vitally important to any athlete. And speed is critical in the Christian life. We must be quick to *hear* God's Word. James instructs us to be "quick to hear, slow to speak and slow to anger" (James 1:19).

We must be quick to *obey* His call. Delayed obedience is no obedience. Mark tells us, "And they immediately left the nets and followed Him" (Mark 1:18).

And we must be as quick to *share* God's Word as Jesus was: "And they went into Capernaum; and immediately on the Sabbath He entered the synagogue and began to teach" (Mark 1:21).

Building Spiritual Endurance

The fourth workout station was *running the stadium bleachers*. Running the long climb to the top of the stadium and then back down was the chosen method of self-inflicted torture. The purpose was to build up our stamina, endurance, and perseverance, not to mention our character. We were ready to die, but we kept pressing on. We couldn't just quit.

The Christian life is likewise a long, uphill climb. It is protracted obedience. Paul urges his Philippian readers to "press on toward the goal for the prize of the upward call of God in Jesus Christ" (Philippians 3:14). Always upward.

All training requires our strenuous effort. We cannot be halfhearted about it. No weak sisters here. Getting in shape for a marathon requires all-out effort and exercise.

Paul states, "It is for this we labor and strive" (1 Timothy 4:10). For what do we labor and strive? For discipline. Spiritual discipline. In other words, I must labor and strive in all my disciplines.

No athlete can effectively train who has an aversion to pain. No pain, no gain. He must labor and strive in his training and workouts. "Labor" means to work to the point of exhaustion. It means to push oneself to the limit. "Strive" is an athletic word meaning to agonize in an athletic contest. It pictures the pain involved in working out and competing. So much so that the first-century marathon was simply called the *agon*. Because it was so agonizing.

All four areas of training are needed. Not two or three, but all four. We must build up our strength through God's Word, prayer, and perseverance under trials. We must develop our body control through our sensitivity to the Holy Spirit's guidance. We must increase our speed by being quick to obey the Word. And we must increase our endurance through our faithful service to Christ, if we want to be champions.

A SURE HOPE

Men, training is hard work—but not without hope. A runner must believe that his training will pay positive dividends. Because it does! No athlete would work out with consistency and intensity if he did not strongly believe, deep down inside, that training would help his chances of winning the race.

He must have hope—a steadfast confidence about the future. He must possess, and be possessed by, a hope that his long hours of training will bring him a reward. It was the hope of winning a crown that kept his fires of motivation burning brightly through the rigors of training.

This is precisely what Paul says as he continues, "Because we have fixed our hope on the living God, who is the Savior of all men, especially of believers" (1 Timothy 4:10). Paul knew his discipline was worth it because it would yield a reward. His hope was set, not on himself, but on the living God.

As we discipline ourselves for godliness, and labor and strive to be godly, we must have hope in God, burning brightly within, that He will infuse and motivate our training.

In a word, hope is a confidence—a God-confidence—that the race will go well. If I train well, I *will* win the race. If I discipline myself, I *will* one day taste His victory.

I had that hope years ago in "two-a-days."

For those of you who have ever played high school or college football, the memory of two-a-days still sends a chill up your spine. It causes you to break out in a cold sweat. Or hives. Or worse.

Those August preseason practices—scheduled twice a day—were so tough, so demanding, so grueling that they separated the men from the boys.

While other students were going to the lake—or on summer vacation—those who were a part of the team went through the ordeal of two-a-days.

I experienced them at two levels. First in high school, then in college. Both were hell. In high school, we went south to Greenwood, Mississippi, for an entire week of two-a-days. We took over a deserted Air Force base—sleeping in barracks, eating in the mess hall, and practicing on the massive marching field.

Have you ever been in the Mississippi Delta in August? Humid. Steamy. Hot. You break out into a sweat just lying on your bunk.

For a solid week, all we did was practice. We scrimmaged against each other. Goal-line offense for thirty minutes. Goal-line defense. Punt coverage. Kickoff coverage. Passing game. Running game. Tackling practice. Blocking practice.

It was unreal.

Actually, we had three-a-days. Seven to nine in the morning. One to three-thirty in the afternoon. Six to eight at night.

No feeling compares with putting on a pungent, sweat-filled jersey. Then, putting on pads that you can squeeze the sweat out of, like slime out of a dirty sponge. Sweat, a few hours old, is the only thing cold on a hot August Mississippi day.

Why would anyone in his right mind subject himself to a week of insanity like this? Only one thing drove us to do so. A commitment to prepare for victory.

Training today means victory tomorrow.

Then, in college, I played for Texas Tech University. That's the good news. The bad news is that Texas Tech is located in western Texas. That meant two-a-days under the blistering, scorching hot Texas sun. In August.

While all my classmates were sitting in air-conditioned homes or offices, we were working out in an empty stadium to prepare for the season.

The first day back meant running the "Red Raider Mile." We had to run it under an individually assigned time—or not have the "privilege" of participating in two-a-days.

We had an Astroturf playing field. Playing on it was like playing on a hot skillet. Literally. As you looked across the field, you could barely see the other goal line because of the August heat rising from the synthetic turf.

No one would dare walk on the field barefoot. Two pairs of socks and taped ankles were the only way to avoid heat blisters. One day we put a thermometer on the field and the mercury shot up to 110 degrees and burst the glass.

So there we were. Practicing twice a day in this inferno. Killing ourselves. Busting our rears. Pushing ourselves beyond danger limits. Suffering sunstrokes. Ignoring dehydration. Ignoring exhaustion. Ignoring leg cramps. Going on despite seeing red, yellow, and orange sunspots. Losing five to ten pounds a day in body liquids. Finding new personal limits every day.

Why would any sane person do this? (It sure made a golf scholarship look pretty good!)

I'll tell you why. Because victory always comes at a price. A high price. You must pay the cost of discipline. Training. Working out. Getting in shape. Sacrifice.

Training today means victory tomorrow.

Men, what is true in the world of athletics is equally true in the Kingdom of God. Spiritual victory always comes at a price. A high price. Like football or any other sport, it requires our discipline, training, and getting in shape. It requires working out and preparing one's self to compete.

Maybe you are saying to yourself, "I don't think I can discipline myself to undergo such rigorous training. I've never gone through this kind of training. The task seems to be too big to get in shape."

My friend, I want to encourage you with some wonderful news. We have a Coach who is in the business of taking raw rookies like you and me and molding us into world champions. He has an unparalleled record at producing winners who submit to His leadership.

His name? Jesus Christ.

Our Lord took some burly fishermen two thousand years ago and, like a coach, whipped them into shape. He disciplined them so much that He called them disciples. And they became worldbeaters.

Jesus can do the same in your life. The only prerequisite is to submit to His leadership. And allow Him to train you for the task. He is able to discipline you and prepare you to run the race to win.

Right now, yield your life to Jesus Christ. Allow Him to make you and mold you into the champion He created you to be. For His glory.

CHAPTER 5

HOMECOURT ADVANTAGE

"**D**EE-fense! DEE-fense!"

The Boston Garden crowd is on its feet. Vocal. Rowdy. In a frenzy. The place is rocking. It's the homecourt advantage.

The Celtics have battled back from a fourteen-point deficit against the Los Angels Lakers. Twelve unanswered points by the Celtics leave Boston only two points back. Momentum is now wearing a kelly green jersey.

"DEE-fense! DEE-fense!"

The Lakers are on the attack, desperately clinging to their lead. Suddenly, Larry Bird strips the ball from Magic Johnson and hits Dennis Johnson with a quick outlet pass. Instantly, the Celtic fastbreak is in fifth gear. Kevin McHale and Bird fill the lanes. Robert Parish is trailing. Only two Lakers are back.

DJ pulls up at the top of the key. He shuffles his feet. Looks left. Then, lightning-fast, he dishes the ball right to Larry Bird. Instinctively, Bird pulls up at the three-point line. He pulls the trigger. The ball arcs a perfect rainbow toward the goal. Bottom! The ref signals a three pointer. The Celtics are now up by one!

The Garden crowd explodes. The roar is deafening. Fifteen unanswered points, and the Lakers are visibly shaken. The Celtic fans have died and gone to Heaven.

"DEE-fense! DEE-fense!"

The Lakers' Magic Johnson works the ball back up court. Dribbling with his right hand, Magic motions the offense with the left. He shouts instructions to James Worthy. But who can hear? Not with this crowd. It's the homecourt advantage.

"DEE-fense! DEE-fense!"

The Celtics overplay their men and cut off all the passing lanes. The Laker offense is shut down. Stalled. Put a fork in them; they're done.

"DEE-fense! DEE-fense!"

The twenty-four second clock has ticked down to three seconds. In desperation, Magic signals for a timeout in surrender. The Celtics come off the court, and the Garden crowd is at a fever pitch. You can just feel the electricity in the air. Cheering, whistling, foot stomping. A standing ovation. It's the homecourt advantage.

This is the Boston Garden. When you are talking homecourt advantage, you are talking the Boston Garden.

There is no place in all of basketball like it. Other cities have new, lavishly furnished arenas with comfortable theater seats. Places that, from the outside, look like upside-down spaceships.

Not Boston. They have the Garden. Built in 1928, this hallowed shrine is the most revered homecourt in the game, now as much a part of Boston's storied history as the Old North Church and Bunker Hill.

So much tradition is here. So much nostalgia. The Celtics' world championship banners hang from the rafters above. Sixteen of them. The retired numbers of Celtics past grace the rafters—Cousey's 14, Russell's 6, Havlicek's 17.

The parquet wooden floor. Checkerboard fashion. Chipped, scarred, and bloodied. The Celtic logo is painted on the center-jump circle. With the green leprechaun smiling and balancing a basketball on his finger.

But most of all, Boston Garden is the crowd. The roar. The noise. The intimidation factor. A multitude—14,890 people—rising to their feet cheering.

Homecourt advantage? You better believe it.

Don't Leave Home Without It

What is this phenomenon? It is playing before home fans who are fanatically cheering. Like crazy. It is the emotion that lifts the home team to a higher level of play. It is a confidence builder transmitted from the crowd to the players. Don't leave home without it.

It is the homecourt advantage. When playing at home, you feel like you can never be beaten. No deficit is too big. No opponent too imposing. No odds too insurmountable. It gets your heart pounding, your adrenaline flowing, your confidence soaring.

Who wouldn't love to play before a hair-raising crowd like this? Be honest. Just once, to hear the roar of the crowd. Cheering for *you*! Just once, to feel the surge of emotion pulsate through your body. Sure you would.

Well, you *can*.

Not at the Boston Garden. But someplace far greater. Before fans more fanatical. You can play before a home crowd far more enthusiastic than the Boston Garden.

I am talking about running before Heaven's grandstands and receiving the applause of Heaven. The homecourt advantage of Heaven causes all earthly applause to pale into insignificance.

The Bible says, "Therefore, since we have so great a cloud of witnesses surrounding us, let us also lay aside every encumbrance, and the sin which so easily entangles us, and let us run with endurance the race that is set before us" (Hebrews 12:1).

Did you get that? God's Word is saying that as we run, we are surrounded by "so great a cloud of witnesses." The imagery is clear. When we become Christians, we enter a heavenly arena. We run before a packed stadium. The crowd is cheering. Like crazy. The roar is deafening. Maddening.

Maybe you are saying, "I don't ever recall hearing Heaven cheer for me. The last time I obeyed God, or resisted a temptation, there was no roar in my ears."

Men, we must be tuned into Heaven's roar. We must hear with spiritual ears. In this chapter, I want to amplify the applause of Heaven. I want to turn the volume up so that it is unmistakable.

THE HEAVENLY CROWD

First, we must identify Heaven's homecourt advantage. Who's in this "cloud of witnesses"? Where are they?

They are *not* angels, sitting on clouds, plucking their harps, playing Heaven's fight song to the tune of the Notre Dame "Victory March." They are *not* seraphim with golden pom-poms and emerald jeweled megaphones, shouting, "Give me a J . . . add an E . . . try an S . . . U . . . S. What have you got? JESUS! Say it again. JESUS!"

Not hardly.

They are *not* B-team believers who did not make the varsity but are cheering us from the sidelines. They are not holding up "John 3:16" signs to us from the grandstands (like that omnipresent person on television who holds those signs up at pro football games and golf tournaments).

I don't think so.

So, who is this "cloud of witnesses"?

These witnesses are members of God's "Hall of Faith" named in Hebrews 11 who have run God's race victoriously. They won Heaven's prize. They are champions—winners of Heaven's Heisman; stalwarts of the faith; God's heroes who have taken their place in Heaven's grandstands.

The picture here is of an earthly saint running life's race in the heavenly arena. As weariness begins to slow him down, he hears the cheers of these great men and women, now in Heaven, shouting words of hope and encouragement. Their applause transmits inspiration and a second wind. Suddenly, he is propelled forward with renewed strength and hope.

This is Heaven's homecourt advantage.

Let's focus now on Hebrews 11. The chapter is called "God's Hall of Fame" or "God's Hall of Faith." It is a record of the Old Testament believers who victoriously lived by faith.

Call the roll of Hebrews 11 and it's like a who's who of the Old Testament. Winners like Abel, Enoch, and Noah. Heroes like Abraham, Isaac, Jacob, and Joseph. Victors like Moses' parents, Moses, Joshua, and Rahab. Champions like Gideon, Barak, Samson, and Jephthah. Conquerors like David, Samuel, and the prophets. These are the "cloud of witnesses."

Heaven's Homecourt

Can you hear them yet? The champions of old. They are cheering for *us*! Heaven is in a frenzy. On their feet. Clapping. Stomping. Whistling. Encouraging *us* onward. This is Heaven's homecourt advantage.

They have faced every formidable foe we face. They won by faith. They *know* we can win by faith. They are yelling, "Go for it! Trust God! You can do it."

Today, we are living at the end of the age. We may well be running the last lap of history. All the saints down through the ages are now in Heaven. Heaven's grandstands have never been so packed. The Apostle

Paul is there. So are Martin Luther and George Whitefield. John Calvin and John Wesley. Your grandfather who knew Christ. Perhaps your mother. Your brother. All these champions are there cheering us on. We may be running the final race of history.

What encouragement this is to run. To not falter. To win!

In school, I ran anchor on our relay team. Every school in Fort Worth, Texas, entered several relay teams in a big, year-end, city-wide track meet.

After each event, athletes who were done competing would sit in the grandstands. Gradually, the stands became fuller and fuller. When it came time for the final race, *everyone* was in the stands. Momentum built as the fastest runners toed their marks for this once around-the-track finale. Before the biggest crowd. To win the most cherished prize.

As anchor, I was running against the fastest kids in town. I was nervous (but I loved it!).

Runners to their mark. . . . Get set. . . . Boom! The runners exploded out of the starting blocks. As they entered the backstretch, it was too tight to determine the lead. Four schools were tied. And one of them was *us*!

Into the last curve came the runners. Stride for stride. Nip and tuck. It was up to me.

I turned my eyes down the track and began to accelerate as the baton was placed into my hand. With eyes riveted on the finish line, I was propelled by the crowd as they rose to their feet and cheered me on. The roar of the crowd scared me! My heart leaped out of my chest. I ran like the wind.

Never looking back, never faltering, one thought in mind—to win—I pushed through the finish tape. Only then did I glance over my shoulder. We had won! The crowd was cheering.

I remember looking up into the stadium. My teammates were cheering and yelling. We won the race, the track meet, and the bragging rights around town. It was sweet!

Men, you and I are running a race—God's race—and Heaven's grandstands are packed and cheering us on. Our hearts ought to leap out of our chests!

Do you hear the crowd? Are you inspired by their urging?

Moses is yelling, "Go for it!" David is waving his fist and saying, "You can do it!" Joshua cups his hands and shouts, "Go forward by faith! Run with all your might!"

It's the homecourt advantage.

THE SILENT CHEERS

"Time out!" I hear you saying. "Are you telling me I'm supposed to hear voices? I've never heard any audible voices. Not once. All I hear are grunts and groans as my feet relentlessly pound the ground." Or, you may be thinking, "Hey, *I've* never won a race! I never hear anyone cheering!"

You are right. There are no audible voices to hear. Heaven's applause is a silent applause. Let me explain.

This passage does *not* say that these people actually watch us from Heaven. It does *not* say they are witnessing the race. I am afraid watching me run would be more hell than Heaven.

Hebrews 12:1 says they are bearing a witness to us. Their lives— the way they ran the race—silently scream encouragement to us. They are not watching us; they are inspiring us by the testimony of their lives. They are demonstrating to us that faith is the victory. They have run God's race by faith—often through impossible circumstances—and have endured victoriously. This should inspire us to follow in their footsteps.

These witnesses—Abraham, Moses, Joshua, and all the rest—put their faith in God and won the victory. So can we. Their examples cheer us on. But it is a silent cheer. It is not their voices we hear. It is their lives we observe which motivate and inspire us.

Since we cannot actually hear the cheers, we need to look carefully at the example of their lives.

A Walk Through Heaven's Grandstand

Let's walk through Heaven's grandstands now and "hear" what these heroes are saying to us.

Hebrews 11 is all about faith. The chapter begins, "Now faith is the assurance of things hoped for, the conviction of things not seen" (verse 1). Faith is the total commitment of one's life to God. It is an inner confidence and conviction that God will fulfill His promises. The word *faith* means belief, trust, confidence. It is taking God at His Word and living daily on that basis.

Chuck Swindoll says, "Faith is confidence in God; the firm conviction that He is at work and will come through on our behalf. Faith is not a blind leap into the dark, nor is it wishful positive thinking or presumption."[1]

Warren Wiersbe adds, "True faith is confident obedience to God's

Word in spite of circumstances and consequences."[2]

As we look at these champions, let's be reminded that these are people like you and me. Warts and all. People who knew failure as well as success.

Noah got drunk. David committed adultery. Abraham told lies. Sarah laughed at God. Moses was a murderer. Jacob was a deceiver. Rahab was a harlot. Despite their momentary failures, they overcame by faith and won the race.

We can overcome by faith, too. Remember, we have the homecourt advantage.

Let's meet the heroes. Let's hear from them.

Abel: "Worship by Faith!"

First, let's hear from Abel, who is seated in Heaven's grandstands. He has had his season tickets forever. The life of Abel inspires us to worship God by faith. Continuing in Hebrews 11, we read, "By faith Abel offered to God a better sacrifice than Cain, through which he obtained the testimony that he was righteous, God testifying about his gifts, and through faith, though he is dead, he still speaks" (verse 4).

God desired that Abel and his brother Cain worship Him through a blood sacrifice. Only through the blood of a sacrifice could a Holy God be approached. But Cain chose to bring the fruit of the fields. He came before God through his own good works. But Abel obeyed God by faith and brought a blood sacrifice. Through a blood sacrifice, Abel acknowledged his sinfulness and God's unapproachable holiness.

A blood sacrifice? That is not intellectually acceptable. That is uncultured. Uncouth. Uncivilized. It does not make any sense.

But, since Adam's fall into sin (which affects us all), it is a blood sacrifice that God requires. Ultimately, Abel's blood sacrifice prefigured the bloody cross of Jesus Christ. Today, our faith must be in the blood sacrifice of Christ to take away our sins.

Most of us who have trusted Christ have been ridiculed. Most of us have taken flack for our faith.

We can identify with the persecution Abel received. Even from within his own household. The same often occurs in our tight circle of relationships. So often, those who love us the most hurt us the most.

Yes, the cold, hardened world will persecute us. We expect that. But when the cold shoulder of sarcastic putdown comes from our own family members, those attacks most often cut the deepest. Those wounds hurt the most.

Abel shouts encouragement to each one of us to personally trust in the blood of Jesus Christ. No matter how foolish this world may consider the Cross to be. By faith, we must come to God through the blood of Jesus Christ.

Enoch: "Walk by Faith!"

Next, the life of Enoch inspires us to walk with God by faith. Hebrews 11 continues, "By faith Enoch was taken up so that he should not see death; and he was not found because God took him up; for he obtained the witness that before his being taken up he was pleasing to God" (verse 5).

Enoch walked with God in an ungodly society (Genesis 5:22,24). He sought a close, personal fellowship with God. He was devoted to knowing God. He kept his heart fixed on God. Despite living in a corrupt society, Enoch would not compromise his walk of faith.

Enoch was a dynamic witness. He proclaimed a message of judgment that his generation resented and resisted (Jude 14-15). He confronted his world and refused to become a part of the godless system.

Men, Enoch inspires each of us to seek God with all our heart. Hebrews 11:6 tells us, "Without faith it is impossible to please Him, for he who comes to God must believe that He is, and that He is a rewarder of those who seek Him."

We must stand out as lights in a dark world. Penetrating, exposing, transmitting. We must be different to make a difference. (I said different, not weird. Some Christians act like a fill-in stunt man for Goofy.)

All the while, we must be insulated from the squeeze of the world's godless value system. Insulated, not isolated. We are to be in the world, not of it. How do we remain pure? By faith. Remaining focused on God. Like Enoch was.

Noah: "Work by Faith!"

Now, let's hear about Noah. The writer to the Hebrews explains: "By faith Noah, being warned by God about things not yet seen, in reverence prepared an ark for the salvation of his household, by which he condemned the world, and became an heir of the righteousness which is according to faith" (verse 7).

God told Noah that He was going to destroy the world through a flood. Noah was to build an ark—a giant ship the length of one-and-a-half football fields—and get his family safely on board.

What a work of faith this was! Noah was 500 miles from the nearest sea. It had probably never rained on the earth before this time. Yet he worked for 120 years—alone—to build this ark on dry land.

Can't you hear the laughing jeers and ridicule of his neighbors? They were all sneering, "His elevator must be stuck in the basement." "He's got rooms to rent upstairs. Unfinished." "His lights are on, but nobody's home."

Noah worked by faith. Despite standing all alone in the world, Noah obeyed God and did God's work.

Men, we, too, must work by faith. Often alone. Are you trying to build a godly family? Are you trying to build a godly business? Noah inspires faith within us to stand alone for our convictions. Even if others around us ridicule us, we must do God's work by faith.

Abraham: "Follow by Faith!"

Here comes Abraham. He is seated on the fifty yard line of Heaven's grandstands. His credentials follow:

> By faith Abraham, when he was called, obeyed by going out to a place which he was to receive for an inheritance; and he went out, not knowing where he was going. By faith he lived as an alien in the land of promise, as in a foreign land, dwelling in tents with Isaac and Jacob, fellow-heirs of the same promise; for he was looking for the city which has foundations, whose architect and builder is God. (verses 8-10)

Abraham lived in Ur, an idolatrous, vile, pagan city. He was a very successful businessman there. God called Abraham to pack his bags and go to an unknown land. There God would establish a nation through his loins.

Abraham obeyed the call of God. Not knowing where he was going or how it would work out, he left behind his home and estate. He severed his family ties. He abandoned the security of comfortable surroundings for an unknown world. Abraham went forward by faith, not knowing where God would lead him.

Men, God may be launching you into a new career. He may be leading you into an entirely new venture. A life of faith may mean leaving your comfort zone and security to launch out in a new direction. It will require making a break with the world's system in order to follow God's direction for your life.

Remember, wherever God guides, God provides. Just follow His leading. You will be safer out on a limb with the Lord than standing on solid ground without Him.

Draw encouragement from Abraham. God will lead you just as He led this patriarch.

Sarah: "Wait by Faith!"

Here comes the head cheerleader now—Sarah. We continue in Hebrews 11: "By faith even Sarah herself received ability to conceive, even beyond the proper time of life, since she considered Him faithful who had promised" (verse 11).

God had promised Abraham that a nation would come through his children. That meant Sarah must bear a child. But she could not conceive. One day, Sarah could wait no longer on God, and she sent Hagar to lie with her husband to help God's plan. Her impatience on God's perfect timing created an Ishmael. And problems for generations.

Years later, when Sarah was ninety years old, God promised a child in her old age. This time, Sarah trusted God to do what was humanly impossible. To give her a baby, despite her being past the age to conceive.

Men, maybe you are growing tired of waiting on God. Impatience haunts most of us. We want instant everything. Perhaps you are in danger of taking matters into your own hands.

Sarah shouts to us, "Wait patiently by faith. God's timing is perfect."

Patience, it has been said, is letting your motor idle when you feel like stripping the gears.

A man was driving home and came to a red light. As he sat there idling his motor, the car behind him began honking emphatically. Honk! Honk!

The man waved in the rear-view mirror, pointing upward to the red light.

Honk! Honk!

The man signaled again, pointing upward to the red light.

Honk! Honk!

That was all the man could stomach. He jumped out of his car and walked back to the car behind him. He was furious. Livid.

"Are you blind? Anyone can see the light is red. Will you stop that honking before you drive me crazy? You are giving me a pain I can't locate!"

To which the man replied, "Your bumper sticker says, 'Honk if you love Jesus.' I was just telling you I love Him, too."

It is hard to let your motor idle. To just sit still.

But Sarah says, "Wait patiently by faith! God's timing is perfect!"

Men, just remember, you'll never be too old to serve God. You are never past your prime in God's economy. It's always primetime with God.

Moses: "Overcome by Faith!"

Who's next in the grandstands? Is that Charlton Heston? No, I'm sorry, that's Moses! Hebrews 11 recaps Moses' life: "By faith Moses, when he had grown up, refused to be called the son of Pharaoh's daughter; choosing rather to endure ill-treatment with the people of God, than to enjoy the passing pleasures of sin; considering the reproach of Christ greater riches than the treasures of Egypt; for he was looking to the reward" (verses 24-26).

Moses grew up in Egypt, the wealthiest, most advanced civilization in the world. He was a prince, the son of Pharaoh's daughter, who lived in the palace. He had all this world could offer—prestige, pleasures, possessions.

At age forty, Moses had to make a choice. Whether to become a full-fledged Egyptian or to join his own people. Moses said no to the honor of the palace; he went to live with slaves.

Moses did not seek the world's prestige. He sought God's will. No rat race for Moses. He chose the right race.

Men, we live constantly in danger of the world squeezing us into its mold (Romans 12:2). Satan is luring us to conform to his system. We must sacrifice present riches for an eternal reward. The world's system looks alluring, but we must say no and choose to pursue spiritual reward.

How will we stay on track in God's race?

By faith. Faith does not buckle and fold under the world's pressures. It keeps looking for the eternal reward, not earthly treasures. It focuses upon the invisible, not what is seen.

Moses' life inspires us to live for eternal reward in the midst of material prosperity. To seek Heaven's applause rather than earthly approval.

There is a man in our church named Ken who is a champion golfer. A few years ago, Ken was on the verge of turning pro only to discover that golf was requiring too much time and keeping him away from his family. It was becoming all-consuming.

From deep conviction, Ken made the painful decision to walk away from a certain career on the tour. He refused to be squeezed into the mold of the world. He chose to follow Moses' example and live for future reward rather than earthly acclaim.

Israel: "Forward by Faith!"

Here's a big section in Heaven's coliseum—the nation of Israel. The writer of Hebrews 11 notes a few highlights of its history: "By faith they passed through the Red Sea as though they were passing through dry land; and the Egyptians, when they attempted it, were drowned. By faith the walls of Jericho fell down, after they had been encircled for seven days" (verses 29-30).

Moses led the children of God out of Egypt to go to the Promised Land. But the journey and conquest were not without challenges. The nation soon found itself in an impossible crunch.

With the Red Sea in front of them and Pharaoh closing in behind them, the nation of Israel had to go forward. No choice here. They had to trust God to defeat their enemy. They knew they couldn't whip Pharaoh's legions.

Once in the Promised Land, it was still forward by faith for the nation. The impregnable walls of Jericho stood between them and advancement into the Promised Land. God called for faith, and He would defeat Israel's enemies. At Jericho, God again defeated their enemy. They advanced by faith.

The Christian life is an advancement forward. Always forward by faith. Forward into the fullness of God's blessing. Forward into Christlikeness. Forward in the conquest of our foes.

What is your Red Sea? What walls are obstructing your spiritual advancement? When impossible obstacles stand in our way, God enables us to advance forward by faith!

Judges, Kings, Prophets: "Fight by Faith!"

Here is another large section in Heaven's arena. These are the spiritual leaders of Israel—probably sitting in the press box high above—encouraging us to fight our foes by faith. Hebrews 11 says, "Gideon, Barak, Samson, Jephthah; . . . David and Samuel and the prophets; who by faith conquered kingdoms, performed acts of righteousness, obtained promises, shut the mouths of lions, quenched the power of fire, escaped the edge of the sword, from weakness were made strong, became mighty in war, put foreign armies to flight" (verses 32-34).

Gideon was outnumbered by the Midianites 135,000 to 300—yet won. Barak triumphed over the Canaanites. Samson slew the Philistines. Jephthah faced impossible odds and won. David fought Goliath and won. Samuel fought against idolatry and immorality and won. The prophets, from Samuel to John the Baptist, stood for God's truth and won. In every case, they were victorious. By faith.

Daniel obeyed God even though it meant being thrown into the lion's den. Because he trusted God, God protected him (Daniel 6). Shadrach, Meshach, and Abednego were thrown into the fiery furnace because they refused to worship the statue of the king. But God protected them (Daniel 3). David escaped the sword of Goliath and Saul. King Hezekiah was about to die, but began to pray to God. God gave him health, and he lived fifteen more years. Elijah and Elisha both raised the dead sons of women. The faith of these prophets brought back those children from the dead.

Men, as Christians, we are facing impossible odds every day. Our race is against the grain of society. Our battles are just as real. The Canaanites outnumber us. The Goliaths are waiting for us to grow weary and falter. The Delilahs are lying . . . well, never mind.

No matter how impossible the odds, we too can triumph by faith. It's our homecourt advantage.

Others: "Suffer by Faith!"
Finally, reverently, here are those martyred for their faith. Unknown on earth, these are the undisputed champions known in Heaven. These are those who . . .

> were tortured, not accepting their release, in order that they
> might obtain a better resurrection; and others experienced
> mockings and scourgings, yes, also chains and imprisonment.
> They were stoned, they were sawn in two, they were tempted,
> they were put to death with the sword; they went about in sheep-
> skins, in goatskins; being destitute, afflicted, ill-treated (men
> of whom the world was not worthy), wandering in deserts
> and mountains and caves and holes in the ground. (Hebrews
> 11:35-38)

Sometimes God does not design the battle to be victorious. Courageous faith continues in the face of suffering. Faith that conquers is a great faith, but faith that continues in suffering is even greater.

Jeremiah suffered mockings, brutal whipping, and imprisonment (Jeremiah 20:2,7). Zechariah was stoned (2 Chronicles 24:20-22). Isaiah was sawed in half, tradition tells us. Others were tortured to deny God. Some were put to a martyr's death. Still others wandered in poverty, having to forsake everything the world had to offer.

There are "men of whom the world was not worthy" (Hebrews 11:38). The world thought these champions unworthy. But God received them into Heaven where they were welcomed home and recognized as having a faith worthy of applause.

Why would former Giants pitcher Dave Dravecky still have any faith? Why would he continue to walk with God?

His baseball career has ended. His arm has been removed. His baseball future, amputated.

It is Dave's unshakable confidence in a God who can only do what is right that continues to sustain him and his family through a time of unspeakable agony.

What keeps Dave going is that he can "hear" with his heart the urging, the encouraging, the compelling applause from this great cloud of witnesses.

This is Heaven's homecourt advantage.

Here are examples of men and women, just like you and me, who ran God's race by faith and won. These champions are screaming encouragement to each of us. Worship, walk, and work by faith! Follow and wait by faith! Overcome and go forward by faith! Fight and, if need be, suffer by faith! That's what these champions are yelling to us.

THE APPLAUSE OF HEAVEN

Some years ago, a great football coach by the name of Lou Little coached Columbia University. A young man who was not a particularly good player tried out for the varsity team. While not nearly good enough to make the team, he had such an irrepressible spirit and contagious enthusiasm that Lou thought, *This boy would be a great inspiration on the bench. He'll never be able to play, but I'll leave him on the team to encourage others.*

As the season went on, Coach Little grew in his admiration and love for this boy. He was especially impressed by the manner with which the boy cared for his father. Whenever his father came to the campus, the boy and his father would always be seen walking together, arm in arm. There was an obvious indication of the close bond between them. They could be seen on Sunday mornings walking to and from the university chapel. It was obvious they possessed a deep faith in Christ.

One day, Coach Little received a telephone call. He was informed that this boy's father had just tragically died. He would have the difficult task of telling the boy. With a heavy heart, the coach informed his player of his father's death. The boy immediately left to go home for the funeral.

A few days later, the boy returned to the campus, only two days before the biggest game of the season. Coach Little walked up to him and said, "Is there anything I can do for you? Anything at all? I'll be glad to do it for you."

To the coach's astonishment, the boy said, "Let me start the game on Saturday!"

Lou was taken aback. He thought, *I can't let him start. He's not good enough.* But he remembered his promise to the boy and said, "All right, you can start the game." Coach Little rationalized, *I'll leave him in for a few plays and then take him out.*

The day of the big game arrived. To everyone's surprise, the coach started this boy who had not played in a game all season. On the very first play from scrimmage, that boy single-handedly made a tackle that threw the opposing team for a loss. Coach Little was shocked.

The boy played inspired football, play after play. In fact, he played so exceptionally that the coach left him in for the entire game. The boy led his team to victory, and he was voted the outstanding player of the game.

When the game was over, Coach Little approached the boy and said, "Son, what got into you today?"

The boy replied, "Do you remember when my father would visit me here, we would walk arm in arm around the campus? My father and I shared a secret that nobody here knew. You see, my father was blind—and today was the first time he ever saw me play!"

As the boy's father's presence in Heaven powerfully influenced his earthly effort, so this "cloud of witnesses" should inspire us to run victoriously. No, Heaven's heroes do not actually watch us as we run. But the examples of their lives influence us profoundly as we run the race.

As we run God's race, let us listen for the applause of Heaven and draw strength. Let me tell you one more time—it's the homecourt advantage.

Shhh, what's that I hear from above?

"DEE-fense! DEE-fense!"

NOTES
1. Charles Swindoll, *Hebrews II Bible Study Guide* (Fullerton, CA: Insight for Living, 1983), page 5.
2. Warren Wiersbe, *The Bible Expository Commentary* (Wheaton, IL: Victor Books, 1989), page 317.

CHAPTER 6

RUNNING BUCK NAKED

★

I have been told I preach like I play golf. Long, to the right, and always near a hazard. With a chapter title like "Running Buck Naked," I could easily hit into some serious trouble. So, pray for me that I will keep this in the fairway.

Come with me to the ancient Greek games. As the fastest runners in the Roman Empire gather at the starting line, the tension and pressure is mounting. They are about to run the race of their lives. The crowd rises to its feet in anticipation.

The runners begin to remove their outer warmup robes. Nothing must slow them down. They then remove their loose-fitting tunics. No garment must cause any wind drag.

Then, in a startling move, the runners remove the rest of their clothing. They strip down. Completely. To the buff.

They are totally nude.

This has become R-rated.

These Greek athletes have stripped down so nothing—absolutely nothing—will slow them down. They will do anything to gain an advantage over the competition. They are willing to risk the embarrassment of public exposure. To run without any encumbrance. All to win the crown.

This gives new meaning to the truism "Less is more."

Their bulging muscles and finely tuned bodies ripple in the open arena. With sculpted torsos that look like they have been chiseled out of marble, they resemble exquisite masterpieces. These are the finest athletes in the Roman Empire.

These naked runners are highly motivated to jump out to a fast start. If you fall behind this bare-bottomed pack, the view can be pretty rough.

Considered offensive by women and Jews, such nudity was the accepted practice of these world-famous athletic games. Nothing must be allowed to impede their speed. Not even clothing. Because winning was everything!

Today, the issue is whether female sports reporters should be allowed into the men's locker room. In ancient times, the issue was bringing the men's locker room out onto the field.

These are men whose burning passion is winning. At any cost. So they remove all encumbrances that would hinder a swift performance. All to capture a crown, if not a cold.

Men, these are the bare facts. Very revealing.

Just as the first-century athletes stripped down to run with maximum speed, we must strip away every spiritual encumbrance that would impede our progress in God's race. Pursuing the ultimate prize requires laying aside anything that would slow us down.

I know what some of you are thinking. "If God wanted us to run naked, we would have been born that way." That's precisely the point.

Hebrews 12:1 says, "Therefore, since we have so great a cloud of witnesses surrounding us, *let us also lay aside every encumbrance*" (emphasis added). This is a call for "spiritual streaking."

Too many of us run as if outfitted with layers of restrictive clothing and with heavy weights. We must strip down and run unencumbered. Take it all off!

In this chapter, we want to look at what it means to "lay aside every encumbrance." What is an encumbrance? Where are they to be found? How can I detect them?

WHAT ARE ENCUMBRANCES?

First, let's consider what an encumbrance is.

Picture with me, if you will, an athlete approaching the starting blocks attired in a three-piece Brooks Brothers suit, an overcoat, and wing tips. How ludicrous! Yet, many of us are running God's race as if under such excess baggage. We are hindered by layers of restrictive clothing and heavy weights.

The word *encumbrance* means a weight, a bulk, a mass of something heavy. It refers to either body bulk or excess weight. It pictures any unnecessary weight that would slow down a runner. In ancient times, an athlete would train by wearing leg weights. But when he approached the starting line, he would shed those weights, along with any warmup clothes.

We're *not* talking about sin here. Hebrews 12:1 contrasts an "encumbrance" with "the sin which so easily entangles us." There is a difference.

The encumbrance is simply something amoral or neutral in our life that works in a counterproductive way. It weighs us down, diverts our attention, saps our energy, and dampens our quest for the ultimate prize.

It is excess baggage. Superfluous.

Legitimate things can become weights to hold us back—love of home and family, love of country, love of comfort, contentment with job, security at work. These legitimate things can become weights to hold us back in the race.

Men, in discerning God's best for our life, not all of our choices are between good and bad. Many of our decisions are choices among what is good, better, and best. An encumbrance may be something good that keeps us from the best. Winning God's race requires choosing the best over the good and the better.

An encumbrance is not a sin. Just anything that prevents God's best.

A runner in training might choose to give up drinking colas. Not because drinking a cola is sinful. But because too much carbonated water might hinder his best performance and affect his mind. In a spiritual sense, watching a football game on television could work the same way. There is nothing morally wrong with watching a football game. In fact, it is a form of recreation that provides beneficial rest and stimulation (at least that's what I tell my wife). But, if watching a football game keeps you from Bible study or prayer, then a good thing has become a hindrance to the best thing. The good becomes the enemy of the best.

The problem is not in what the encumbrance *is*, but in what it *does*. *Good* things become *bad* things when they keep us from the *best* things.

The question we must ask is, "How fast do I want to run God's race? Fast, faster, or fastest?" If fast, then I can carry some excess baggage. If faster, I can carry a little baggage. But if I want to run my fastest, then I must lay aside *every* encumbrance.

The Bare Essentials

The story is told of a group of people who were preparing to climb Mount Blanc in the Swiss Alps. On the evening before the climb, the guide outlined the prerequisite for reaching the top. Due to the difficulty of the climb, one could reach the top by taking only the bare essentials of equipment. All unnecessary accessories must be left behind.

A young Englishman refused to listen. He proceeded to bring along an extra blanket, a cap, and a fancy notebook in his backpack.

On the way to the summit of Mount Blanc, the guide began to notice certain items left behind in the snow. First the blanket. Then the notebook. Later the cap.

Finally, when they reached the top, they discovered this Englishman had jettisoned everything unnecessary along the way.

This epitomizes what must happen in our lives spiritually if we are to win the race. Every unnecessary weight must be cast aside if we are to make it to the top. We must let go of the good if we are to achieve the best.

Running with maximum speed requires stripping down. Even small encumbrances can keep us from victory. The difference between victory and defeat is often very small.

The famous runner Gil Dodds was once preparing to run a race. After a series of stretching exercises, Dodds ran several warmup laps around the track in preparation for the race. Just before the race began, he stopped and quickly changed into some other track shoes.

One of the onlookers asked why he was changing shoes. Dodds tossed to the inquirer one of his warm-up shoes. Then one of his racing shoes.

The man was still puzzled. There was no detectable difference in the two shoes. Both looked the same. Both seemed to weigh the same.

Then Dodds explained. There was indeed a difference. The warmup shoes were slightly heavier than his racing shoes. Though only a small difference, saving even that amount of weight for the race could spell the difference between victory and defeat.

Men, the same is true in our spiritual lives. No encumbrance, large or small, can be tolerated in our life. Not if we are to win. The Word of God says "lay aside *every* encumbrance" (Hebrews 12:1, emphasis added). Not some, but *every*. So every encumbrance must go. Anything that would hold us back must be relinquished.

Men, are you ready to strip?

WHAT MUST BE LAID ASIDE?

If stripping down is really a factor in winning, then let's identify some areas of potential "excess baggage" in our lives.

I think we have to admit that most of us suffer from too much baggage. Too many irons in the fire. Too many balls in the air. Too many competing demands. Too many good things crowding out the best things.

Let's examine three key areas where encumbrances may need to be laid aside.

Hindrance 1: Career Crunch

First, let's talk about our work life and the demands we face there. We must guard against becoming so caught up in our work that our spiritual and family life begin to suffer. The squeeze of the marketplace can be a death grip.

Work, in and of itself, is not bad. In fact, work is good. The Bible teaches that hard work is honorable. God lovingly assigned man the responsibility to work and manage the earth (Genesis 1:28). This divine assignment was made before the entrance of sin into the world. Work was a part of paradise. Now, after the Fall, man still works for the glory of God (Colossians 3:22-24). And he can find great enjoyment and fulfillment from his professional pursuit.

However, the growing demands of time on the job and the drain of emotional energy at the office can become heavy weights. Encumbrances. Hindrances. Excess baggage.

When that happens, the good crowds out the best. We soon find ourselves winning at work but losing in God's race.

Our work can become a big, heavy weight that holds us back in running God's race victoriously. When we become so wrapped up with our careers that we have little time and energy left for God, His Kingdom, and our families, we are hindered severely in the race.

No one is immune from this trap. Not even ministers. Even something as noble as doing God's work can become a hindrance to doing the more important things in life. For me, I can become so busy with my ministry that I neglect time alone with my family.

Let me show you how I can blow it.

Recently, my wife asked that I be home by 5:00 p.m. She and our boys needed to leave home by 5:30 to get to the church for a children's program rehearsal. She knew she had to ask me because I had been coming home later and later each evening. Sure enough, I was met with a church emergency at 4:30 and I came dragging home at 5:45. As I drove home, God's Spirit convicted me that I should have postponed solving the emergency until the next day. (Most "emergencies" can wait until the next day.)

As I walked into our kitchen, my sweet wife burst into tears. "You promised you would be home by 5:00. John almost killed himself by falling out the back door. Andrew and James are being rowdy. Grace Anne needs your attention. And I'm burning dinner!"

"But, sweetheart," I replied, "I was taking care of an emergency at church that came up and would not go away without my help. I had to help a person."

Still hurt because I was becoming too absentee, she said (tongue in cheek), "Well, maybe I need to set up an appointment to see you. That's the only way I'm going to be able to talk to you."

Ouch! (She was right.)

Men, our work *can* crowd out more important matters in our life. Like family. Like God. Maybe God Himself needs to say, "Well, maybe I need to set up an appointment to see you. That's probably the only way I'm going to be able to talk to you."

Maybe you can relate to how I blew it. We can let the tyranny of the urgent crowd out the best. When that happens, repeatedly buckling to the demands of work becomes a hindrance.

We must not allow the crunch of career demands to crowd out what is truly best in life. If we make that tradeoff, we will surely lose the race.

Our passion for the marketplace too often crowds out what is most important in our lives. When that happens, these imbalances become an encumbrance. A ball and chain.

Have you ever wrestled with this tension? Have you ever felt the growing demands at work subtly crowding out your devotional time with God? Squeezing out your family time? Pushing out time to serve God? Are you too busy to notice?

Well, this is too convicting. Let's move on.

Hindrance 2: Pastime Passions

Let's talk about how we spend our free time. Recreation is not sin. Hobbies and entertainment are not sin. But they can become an encumbrance if not checked, which will slow us down in the pursuit of Heaven's prize.

It could be fishing or hunting. It could be golf or tennis. Or working around the house. Whatever you like to spend your spare time doing can become a hindrance. If it begins to crowd out the best.

Sure, recreation is good and needed. I believe it is a part of the Sabbath principle taught in the Bible. Just as God worked six days on Creation and then rested, so we must have regularly scheduled rest from the stress of the marketplace. We need physical rest. Emotional rest. Spiritual rest. Without it, we will snap and break, like a tightly wound rubber band.

But recreation, something good, can keep us from the best things. In other words, recreation is a means to an end. But not an end in itself. Our passion for recreation can displace our passion for winning God's crown.

For me, it's golf. That little white ball is my addiction. If there is AA for alcoholics, then surely we need a GA for golfaholics. I may need to check myself in for treatment soon. I confess I love golf. With a passion. My children recently gave me a toothbrush that says, "I love golf." That says it all.

Can you imagine a greater way to be outdoors than to be on a beautiful golf course? Riding in a cart? When I die, I want it to be on a golf course, so I can go from glory to glory.

I recently took Jeff Kinley, my youth pastor, to play golf. We decided to drive to a golf course about two hours away. The night before, I went into my religious ritual to get ready, like a bride preparing herself the night before her wedding day.

I got my golf clubs out and cleaned them. Again. They were clean enough to eat off. I took the car up to the corner and filled it with gas. Had the oil checked. I cashed a check at the grocery store. Got to be ready for any emergency. I laid out my golf clothes for the next day. Even packed an extra shirt in case I spilled something. I polished my golf shoes. Tightened my spikes. I called the golf course to ask exactly how long it took to drive there. To the minute. I reviewed the directions with the receptionist. I then watched the weather forecast and earnestly prayed and fasted for good weather the next day.

As my wife and I retired to bed that night, I think she felt a bit neglected. She said gently, "Why can't you get this excited about our family time together? You are never this organized for our vacations."

Ouch! (She was right again.)

I can let golf get out of hand. When it does, it becomes an encumbrance in my life. It holds me back from running God's race. It can paralyze my real priorities. Like time with my family. Like time with God.

Men, is there any hobby or entertainment in your life like that? Could it be in danger of crowding out the best in your life?

Another recreational hindrance can be television. Personally, I have made the choice not to hook our house up to cable television. My kids think we are the Beverly Hillbillies. Before they discovered oil.

I have made this "radical" decision for two reasons. First, because I do not want many of those cable programs available to my children. But second, because I know I would become addicted to ESPN (the all-sports network). If I had access to ESPN, it would ruin my life. I know it would. I would be tempted to watch it every night. No, I *would* watch it every night. To the neglect of my family. To the disregard for time in God's Word. For me, it would become an encumbrance, slowing me down in the best things.

You ought to see us on family vacations. The moment we check into a hotel, we immediately flip on ESPN. I tell my wife that I am spending personal time with my boys.

Men, what is your pastime passion? Working on your car? Grooming your yard? Building something in your workshop? Being mesmerized by your PC?

Now, these are not sins. They are innocent things. Legitimate. Good things. But they can become encumbrances. And detract us from the goal.

Hindrance 3: Ministry Overload

Here is a third hindrance that must be stripped off. We carry excess baggage when our ministry for Christ becomes too consuming. If it pushes out our time alone with God, our ministry becomes a hindrance to the best. Our work *for* God must never take away from our worship *of* God. That, my friend, is a bad tradeoff.

Don't get me wrong. Ministry is important. As a pastor, I am committed to ministry. My job is to equip the Body of Christ to do ministry (Ephesians 4:11-12). Every believer must serve in God's Kingdom. Christlikeness requires girding oneself with a towel and serving others (John 13:1-17).

But this must never crowd out my worship of God. The most important thing about us is our knowledge of Christ (John 17:3). We must constantly grow to know and love Him in a deeper, fuller, richer way (2 Peter 3:18). So, my service for Christ must flow out of my personal walk with Christ. Worship first; work second.

Sometimes we get so busy serving Christ that we neglect our heart devotion with Him. Our quiet times get put on the back shelf for the busy hustle and bustle of ministry. That is the good competing with the best. That is buy high, sell low.

I know this is a men's book, but there are two ladies who can teach us a lot about this lesson. They are Mary and Martha (Luke 10:38-42). One day Jesus came to their house, and Martha began serving Jesus in the kitchen. She rolled up her sleeves and got after it!

Guess what Mary did? She just sat there. At Jesus' feet. She spent time alone there, drinking in the words of Jesus, adoring His majesty.

Martha was not pleased to be serving solo. She got hot and bothered. "Lord," she complained, "do You not care that my sister has left me to do all the serving alone? Then tell her to help me" (Luke 10:40).

Jesus gently rebuked her by saying, "Martha, Martha, you are worried and bothered about so many things. . . . Mary has chosen the good part."

In other words, "Don't just do something. Sit there!"

Jesus made it very clear. He put the cookies on the bottom shelf. Do not sacrifice your personal worship on the altar of ministry. Serving Christ is good. In fact, *very* good. But worshiping Christ is the best. The *very* best.

Men, I must confess to you that I struggle with maintaining this priority. As a task-oriented, impatient, take-charge kind of person, my tendency is to *do* for Christ. Often at the expense of worshiping Him. Sitting still at His feet is not my natural tendency. But it is what He wants. I must not let ministry mania crowd out my time alone with God in devotions, prayer, or personal worship.

God does not want a performance. He wants a relationship. We must be careful not to discard the best for something as noble as serving God.

What about *you*?

Does ministry madness ever crowd out your heart relationship with Christ? If so, it is a hindrance in running the race. A heavy weight.

Men, watch over your heart. Do not allow your heart to grow cold and distracted from God. Choose the best. Choose worship.

HOW TO IDENTIFY YOUR OWN BAGGAGE

Men, it's not enough for us to talk about encumbrances in broad categories. We must get specific about identifying those hindrances in each of our lives. I want to give you some principles that will help you identify them.

In an airport each traveler must identify his own baggage after his flight and match his claim check with his own baggage. Over the loud speaker, the voice warns us not to pick up someone else's baggage. Be sure to identify your own baggage.

The same is true spiritually. We need to identify our own baggage. Our *excess* baggage. So that we can lay it aside. It would be presumptuous for me to specifically identify your baggage. Legalism occurs when I attempt to tell you what is excess baggage in your life. What is a hindrance for me may not be a hindrance for you.

Each Christian must individually decide which encumbrances must be laid aside. Only the Spirit of God can point out theses weights to each believer.

Here are some biblical principles that, when properly applied, can determine personal hindrances which must be laid aside. Here is how to identify your own baggage.

The Bible is very explicit about sin. It is black and white. But encumbrances usually are gray. The Apostle Paul assists us with identifying these "gray areas" in 1 Corinthians 6–10.

Men, you must decide for yourself what must be removed. Ask the Spirit of God to point out these weights. Then resolve to take proper action. Only then can you run buck naked. Apply each of the following questions to every area of your life.

Is It Profitable for Winning?

Paul writes, "All things are lawful for me, but not all things are profitable" (1 Corinthians 6:12; see also 10:23). Profitable means "advantageous, beneficial, helpful." Is this thing to my advantage? The price of doing some things is terribly high and thus unprofitable.

An athlete must do only those things that will bring victory. Areas of his life that are not expedient to winning, he will monitor and restrict.

"All things are lawful" does not mean that "anything goes." It means that all things that are not unlawful are lawful. The Bible explicitly teaches that some things are unlawful. For example, "You shall not commit adultery" (Exodus 20:14). Period. Paragraph. I do not have a right to take anyone other than my own wife. You will recall that there are a few more of these commandments.

All other things in my life are lawful. God has made all things for me to freely enjoy. But not all things that I have a right to do are profitable for winning the race.

A champion runner must say no to things to which he has a right to say yes. A marathon runner will deny himself certain foods and activities simply because they will not contribute to winning. They may, perhaps, even hinder his winning.

I must ask myself: Will doing this enhance my spiritual life? If not, strip it. Will it cultivate godliness? If not, strip it. Will it be to my advantage? If not, strip it. The question is not, "Can I do this and get away with it?" Rather, I should ask, "Will this profit me spiritually?" If not, strip it.

Will It Bring Me into Bondage?

Paul writes, "All things are lawful for me, but I will not be mastered by anything" (1 Corinthians 6:12). This means nothing must be allowed to control or dominate my life except God and His will for my life. My body, my passions, and my drives must be controlled by God alone. And not by work, recreation, ministry, or anything else.

A championship runner must not allow anything to master him. Nothing must control his body or dull his senses. His body must be free of all substances if he is to compete victoriously. No drugs, nor alcohol, nor any controlled substance must bring his body into bondage. Addictions destroy.

A believer could become enslaved by something in which he has freedom to indulge. If he is to win the race, he must not allow anything to hold such a grip on his life.

Men, do not allow anything to master your life. Not sports. Not work. Not alcohol. Not anything.

If something like this is controlling your life, yield your life to Christ and, by the power of the Holy Spirit, lay it aside. Strip it off.

Will It Cause Others to Stumble?

Paul writes, "But take care lest this liberty of yours somehow become a stumbling-block to the weak" (1 Corinthians 8:9). A stumbling block is something that causes another person to trip and fall in the course of the race.

A runner who interferes with the progress of another runner will be disqualified. It matters not how well or how fast he is running if he causes another to trip and fall. He will be put out of the race.

Men, what in your life may cause a weaker runner to stumble?

For me, it can often be the use of my tongue. Unfortunately, I have too often caused another to trip over my long, flapping tongue.

Once in our Sunday evening worship service, I asked the congregation to stand and greet one another, especially being sensitive to visitors. After a few minutes of warm hospitality, I said, "All right, everybody be seated. Now, who met somebody who is visiting tonight?"

Boom—a hand shot up immediately in the very back of the sanctuary.

"Yes," I said. "Who did you meet? Please introduce them to us."

As the entire congregation turned around, straining to see, one member graciously said, "Pastor, I would like to introduce a visitor."

"Great," I cheerfully responded, although I couldn't see well all the way to the back.

This visitor, who was sitting all by himself, happened to be an enormously large man. He was huge. Gigantic. To say the least, on the heavy side.

I inquired, "Tell us, who is that with him?"

Unfortunately, I couldn't see that this large man was alone. (The congregation was beginning to chuckle.)

"Pastor, he's by himself tonight," our greeter explained.

Realizing now why my remarks caused the chuckles, but unable to control my tongue, I blurted out, "Oh, I'm sorry. I thought he was an *entire family*."

The laughter was explosive. Out of hand. People were lying down in their pews, they were laughing so hard.

Needless to say, this fellow believer never came back to visit our church. I am sure my tongue caused him to stumble.

The next week, I publically apologized to the church family for the improper use of my tongue. Unfortunately, this brother hadn't filled out a visitor's card (would you?), so I could not personally call him and ask his forgiveness.

We must be careful not to cause other brothers to stumble.

Will It Weaken My Faith?

In 1 Corinthians 10:23 the word *edify* means "to build a house." It refers to building up other people to increase or strengthen their faith. Whatever contributes to spiritual growth is profitable.

A marathon runner must be strong if he is to run God's race to win. Weak legs will never cross the finish line first. So anything that weakens him must be laid aside. It is not worth it.

Will It Keep Others from Entering the Race?
Paul writes, "Give no offense either to Jews or to Greeks . . . just as I also please all men in all things, not seeking my own profit, but the profit of the many, that they may be saved" (1 Corinthians 10:32-33). We should not abuse a freedom that would lead to offending an unbeliever or repel him from entering the race.

It is important that I run my race in a way that encourages others to enter the race. It must not keep them from entering the race. How important it is to God that others be saved and enter the race. So it is important to us, as well.

Think about it. Most people are led to faith in Christ through the witness of another. Rare is the conversion that occurs in a human vacuum. Usually, God uses one life touching and impacting another life to bring that unbeliever to faith in the Savior.

How I conduct my life, therefore, is of monumental importance. By my life, I can influence a seeking unbeliever closer to Christ. Or, tragically, I can influence another away from Christ.

By the way, what kind of an impact are you making? Don't give someone else an excuse to continue rejecting Christ.

Will It Glorify God?
Paul writes, "Whether, then, you eat or drink or whatever you do, do all to the glory of God" (1 Corinthians 10:31). Here is the all-inclusive principle that governs and guides all our actions. It is that God should be glorified in everything that is done. We must test all things in our life by whether or not they bring glory to God. Is this glorifying God? Will it exalt God? Will it honor Him?

Runners in the Olympics have a higher motive for running than selfish desire. Uniquely, they run for the glory of their country. In the Roman Empire, they ran for the glory of the emperor. Likewise, we run with a higher motive than personal glory and reward. Our highest passion must be to run for the glory of our great God.

Men, these are all significant principles, but they will be utterly useless if not personally applied and practiced. Right now matters forever! No encumbrance is too precious to discard. Nothing must slow us down!

IT IS TIME TO STRIP DOWN!

Men, you can get out of the rat race and be in the right race. You can set your heart on Heaven's Heisman. You can train and discipline yourselves for godliness. You can hear the roar of Heaven's grandstand and be inspired to push to the finish line. But, if you are encumbered and hindered by excess baggage, everything else is to little avail. You are merely plodding. You are not running to win!

Men who win are men who have stripped away all unnecessary encumbrances. They have laid aside all excess baggage. They have rid themselves of all expendable weights.

Listen, until there is a fire burning in your heart to count the cost, to pay the price, to lay aside the hindrances—none of this matters. The passion to win for the glory of God must be an all-consuming fire that energizes you to sacrifice, discard, and divest yourself of petty hindrances that are keeping you from God's best.

Have you stripped down?

Are you running buck naked?

CHAPTER 7

STARTING BLOCKS
AND STUMBLING BLOCKS

★

A determined runner is crouched and coiled at the starting line, ready to explode. He nervously shakes the stiffness from his legs. In the pit of his stomach, he feels this is *his* race to win.

"Runners to your mark . . . set . . . go!"

As the runners launch from the starting line, he jostles for the lead. His legs are strong. His stride fluid. His breathing effortless. His arms relaxed. His eyes focused. His head still. He is running like a well-oiled machine. All systems are go.

His feet are barely touching the ground. He passes one runner after another and moves to the front of the pack. Every runner he passes gives another burst of energy just as he goes by.

He can hear the crowd cheering. A rush of adrenaline shifts him into a higher gear. This is *his* race to win!

The runners leave the stadium and wind through the streets of the town. This runner pushes himself to new limits. He discovers hidden reservoirs of previously untapped energy.

Returning to the stadium, he finds he is the lone leader. His dreams are about to become reality. Victory is sure! Months of training have paid off. The crowd is on its feet cheering. Fanatically.

He glances over his shoulder to confirm that the lead is all his. He is all alone. The only runner back in the stadium. He savors the moment. This is *his* race to win!

Suddenly, the unthinkable happens. A loose object lies on the track. A small stone. Unseen. Undetected.

As the runner approaches, his foot comes down directly on the stone. His ankle twists. He stumbles.

Frantically, he tries to gain his balance. But it is too late. His stride is broken.

He extends his hands to brace his fall. But to no avail. He crashes headfirst into the track. Hard. His body rolls over several times. Wipeout.

As he skids to a stop, his entire body is jarred. His knees are ripped open. His flesh torn.

His competitive drive screams to get back up. Instinctively, he scrambles to his feet. But he immediately collapses back to the ground. His ankle is twisted too severely.

The other runners now reenter the stadium. He can hear the crunching of the cinders as their feet sprint past him. He can taste the blood flowing from his cut lip. The sweat streams down his dejected face. He drags himself off the track. Dejected. Shattered. Defeated.

The sound of the crowd cheering for another winner is a dagger thrust into his heart. Tears of remorse flood his eyes. The sting of defeat fills his heart. Victory was *his*! Until this fatal fall.

A look of anguish covers his face. Bitterness sours his spirit. Months of training, now wasted. Boyhood dreams, a nightmare. Life-long hopes, dashed.

From the edge of the track, his eyes search for that dread object, for what caused his fall. He sees it.

A small stone. A rock.

He limps over to the stone. He glares at it. A simple stone. He picks it up in disgust and throws it off the track. The margin between victory and defeat is this hellish stone.

How could anything so small have caused such devastating consequences? It is just a small stone.

Or is it?

POINTING OUT THE STUMBLING BLOCKS

Let me ask you: If you were sitting in the stands that day and knew the stone was there, wouldn't you have warned the runner? Especially if you wanted to see him win? Wouldn't you have pointed out the stumbling stone?

Surely you would have.

To spare him the pain. The humiliation. The loss.

If you cared anything at all for the runner, you would have warned him and pointed out the stone.

Men, as we run the race of life, there are stumbling blocks in our path. Small. Imperceptible. Yet destructive. Dangerous. Fatal. From where God sits, He sees them all. And in His Word He has revealed them to us. To warn us. To prevent our stumbling. Why? Because He wants us to win!

Listen, it is possible to be running God's race—with victory certain—and then to suddenly, without warning, stumble and fall. What tragedy! One moment running full speed. Wide-open. Unhindered. Then in the next split second—BOOM!—to stumble and fall. And land flat on our face.

This is the bone-jarring reality of the Christian life. It happens.

Hebrews 12:1 warns, "Therefore, since we have so great a cloud of witnesses surrounding us, let us lay aside every encumbrance, and *the sin which so easily entangles us*" (emphasis added).

It is bad enough to be slowed down by a heavy weight. We discussed that in the last chapter. But it is even *worse* to stumble and fall because of an entanglement. Far worse! The tragic stumbling because of sin will be the focus of this chapter.

I must warn you. This chapter is a hard-hitting look at sin. But no less hard-hitting than what sin hits us with. So strap it on. Here comes a hardball look at sin.

First, let's look at this little three-letter word called *sin*. S-I-N. It's just a small stone. What does God say about sin? I fear we have been so desensitized toward sin that we no longer take the small stones seriously.

The word *sin* (*hamartia*) means to miss the mark. To miss the way. To deviate from the path. To go wrong. Sin is missing God's standard of right and wrong. It is falling short of God's glory (Romans 3:23). This is no small stone.

Sin is pictured as a fall. The original sin of Adam is called "the Fall." Sin trips us up and causes us to stumble. It knocks us off our feet, puts us on the ground, and brings defeat. Sin is a crippling hindrance to running life's race.

Men, as we run God's race, there are stumbling blocks that can "so easily entangle us." These stumbling blocks either lead us into sin or bring its devastating consequences upon us.

What is a stumbling block? The word (*skandalon*) originally meant the trigger stick of an animal trap where the bait was placed. It means to lure or ensnare into destruction. It was a snare, a trap. A cause of disaster. A temptation to sin. An occasion to sin.

We Christians encounter various stumbling blocks. James 3:2 says, "For we all stumble in *many* ways" (emphasis added). What are the different ways we stumble? To answer that question, we need to consider the different stumbling blocks we will encounter: Satan, the world, our flesh, other believers, and God Himself. Wise is the man who is aware of each.

Stumbling Block 1: Satan

First, Satan lines our path with stumbling blocks. The Bible teaches that there is a real Devil who opposes the work and people of God. The word *devil* means "one who slanders," or "one who trips up." The Devil is a stumbling block who trips us up in the race.

As we run God's race, we are sure to encounter the Devil's snares and traps, shrewdly camouflaged and strategically placed.

What are these devilish snares?

Temptation. Temptation to abandon God's will. To put our self-interests before God's. To seek our own will rather than God's. To work our own agenda, not God's.

The temptation itself is not sin. But it is the stumbling block that can lead to sin.

Peter's Plan

In Matthew 16, Jesus predicted His own death. He told the disciples that He would be going to Jerusalem to suffer, be killed, and be raised on the third day (Matthew 16:21). This was all a part of God's plan.

When Peter heard this, he took Jesus aside and rebuked Him: "God forbid it, Lord! This shall never happen to You" (verse 22). In other words, "Lord, I love You and I have a wonderful plan for Your life." Peter was attempting to divert our Lord from God's plan—"Surely God does not want You to face this," he was saying.

Jesus saw through these words to the deadly source—Satan! Jesus responded immediately, "Get behind Me, Satan! You are a stumbling-block to Me; for you are not setting your mind on God's interests, but man's" (verse 23).

Peter's well-intended words, prompted by Satan, were a stumbling block. A temptation to abandon God's plan. An enticement to pursue His own will, not God's.

Men, Satan will do the same in our lives. The Devil will attempt to wreck our race. To disrupt our running. To divert our direction. And he'll do it by enticing us to follow our own desires, to go our own way, to make our own path.

Satan's chief temptation is just to leave God out of the picture. He wants us to forsake God's eternal perspective and merely see life from our human, temporal perspective. To focus upon man's interests, not God's.

For Christ, His temptation was to abandon the cross and pursue earthly success. It will be the same for us. To abandon Heaven's reward for men's applause.

We must always maintain an eternal perspective. Every decision must be made in light of God's eternal plan for our life. We must always ask, "Which decision will leave the greatest mark on eternity and bring the greatest glory to God?" Satan would have us think solely about what is personally expedient. This is a stumbling block we face day after day.

False Teaching

Here is another stumbling block of Satan: false teaching—anything that does not square with God's Word.

Mark it down. Satan is a liar and the father of all lies (John 8:44). He is the architect of doctrines of demons (1 Timothy 4:1). Satan will tempt us to abandon God's Word and follow his lies. This has been his *modus operandi* since the garden.

Even within the safe confines of Christian fellowship, Satan's stumbling blocks of false teaching can be found. Jesus said to the church at Pergamum, "I know where you dwell, where Satan's throne is. . . . But I have a few things against you, because you have there some who hold the teaching of Balaam, who kept teaching Balak to put a *stumbling-block* before the sons of Israel to eat things sacrificed to idols, and to commit acts of immorality" (Revelation 2:13-14, emphasis added).

This devilish doctrine of Balaam He refers to was hatched in hell. Specifically, it taught that God's people should marry unbelievers and join their idolatrous worship. Christ strongly warned against this worldly compromise because, since He indwells believers, such practices brought Him into union with Satan.

This same stumbling block is still laid by Satan today. It is the temptation to fellowship with the world. The lure to become like the world. To adopt its standards. To follow its lifestyle. To laugh at its jokes.

Men, where are you being lured away from the authority of God's Word? How are you in danger of compromising God's Word, and therein losing the race?

Stumbling Block 2: the World

Let's just stop here for a moment to catch our breath. Before I point out the second stumbling block, I already know some of you are not going to want to hear this. You are going to want to turn the page. Maybe even close the book.

But before you do, let me just remind you of the title of this book: *Men Who Win*. We cannot be winners in God's race unless we deal successfully with this second stumbling block. Head on.

The second stumbling block is the world. Like Satan, the world lays its obstacles before us as we run God's race.

Jesus said, "Woe to the world because of its stumbling-blocks! For it is inevitable that stumbling-blocks come" (Matthew 18:7).

The world is the invisible system of evil in society that is opposed to God. It is the organized system, headed by Satan, that is hostile to God and founded on self, greed, and pride. It opposes and contradicts all that is godly and Christian. God is ignored, forgotten, and ultimately denied by all participants of this world system.

As we Christians run the race, the world is contending for our minds, our hearts, and our souls. With evangelistic fervor. The world is relentlessly seeking to squeeze us into its mold. To prompt us to adopt its godless values and lifestyles. To trap and ensnare us as we run God's race.

But we cannot love the world and God at the same time. The two are mutually exclusive. The Apostle John tells us, "If any one loves the world, the love of the Father is not in him" (1 John 2:15).

In the next verse John describes the seductive lure of the world: "For all that is in the world, the lust of the flesh and lust of the eyes and the boastful pride of life, is not from the Father, but is from the world." With this threefold enticement, the world stirs up within our hearts a strong desire for satisfaction through wrong desires.

"The lust of the flesh" is the world's appeal to our physical desires. Sensuality. Immorality. Pornography. Drugs. Alcoholism.

"The lust of the eyes" is the seduction of our eyes with the world's goods. It breeds a materialism that must have more and more of the world. Lust causes us to become obsessed with the glitter of "things."

"The boastful pride of life" tempts us to self-elevation, arrogance, egotism, and obsession with our own importance. It is the drive for popularity and prestige.

Men, we all encounter these stumbling blocks. There seems to be no end to their seductive attempts to mislead and corrupt us. We must resist the attraction of the world (Romans 12:2). We must not become entangled with the world's values, lifestyle, and godless philosophy. These are dangerous stumbling blocks.

Let me tell you quite candidly, I struggle with this attraction of the world. These have been allurements in my life. And still are.

Having once had a taste of the world's "good life," I know how hard it can be to resist the attraction. Materialism can spin its web around my heart. It is hard to cut the cords and remain unstained.

Stumbling Block 3: Our Flesh

Here is a third stumbling block: our flesh. This one is not so obviously seen because it arises from within. It is hidden within our own hearts. It is our sinful flesh.

When the Bible says flesh, it docs not mean the skin that covers our body. The flesh is our sinful human nature. It is called the old man, the old self, the body of sin. It contains our self-centeredness that leads us away from God. It is the evil inclination that lurks within us, a propensity for evil that pulls us toward sin.

Let's disclose four sometimes subtle but always deadly ways the flesh rears its ugly head.

Pride

First, *pride* can cause us to stumble. This is the chief destructive obstacle within our flesh. Solomon records, "Pride goes before destruction, and a haughty spirit before stumbling" (Proverbs 16:18). Pride causes us to run God's race with our nose in the air. No wonder we fall.

It comes in many disguises: male ego, the drive to be number one at all costs, glorying in the world's approval, the quest to be the best regardless of whom it hurts. The attention is on me, my, and mine.

Muhammad Ali once spoke of himself before his 1971 title fight with Joe Frazier thus:

There seems to be some confusion. We're gonna clear this confusion up on March 8. We're gonna decide once and for all who is king! There's not a man alive who can whup me. [He jabs the air with half a dozen blinding lefts.]

I'm too smart. [He taps his head.]

I'm too pretty. [He lifts his head high in profile, turning as a bust on a pedestal.]

I AM the greatest! I AM the king! I should be a postage stamp—that's the only way I could get licked.[1]

By the way, Ali lost to Frazier. Need we say more?

Greed

Second, *greed* is another stumbling block within. It is the drive for more and more and more. It is never being content with what you have, the restless passion to always have more.

The Bible says, "They shall fling their silver into the streets, and their gold shall become an abhorrent thing. . . . They cannot satisfy their appetite, nor can they fill their stomachs, for their iniquity has become an occasion of *stumbling*" (Ezekiel 7:19, emphasis added). Despite having silver and gold in abundance, the heart's appetite is not satisfied. It must have more. Always more. The sin of greed is a sure occasion of stumbling.

Years ago, a great ship struck a reef and began to sink. The people on the ship had only a few minutes to escape. So they abandoned all their belongings and fled to the lifeboats.

One man, however, ran back to his stateroom and filled his pockets with his money and jewelry. This took just long enough to ensure that no room was left in the lifeboats for him. The man put on a life jacket and jumped overboard with his pockets full of his personal belongings. But, as his friends looked on from their lifeboats, they saw him hit the water and plummet to the bottom like an anchor.

The weight of the money and jewelry was too great to allow him to float. He sank to his death.

Greed often fills us with what becomes our own destruction.

H. L. Hunt, at one time the world's richest man, was once asked how much was enough money. To which he replied, "Just a little bit more."

It is this mentality: Get all you can, can all you get, sit on the lid, and let the rest of the world go to hell.

Men, are you driven by the desire for more? Always more? Always bigger? Always better? This is greed. A stumbling block.

A Loose Tongue

Third, *a loose tongue* can cause us to stumble. In the previous chapter, I gave a painful illustration of how my tongue caused another to stumble. But listen, that's *not* what I am talking about here. *Now* I'm talking about my tongue causing *me* to stumble. Ouch! James writes, "If any one does not *stumble* in what he says, he is a perfect man, able to bridle the whole body as well" (James 3:2, emphasis added).

Few stumbling blocks can trip a believer more easily than a dangling tongue. Our tongues can get so long, we can actually trip over them as we run.

A woman once came to John Wesley, convicted of her gossiping. She confessed that she wanted to put her sinful tongue on the altar. Wesley replied curtly that he did not think the altar was large enough.

Another time, a young lady said to Wesley, "I think I know what my talent is."

Wesley said, "Tell me."

"I think it is to speak my mind," she replied.

"I do not think God would mind if you buried that talent," Wesley said.[2]

Men, this is not just a problem for women. Our tongues, too, can cause us to stumble.

We hurt ourselves when we hurt others with our tongue. Like the man who knocked himself out trying to throw his boomerang away, our hurtful words come back to haunt us. And hurt us. What goes around, comes around. Especially with our words.

Always speak as if you were in the presence of Christ. Say nothing that would be inappropriate if He were present. Because He is.

Sexual Lust

Fourth, *sexual lust* is another fleshly stumbling block that we must avoid. Jesus said, "Every one who looks on a woman to lust for her has committed adultery with her already in his heart. And if your right eye makes you *stumble*, tear it out, and throw it from you. . . . And if your right hand makes you *stumble*, cut if off, and throw it from you" (Matthew 5:28-30, emphasis added).

Don't misunderstand. Jesus is not calling for self-mutilation. Even a blind man can lust. He is saying we must deal radically with lust in our heart. We must take drastic steps to remove it.

I will deal with this subject of lust more fully in chapter 11. In fact, I will devote the entire chapter to it. But, let me say now that sexual lust must be mastered.

I have found the best defense is a good offense. Both in football, and with lust. Defeating lust requires an all-out, aggressive saturation of my mind with the Word of God.

I am an intently single-minded person. Very monothematic. When my mind is dwelling on God's Word and His holy character, then it is not free to wander onto what is wrong. Meditating on God helps avoid this major stumbling block.

Paul writes, "Whatever is true, whatever is honorable, whatever is right, whatever is pure, whatever is lovely, whatever is of good repute, if there is any excellence and if anything worthy of praise, let your mind dwell on these things" (Philippians 4:8).

These are the entrapments of the flesh: pride, greed, a loose tongue, lust. They are hideous, ugly, and deadly. They head the résumé of everyone who loses God's race.

It is not enough to just recognize them. We must resist and replace them with what is holy and righteous. If we are to say no to these enticements, we must say yes to Christ. Yes to His lordship. Yes to His power. Yes to His holiness.

Stumbling Block 4: Other Believers

The fourth stumbling block is very subtle. Would you expect your own teammates in the race to cause you to fall? Probably not. But by their actions and attitudes, they can do just that.

Let me remind you again that we are not racing against one another. My victory does not depend on me "beating" you. Nor vice versa. We are racing against ourselves and the track, not against other believers. Therefore, we can encourage one another to excel without fear of personal loss.

Nevertheless, the influence of other believers is a very real and powerful force, either for good or for bad.

The Bible clearly warns us against causing another believer to sin: "Therefore let us . . . determine this—not to put an obstacle or a stumbling-block in a brother's way" (Romans 14:13). This is a serious offense against Christ, as well as against that Christian.

Conversely, this verse implies that we must be careful not to allow the influence of another believer to cause us to stumble. This influence can arise from their Christian liberty (1 Corinthians 8:9). Or it may be something that is clearly sinful (1 Corinthians 15:33). But fellow runners can trip us. And cause us to fall.

The 1984 Olympics will always be remembered for a tragic event. It focused on Mary Decker of the United States and Zola Budd of South Africa (but she was running for Great Britain) in the women's 3,000-meter run.

Midway through the race, Decker and Budd were running even. Stride for stride. Budd, who was running barefoot, slightly clipped the back of Decker's heel. Unintentionally.

Decker went down hard as if she were shot. She was too injured to complete the race. Her stumble caused her to lose in her attempt to win the gold medal.

Not only did it cost her this race, but she also did not run competitively for an extended period of time. It cost her many victories.

Men, the same can happen to you and me. Unintentionally perhaps, other runners can cause us to stumble and lose the race. Just as we must not be a distraction to others in the race, neither should we allow another to cause us to fall.

That is why we must keep our eyes riveted upon Christ as we run. If we become too focused upon others—their shortcomings, their failures, their opinions, their successes—then we will surely trip and fall over their life.

Throughout the day, Jesus Christ must remain preeminent in our hearts and minds, the object of our adoration and thoughts. Others will fail us often, causing us to fall. But Christ will never fail us.

Stumbling Block 5: God Himself

Here is the final stumbling block: God Himself. Would you believe God Himself can be a stumbling block? Yes, I said God. I have purposefully reserved this one for last. Because it is the most serious stumbling block of all.

Let me first make a disclaimer. I am not saying that God is the author of sin. Nor am I saying that He tempts us to sin. What I am saying is that God allows us to suffer the consequences of our sin. He places stumbling blocks in our path to knock us on our back. From there we can humbly look up to Him.

In other words, we are knocked down to look up. There can be a time in a believer's life when God must discipline him. God, in love, disciplines us for our good. Yes, God loves us and accepts us, just the way we are. But he loves us too much to let us remain in our sin.

His loving discipline seeks to remove us from our sin. Consequently, when we go too far into sin, He will place a stumbling block before us to discipline us. The purpose is to cause us to fall. Often, it takes being knocked flat on our backs before we look up to God. He allows us to stumble, not to harm us needlessly, but to bring us back to Himself.

Israel's Discipline

Such was the case with God's people, the nation Israel, in the Old Testament. Their worldliness and immorality became a cause for His divine discipline in the form of stumbling blocks.

In Jeremiah 6:21, God Himself says He will place stumbling blocks before His willfully disobedient and unrepentant people: "Thus says the LORD, 'Behold, I am laying stumbling blocks before this people. And they will stumble against them.'"

In Ezekiel 3:20, God states that He will lay a stumbling stone before a once-righteous man who has fallen into apostasy: "When a righteous man turns away from his righteousness and commits iniquity, and I place an obstacle before him, he shall die."

Isaiah wrote, "It is the LORD of hosts whom you should regard as holy. And He shall be your fear, and He shall be your dread. Then He shall become a sanctuary; but to both the houses of Israel, a stone to strike and *a rock to stumble over*, and a snare and a trap for the inhabitants of Jerusalem. And many will stumble over them. Then they will fall and be broken. They will be snared and caught" (Isaiah 8:13-15).

Either the Lord is the cornerstone of our lives, or He is a rock over which we stumble and fall. When we fail to build our daily lives upon His wisdom and truth, we are subject to His stumbling blocks. Maybe too often, we give Satan credit when it is actually God who is at work in our lives.

Similarly, Jesus Christ will be either a cornerstone or a stumbling block. The Apostle Peter writes,

> And coming to Him as to a living stone, rejected by men, but choice and precious in the sight of God. . . .
>
> "Behold I lay in Zion a choice stone, a precious cornerstone, and he who believes in Him shall not be disappointed." . . . But for those who disbelieve, "The stone which the builders rejected, this became the very cornerstone," and "A stone of stumbling

and a rock of offense"; for they stumble because they are disobedient to the word. (1 Peter 2:4,6-8)

Ultimately, these verses say that when we receive Christ by faith,
we build our lives upon Him (Matthew 7:24-25). He becomes our
cornerstone, who holds us up and gives strength to our entire life. If
we refuse to trust in Christ, then we stumble over Him and are eternally
destroyed.

Practically, as we run God's race, we must run in close fellowship
with Christ. We must continually trust in Christ, much as a building
constantly rests upon its cornerstone. When we fail to do so, we stumble
through our disobedience and fall into serious consequences.

Men, these are the five stumbling blocks we will face: Satan, the
world, our flesh, other believers, and God Himself. We must be ever
on the alert as we run God's race and not allow ourselves to falter and
suffer loss.

NEVER SAY NEVER!

Some of you are saying, "This would *never* happen to me. Why are you
talking to *me* about this? I'm not going to fall." Such naive thinking
only assures the probability that you will fall. Stumbling is an ever-
present danger for all of us. No one is immune. No one is safe.

The Bible warns, "Let him who thinks he stands take heed lest
he fall" (1 Corinthians 10:12). When we have just come off a spiritual high or victory, we are prime candidates for catastrophe. Many
times, our most tragic defeats come on the heels of our greatest spiritual
victories.

Peter learned that lesson. Painfully.

The scene is the Upper Room, the night before Jesus was crucified.
Our Lord tried to prepare His disciples for what was to occur by saying, "You will all *fall away* because of Me this night" (Matthew 26:31,
emphasis added). To fall away means to stumble. Jesus was saying, "You
will all stumble tonight. You are headed for a devastating fall tonight.
Your world is about to be turned upside-down through a fall."

But Peter—who always suffered from foot-in-mouth disease—
shot back, "Even though all may *fall away* because of You, I will
never *fall away*" (verse 33, emphasis added). Peter thought he would
never fall. He certainly never meant to fall. Especially not that night.
He was saying, "Other runners may stumble and fall flat on their face,

but not me, Lord. I will never stumble in the race."

Knowing the human heart, Jesus sadly replied, "This very night, before a cock crows, you shall deny Me three times" (verse 34). In other words, "Peter, you say you won't stumble? You may be running fine now, but tonight you will fall flat on your face. Three times!"

Men, you know what happened to Peter. The Bible records that he did just as Jesus had said. He fell flat on his face. Three times.

Never presume that you are incapable of stumbling into sin. Never. Satan is too cunning. The world is too seductive. Our flesh is too weak. Other believers are too influential. Distractions are too numerous. God is too concerned.

Never say never!

GET BACK INTO THE RACE!

If you are like me, you are saying, "Good grief, I stumble and fall all the time. Is there any hope for me?" We all stumble. None of us makes it through the race unscarred by sin.

And you ask, "After I fall, can I get back in the race?"

Sure. Here is how.

First, you must *confess your sin*. First John 1:9 says, "If we confess our sins, He is faithful and righteous to forgive us our sins and to cleanse us from all unrighteousness."

To confess one's sin means to agree with God about one's sin. To acknowledge that it is wrong. To tell God that you have fallen short of His glory.

When we confess our sins, God cleanses our sin by the blood of Christ. He loves to forgive our sin. Fully. Completely. Freely. It is His nature to forgive. Once confessed, our sin will never be brought up again.

Second, you must *forsake your sin*. You must not commit a sin, confess it, and then return to it—only to fall again. Proverbs 28:13 says, "He who conceals his transgressions will not prosper, but he who confesses and forsakes them will find compassion." This is a call for repentance. To run from your sin. To forsake it.

Third, you must *get back into the race*. You must get back on your feet and continue running the race. God is a God of a second chance. And a third. And a fourth.

Peter fell, but he got back in the race. After he denied the Lord, he confessed his sin (John 21:15-17) and resumed his place of spiritual leadership (Acts 1:15). He was the powerful preacher on the day of Pentecost. He preached, and three thousand souls were saved (Acts 2:3-41).

Jonah fell, but he got back in the race. God told him to go to Ninevah to preach, and he went the opposite direction. He stumbled and fell. But he spent the night on a foam-blubber mattress in the belly of the whale, and he confessed his sin and got back in the race. He went to Ninevah and many thousands were saved (Jonah 3).

So, can you get back in the race if you have stumbled and fallen? Yes, you can. Confess your sin. Forsake it. And get back in the race.

Get up and run.

The movie *Chariots of Fire* depicted the life of Eric Liddell and his quest for the Olympic gold medal. Early in the movie, Liddell is running a race in the Scottish Highlands. Many local Scots have turned out to see this "Flying Scot" run.

As the runners make the first run, Liddell trips and falls. Flat on his face. The crowd gasps and groans as the race appears lost for Liddell. It is a moment of personal decision for the "Flying Scot." Will he stay down? Will he concede the race? What will he do?

To everyone's astonishment, he gets back up and reenters the race. Far behind the pack, Liddell runs as fast as he can. Gradually, he overtakes one runner. Then another.

Finally, he captures the lead. Eric Liddell speeds down the final straightaway and breaks the tape at the finish line. He is exhausted, bent over, gasping for air, collapsed. But victorious. He fell, but got back up. He came back to win the race.

That is the message of grace in the gospel of Jesus Christ. Though we fall, we may get back into the race. There are many stumbling blocks lurking in our path as we run God's race: Satan, the world, our flesh, other believers, and God Himself. There is not a one of us who will not fall at various points in the race. We are all prone to sin.

But when we do fall, it need not mean that we will automatically lose the race. If that were so, we would all lose. When we become entangled with sin, we must confess it, forsake it, and get back in the race.

Please do not misunderstand. There are serious consequences to our sin. But that doesn't mean there no longer remains any chance for victory. We may overcome our stumbling blocks through the grace of God. We may overcome isolated defeats and bounce back to experience His ultimate victory.

Maybe you have been knocked down in life's race. Hard. Perhaps you are lying on the track hurt, disappointed, discouraged. Maybe you think you can never win. You may have lost your will to even finish the race.

I have good news. Failure is never final as long as there is the grace of God. If you have fallen, you *can* overcome defeat. If you have stumbled, you *can* still win the victory.

Get back up!

Get back in the race!

Don't lie there!

Failure is never final.

NOTES
1. Michael Green, ed., *Illustrations for Biblical Preachers* (Grand Rapids, MI: Baker Book House, 1989), page 289.
2. Green, page 379.

CHAPTER 8

YOU DON'T HAVE TO GO TO BOSTON TO RUN A MARATHON

★

T he third Monday in April. If this date means anything to you, you are definitely a serious marathoner.

On this date the Boston Marathon—the world's oldest, longest-standing, and most prestigious race—is run every year. On this date, the finest runners from around the globe gather to run this marquee event. There is nothing like Boston. Nothing. No other race generates such electricity, nor exudes such mystique.

This third Monday in April is also Patriots Day in Massachusetts. A state holiday. Thus, over a million spectators line the course to witness this sports spectacle.

With media-filled helicopters hovering overhead, approximately six thousand of the world's elite runners bunch nervously at the starting line in Hopkington, Massachusetts. Their destination—downtown Boston, twenty-six-plus miles away.

Landmarks of Tradition
Along the route, two memorable landmarks have become ingrained in the rich tradition of the Boston Marathon.

The first is the all-girls school Wellesley College, located at the halfway point. The student body of this college lines both sides of the course to cheer the "old men" along. The sight and sound of attractive coeds provide a much-needed emotional lift and encouragement to the drained runners.

The second landmark is Heartbreak Hill. After passing Wellesley College, the runners face a series of five ascending hills spread out over the next eight miles. Climb, plateau; climb, plateau; etc. Gut-check time. The fifth and climactic hill is the shortest—but it's also the steepest. And it comes at the twenty-one mile mark. Heartbreak Hill is exactly that—a heartbreaker. A lungbreaker. A backbreaker.

The difficulty is not in the steepness of Heartbreak Hill, but in its location. It comes at a point in the race when legs are already exhausted and lungs are ready to burst.

Once past this "cardiac climb," the race leads downhill into the heart of downtown Boston, amid the skyscrapers and many historic buildings.

Approaching the Finish Line

Over the last five miles, anxiously awaiting spectators line both sides of the course, peering into the distance to catch the first glimpse of the oncoming runners. They shout to the weary racers encouraging words of inspiration: "You can do it!" "You're looking good!" "You're almost there!"

As the runners continue their odyssey, they anxiously search the horizon for the red Citgo sign perched high above. When they reach it, they know only one mile remains between them and the end of the race. A sharp right. A turn left. Before them lies the most strenuous straightaway in all of sports. Six hundred agonizing strides, down a corridor framed by towering buildings and packed bleachers, toward the finish line of the Boston Marathon.

Amid the shadows of the tall office towers looms the finish line at Copley Square, just in front of the Boston Public Library. Here, in bleachers nestled between the tall buildings of downtown Boston, over one-hundred thousand supporters await their heroes.

The flashing lights on the motorcycle escort signal to the crowd the advancing runners as they stride for the finish line. The crowd rises to its feet and responds with a deafening roar of approval. The runners can feel the roar of the crowd surge throughout their numb bodies. Every runner is a hero. If you run and finish this race, you are an undisputed champion.

The Boston Marathon is now over. Another page of history is

recorded. These gallant runners have run the race. They have met the challenge. They have finished the course. They have won the prize.

Can't you sense the exhilaration as these runners come to the finish line? Can't you feel the vibration of the crowd's roar? Can't you hear the motorcade at the finish? Can't you smell the sweat of the athletes? Can't you just taste the victory?

Must We Run in the "Big Races"?
In the world of competitive marathoning, world-class runners must run in the "big races." Marathons like Boston, New York City, London, Rotterdam, the Olympics.

You cannot be a champion marathoner by just competing against the local talent. You must go where the big-time runners are.

You cannot be a recognized champion and stay home. To be the best, you must beat the best. You must travel great distances to face the stiffest competition.

If you are not willing to travel, you will always just be a second-class runner. No matter how fast you think you are.

Men, some people think the Christian life is the same way.

They think the "big race" is out there somewhere. They think to be a big-time Christian you need to go across the ocean. To the mission field. To Africa. To Europe. Or at least across the country—to seminary.

But the truth is, you do not need to go out looking for God's race. It is right in front of you. The Bible says, "Let us run with endurance the race that is *set before us*" (Hebrews 12:1, emphasis added). It is set by God right before us. It is right under our noses. Not "out there" somewhere. But right where you live.

In the Christian life, you do not have to go to Boston to run a marathon. God has a championship race for you to run at home. Right where you are. In your office. In your family. In your neighborhood. In your school.

Some people think that unless they go across the country, or halfway around the world, they will remain a second-class Christian. You know, "*Just* a businessman." Or "*Just* a layman."

Daily Olympics
Nothing could be further from the truth. In the Christian life, the "big races," the Olympics, are held every day in your home, in your office, in your school.

You do not have to go to the mission field. Nor to seminary. Nor into the ministry. Certainly, God will call a few of us to do that. But most Christians will run God's race right where they are.

It is not the place that counts. It is the race.

Is this not liberating? This truth gives new significance to the day-to-day grind of life. Nothing in my life is meaningless. It is all important. Because it is a part of God's race for me.

God's race before me is very simply God's will for my life. No more, no less. God's will is the track on which we run this race of faith. It is important that we understand what this track is and how we can discover it!

God has placed a race—a track—right before each of us. Christians run on a specially prepared track called God's will. God has a plan for each of our lives—a blueprint. It is called His will. There are several features of God's will that we must grasp if we are to recognize God's track before us.

It was just such a race, much like the Boston Marathon, that the writer of Hebrews had in mind when he wrote, "Therefore, since we have so great a cloud of witnesses surrounding us . . . let us run with endurance the race that is set before us" (Hebrews 12:1). In this chapter, we want to focus on the last part of this verse: "Let us run the race set before us."

While you may never make it to the Boston Marathon, God has a race for you to run right where you are.

What strategy do you need to follow to run this race? I want to give you four key strategies that will show you how to run God's race. You can run like a winner!

RUN YOUR OWN RACE!

Here is the first strategy: Run your own race! God has an individual race for each of us to run. No two races are run exactly alike. No two runners are exactly alike. I do not run your race. You do not run mine. You do not have to copy another believer's pace. We each run at our own pace.

In competitive marathoning, some runners like to get a quick start. Others like to lag behind and make their push at the end. Some like to run in a pack. Others like to run alone. Some like to set the pace. Others like to follow the pace. The point is, no two runners run exactly the same way.

Many factors determine how one's individual race is run. Speed.

Body strength. Personality. Emotions. Health. Familiarity with the course. Other runners. Past successes. The last race. Weather.

No two runners are exactly alike; no two races are run exactly alike.

A number of different factors determine our different races. Different spiritual gifts. Different callings. Different temperaments. Different natural talents and abilities. Add to that different backgrounds. Different passions. We are all wired up so differently.

Men, God has an individual race for your life. No one else is meant to run your race. If I were to run your race, I would miss God's individual race for my life. God has a tailor-made race for each of us.

Please do not misunderstand me. I am not saying there are different roads that lead to Heaven. Jesus Christ claims that He alone possesses exclusive passage to the Father: "I am the way, and the truth, and the life; no one comes to the Father, but through Me" (John 14:6). Only one road—the bloody cross of Jesus Christ—leads us to the Father. I believe that with all my heart.

What I am saying is that there are different individual races for each of us to run. Different paces. Different speeds. Different places in the pack. God has not cut us out with a cookie cutter. We do not all look alike or sound alike. Neither do we run alike.

I find this truth very liberating. I must allow God to be as unique with me as He is with you. You can be who God uniquely made you to be.

Don't Run Someone Else's Race
Let me illustrate. When I was in college, there was a professor who had a tremendous impact upon my life. He was a lawyer who was teaching a business-law course. He was successful, smart, sharp, and explosively funny, the kind of person to easily influence an impressionable student like myself.

I soon found myself wanting to be just like him. I figured the way to be successful, smart, and sharp was to be a lawyer. So, guess what? I headed off to law school. To be like my prof.

Once I got what I wanted, I did not want what I got. I was miserable in law school. Absolutely depressed. I hated it.

I took a leave of absence to work for this professor in his bid for the Texas state senate (which he won and eventually went to Washington as a U.S. congressman).

It was there, working in his political campaign, that I made a sobering discovery. I was not running God's race for my life. I was running someone else's race. I was trying to be my professor, not the person God had called me to be. I had gotten off track.

This was a painful lesson to learn. But a much-needed one.

I must run my own race. Not somebody else's.

Men, this is a key strategy we must follow. Run your own race! Do not run somebody else's race. Be the person God uniquely created you to be.

FOLLOW GOD'S TRACK!

Here is the second strategy: Follow God's track! Picture God's race being run on a divinely prepared track. Call it God's will for your life. You do not make up your own route to run. You do not find your own way to the finish line. God has divinely prepared the track that He has chosen for you to run.

God does not say, "You are here, at point A. I want you to get over there to point B. Now, go find a way. Get there somehow, some way." I am glad to say God already has designed a route to get me where He wants me. I simply run God's track, which He has already prepared.

It Was Designed in Eternity Past

The Bible teaches that in eternity past—before I was even born—God planned the path I should take. He laid it all out. With infinite wisdom He weighed and considered all the possible options and chose the best race for me to run.

Before I even entered the race, God laid out my track to run. When in history I should be born. Where on the globe I should live. Who my parents would be. Who my spouse would be. What my vocational calling would be. My personality makeup. My spiritual gifts. Where I would serve Him. All this—and much more—was a part of His predetermined plan for me.

This predetermined plan was certainly true for Jeremiah. God chose him to run a divinely prepared race that was mapped out ahead of time. This race was planned long before Jeremiah was born. God explained to the prophet, "Before I formed you in the womb I knew you, and before you were born I consecrated you; I have appointed you a prophet to the nations" (Jeremiah 1:5).

It was also true for the Apostle Paul. The apostle came to realize he was running a sovereignly prepared race. A race prepared long before his birth. Every step he ran was a step of destiny. Paul testified, "He who had set me apart, even from my mother's womb, and called me through His grace, was pleased to reveal His Son in me, that I might preach Him among the Gentiles" (Galatians 1:15-16).

Men, this is no less true for you and me.

Our race has been specially designed by God from before the foundation of the world. We run with a sense of destiny. Everywhere I run, I arrive by divine appointment. God has a reason—a divine purpose—for everything that happens in my life. God has prepared good works for each one of us in which to walk (Ephesians 2:10).

Every day when I get out of bed, I am running into a day specially designed by God to fulfill His purposes. It is all a part of His master plan. Every step is divinely appointed.

This is a track forged in the heart and mind of God from before time. With my name on it.

It Is Constructed on God's Character

A second aspect of this track is its divine character. This track—God's will for my life—is constructed on God's character. The character of the Designer is revealed in the track itself. Because God is *good*, His will for me is good. Because He is *perfect*, so His track is perfect.

The Bible teaches that the will of God is "good and acceptable and perfect" (Romans 12:2). That means it is the very best track on which to run. "Good" means devoid of any evil. God will not lead us to sin. His will is also "acceptable," meaning that when we discover it, we will like it. It will be acceptable to us.

Back in my college days, I used to fear that if I followed God's will for my life I would have to marry someone ugly and go to Africa and help people with monkeys on their heads. If any of that is what God wants me to do, then great. He will put the desire in my heart for His will. He will make it acceptable for me. I would be miserable doing anything else.

His will is "perfect." It cannot be improved upon. If I had a thousand lifetimes to redesign God's track, I could never improve upon it. Because He is perfect, it is perfect.

I hear people talk about surrendering to the will of God. They talk like it is surrendering to defeat. "Well, I guess I'm *stuck* with doing God's will." Get those notions out of your brain. God's will is something good that you get in on.

The Lord says, "I know the plans that I have for you; . . . plans for welfare and not for calamity to give you a future and a hope" (Jeremiah 29:11).

Who wouldn't "surrender" to this?

It Encompasses All My Life

Third, everything that God designs for my life ought to happen on this track. Everything!

No part of my life is excluded from His plan. Paul tells us that God "works all things after the counsel of His will" (Ephesians 1:11). This truth is an all-inclusive statement.

Some people make a false dichotomy in life between the spiritual and the secular. They assume that only the spiritual is a part of God's race, that is, Bible study, prayer, witnessing, church work. The secular, they reason, must not be a part of God's race. Things like work, parenting, recreation.

As a result, a gross misconception arises about the race, that only certain parts of my life are run on the track. No way! God has designed all of it. Every area of my life is to be included in the race.

This race is not run only on Sundays with a few spiritual pit stops during the week. No way. Everything I do is a part of God's race. Everything.

God's race includes my spiritual life, my church life. Sure. But it also includes my family life, my professional life, my social life, my recreational life, my community life, and my financial life. Everything about my life is a part of God's race.

It Leads Me into the World

Fourth, this track leads into the world. For the most part, it is not run behind the cloistered walls of the church. It is run out in the world.

In the Olympics, only the first lap of the marathon is run in the stadium. Almost the entire race weaves through the streets of the city—by the banks, through the marketplace, next to the schools, past the hospital, by the factory. The course snakes through the entire community. Finally, the race reenters the stadium for one final lap before the crowd for what has been called "the most dramatic moment in sports."

Men, God's race is like this. It takes us into the world. Through neighborhoods. Into the business districts. Into the classroom. Into the marketplace. We do not run our laps continuously behind the four walls of the church.

God's track leads us into the real world, where real people need Him. We do not stay within the secluded confines of Christian fellowship. Mostly, we run into the world to impact our community with the gospel of Jesus Christ. We must "take it to the streets."

Jesus commanded his first runners, "Go into all the world" (Mark 16:15). He said, "Go therefore and make disciples of all nations" (Matthew 28:19). He prayed to His Father for us: "I do not ask Thee to take them out of the world, but to keep them from the evil one" (John 17:15).

We are to be in the world, but not of the world.

READ THE SIGNS

Men, I am assuming you are with me. Most of you are saying, "Great! I want to follow God's track. But I am not certain where it is. How do I recognize His track for my life?"

Before runners run a marathon, they study the markings and signs along the way. They know that to lose sight of the course for very long will probably mean losing the race. It means loss of energy, loss of time, loss of opportunities. Perhaps loss of victory.

Even so, God has clearly marked His race for our lives. The key to knowing God's race for our life is knowing how to read the signs along the way. What are the signs that reveal the way?

Here are seven key signs that reveal how to follow God's track.

Follow God's Word
First, the Bible leads us along God's track. As we run in this world of darkness, we need light to see the way. God's Word is this light—"a lamp to my feet, and a light to my path" (Psalm 119:105). Scripture shines a spotlight before us and reveals the direction in which we should run. His individual will for me is always found within the wisdom and morality revealed in His Word.

How exactly does the Bible—an ancient book written thousands of years ago—reveal God's way to modern men today? There are several key questions we must ask, the answers to which reveal to us the way. Here they are.

One, "Is there a command to obey?"

The Bible is filled with the divine commands to you and me. There is no question what God's will is in these areas. Our obedience to His commandments leads us precisely into the center of His will.

For example, "Do not get drunk with wine, for that is dissipation, but be filled with the Spirit" (Ephesians 5:18). This is clear-cut. Nonnegotiable. Black and white. There is no doubt what God's will is in this matter. His track will always—I repeat, always—be found within the boundaries of obedience to His commandments.

Two, "Is there an example to follow?"

The great majority of the Bible is written in story form—narrative and biographical literature. The first seventeen books of the Old Testament are narrative; the first five of the New Testament are biographical and narrative. These historical books contain the lives of real people who followed God. Their godly lives are recorded as an example for us to follow (Romans 15:4). As we model their lives, their walks of faith point out God's track to us.

Take Daniel, for example. As I read that this exiled prophet placed a higher allegiance on obeying God than obeying government, his life reveals God's way to me today. When I am confronted with a similar tension between the earthly and the heavenly, I must choose to obey God, not men. Always.

Three, "Is there a promise to claim?"

As a father's will governs the management of his vast estate, so too is the Bible filled with promises from God to His children—to bless, to enrich, to satisfy. God's estate is a huge reservoir of spiritual riches, able to meet all the needs of our life. Charles Spurgeon once compared these divine promises to blank checks issued by God to His children. Already signed by God, they are to be cosigned by His children, brought to Heaven's treasury, and drawn against the wealth of Heaven's account.

For example, Jesus says, "Whatever you ask in My name, that will I do, that the Father may be glorified in the Son" (John 14:13). Just think about the vast inheritance that Christ desires to share with us. Of course, the key is praying in Jesus' name—for those things which honor and glorify His name.

Four, "Is there a sin to avoid?"

The Bible holds up before us certain sins that must be avoided. At all costs. They are clearly out of bounds. For example, "For this is the will of God, your sanctification; that is, that you abstain from sexual immorality" (1 Thessalonians 4:3). God's will is always found where sexual purity is maintained. This is a no-brainer, guys. Any step toward immorality is definitely out of bounds and off track.

Five, "Is there a principle to follow?"

A principle is a timeless truth tightly stated. It is a short, pithy, practical statement of truth drawn from a passage and used to guide our life. Principles are broad statements of truth that universally apply in every situation of life. For example, Joshua led the children of God in a march around the city of Jericho, giving a shout of victory as they trusted God to fight for them. The principle is that we should worship before we go to war. Praise God in the face of the impossible and watch Him act on our behalf.

Obviously, the better we know God's Word, the better God communicates His will to us.

Follow the Spirit's Witness

Second, God's Holy Spirit sets the pace for us along God's track. The Bible says, "For all who are being led by the Spirit of God, these are the sons of God" (Romans 8:14). Just as there is the outward objective witness of God's Word, so there is the inward subjective witness of the Spirit.

While this verse primarily addresses the Spirit leading us to put to death the sins of the flesh, it does speak, in a general way, to the Spirit leading us in our daily life. The witness of the Spirit is the inner "tugging" we may feel in our heart. It is the divine pressure of the Holy Spirit that urges us to pursue a particular action.

A little boy was out flying his kite on a windy day. The blowing breeze pushed the kite higher and higher until it disappeared above the clouds.

Soon, one of his buddies came up. He looked up and saw only string ascending into the clouds. But he saw no kite. "Why are you holding onto that string?"

The little fellow replied, "I've got a kite up there."

His friend looked up again. But he still could see no kite. "I don't see it. How do you know there is a kite up there?"

"Well, I know it's there," he said, "because I can feel the tug."

Men, that is precisely how the inner witness of the Holy Spirit works within our hearts. While we do not see God visibly, we feel the inner tug of the Spirit leading us into God's will. We are constantly in touch with God, sensing His leadership in our lives.

Often, this witness of the Spirit of God is received and recognized through prayer and meditation. The Bible says, "If any of you lacks wisdom, let him ask of God, who gives to all men generously and without reproach, and it will be given to him" (James 1:5). Prayer helps us sense the Spirit's inner witness in our heart.

Wisdom, according to J. I. Packer, is the best means to achieve the highest goal. It is the earthly living of heavenly truth that the Spirit applies to our hearts.

When we are confused and do not know which course to pursue, God invites us to pray. To ask for His wisdom. To seek His counsel. Jesus says, "You do not have because you do not ask" (James 4:2). The Holy Spirit gives us the wisdom to discern the course to pursue.

God does not answer begrudgingly. Just as any earthly coach gives counsel to his athletes, so God desires to give wisdom to His runners. When we ask for it, God delights in bestowing such wisdom.

Listen to James again: "But let him ask in faith without any doubting, for the one who doubts is like the surf of the sea driven and tossed by the wind" (James 1:6).

We must ask for wisdom in faith without a wavering doubt. This means without being divided within oneself, without being pulled in two directions. We should not think, *God can! . . . No, He can't.* We must believe that God is infinitely wise, unconditionally loving, and ultimately sovereign. Thus, He knows best, wants our best, and is able to bring it to pass. No matter how impossible it seems.

Lloyd John Ogilvie wrote, "Prayer does not overcome God's reluctance to guide us; but it puts our wills in condition to receive what He wills for us."[1] Prayer does not so much change God's will as it finds God's will.

Follow "Sanctified" Common Sense

Third, God's track is followed through "sanctified" common sense. Now, all too often, common sense is just that—common. But what I am talking about is *sanctified* common sense. A Spirit-enlightened common sense through a renewed mind.

God has given us a mind with which we are to make decisions. We are to think rationally, logically, and perceptively in discerning His will. Because we are created in the image of God, He has given you and me the capacity to think, reason, and choose. We are able to sort things out, analyze situations, think things through, make evaluations, have insights, and draw conclusions.

Too often, we think God's will is found through some bizarre, unconventional way. But that is not usually the case. It is through a renewed mind that His will is discovered (Romans 12:2).

I read about a lady who received a brochure advertising a tour of the Holy Land. Because going to Israel was one of her lifelong dreams, she really wanted to go. She had the money, the time, the interest, and the strength. But was it God's will?

Before going to bed, she read the pamphlet once more and noticed that the airplane they would be traveling on was a 747 jumbo jet. After spending a sleepless night wrestling with the pros and cons, she awoke the next morning. She opened her eyes and *there* was the answer. She just knew it was God's will for her to go to Israel.

How did she know for sure?

When she awoke, she glanced at her digital clock and it read 7:47. That was her "sign" from God. (In reality, her mind was already made up and she was grasping for any "sign.")

I wonder what would have happened if she had awakened in the middle of the night only to read 1:47. Maybe that would have been a sign to take a smaller plane, like a crop duster.

Listen, God has given us brains (although that could be debated based on a lot of religious television programs). He expects us to use them with sanctified common sense.

How did the early Church know God's will? Most often, the Holy Spirit worked through a renewed mind. In Jerusalem, the church leaders discovered God's will through what *seemed* good and right: "Then it seemed good to the apostles and the elders, with the whole church, to choose" (Acts 15:22). The apostles concluded that "it seemed good to us" (verse 25). This rational thinking was in conjunction with the inward witness of the Spirit. It was the Holy Spirit working through the thinking capacity of men yielded to God. And that's how the early Church made its decisions: "For it seemed good to the Holy Spirit and to us" (verse 28). His will just seemed right. Logical. Prudent.

God also led Paul in much the same way. By his sanctified common sense, he sent Epaphroditus to the Philippians: "I thought it necessary to send to you Epaphroditus" (Philippians 2:25). He simply *thought* it best. No bells and whistles.

A. W. Tozer remarks, "The mind is good—God put it there. He gave us our heads and it was not his intention that our heads would function just as a place to hang a hat."[2]

Follow Your Heart

Fourth, God leads through our hearts just as He works through our minds. The biblical view links our minds with our hearts.

A strong compulsion within to pursue a course of action is often

God revealing the way. J. I. Packer advises us to "note nudges from God that come your way—special concerns of restlessness of heart."[3]

God worked through Nehemiah's heart to lead him into His will. Nehemiah recorded, "I arose in the night, I and a few men with me. I did not tell anyone what my God was putting into my mind to do" (Nehemiah 2:12). Literally, mind here is the word *heart*. God led Nehemiah by putting into his heart what He wanted him to do. This godly man felt a strong passion and desire to do this for God.

When I consider my own call into the ministry, the leading indicator of God's will for me was this strong desire. It was not something I merely wanted to do. It was something I *had* to do. A holy passion. A heavenly compulsion.

When Paul wrote Timothy, he told him this strong compulsion would accompany God's leading men into the ministry: "If any man aspires to the office of overseer, it is a fine work he desires to do" (1 Timothy 3:1).

The verbs employed here are very strong. *Aspires* (*oregomai*) means a strong aspiration to covet after, as one would for Heaven (Hebrews 11:16). *Desires* (*epithumea*) is even stronger. It is a great desire to long for, to covet after (Luke 16:21, 17:22, 22:15).

So, God puts His desires into our hearts. They then become our desires, which lead us into His will and along His track.

Follow Open Doors

Fifth, God's track is also followed by open doors of opportunity. We believe that nothing occurs by random chance. God is the sovereign Lord of Heaven and earth who ultimately controls every circumstance of human history. He governs all the events of our lives. As R. C. Sproul says, "There are no maverick molecules on this planet. All are under His control."[4]

Consequently, our sovereign Lord opens doors before us through which we are to run. He prepares a way to travel where there is no way. He lays the track for us to run. And removes the obstacles. These opportunities we call "open doors."

In the New Testament, the phrase "open door" is used five times. In each instance, it refers to an opportunity. Jesus told the church at Philadelphia, "Behold, I have put before you an open door which no one can shut" (Revelation 3:8). For Paul, God created opportunities for service and ministry by placing open doors before him (1 Corinthians 16:8-9).

God does the same for you and me. He opens doors, which permits us to follow His track.

Follow Your Strengths

Sixth, God leads through our strengths. Before I can make proper decisions, I must properly know myself. I must know my strengths and weaknesses because God generally leads me to exercise my strengths.

Paul told young Timothy, "Pay close attention to yourself" (1 Timothy 4:16). In other words, watch over yourself. Know yourself. Know your gifts, your strengths, your abilities.

The apostle writes, "I say to every man among you not to think more highly of himself than he ought to think; but to think so as to have sound judgment" (Romans 12:3). We should know and think about our strengths. We must not overestimate them; nor should we underestimate them. But we should know them! The verse immediately before this one talks about how to know God's will. I can only conclude that knowing my strengths and gifts is a part of knowing God's will and following His track.

Each of us has an array of God-given strengths and spiritual gifts that we bring to any situation. When presented with a choice concerning where to work or where to serve Christ, go with your strengths. Know your strengths and go with them.

Knowing God's will involves developing and using one's spiritual gifts and natural abilities. It is a matter of stewardship. We must be faithful to utilize and maximize what God has entrusted to us.

Jesus told a parable about a king who went on a journey (Luke 19:11-27). Before he left, he gave ten of his slaves ten minas each. "Do business with this until I come back," he told them.

When the king did return, each slave was called to give an account of what business he had done with the king's money.

One invested well and made ten minas. To which the king replied, "Well done, good slave."

Another made five minas. "Well done, good slave."

But the last failed to invest the king's money. He sat on it, and it brought no return. The king was greatly displeased. He ordered his initial investment taken from this overly cautious slave and given to the others.

The slave was not judged for what he did not have, but for what he *did* have. Not for his weaknesses, but for his strengths.

The lesson of the parable is this: God has entrusted to every believer a certain stewardship. Every believer must be faithful to invest God's entrustment, or face His displeasure.

What gifts, talents, and resources has God entrusted to you? Your wise and aggressive investment of what He has given to your care will lead you into God's will.

No two of us are exactly alike. Each of our individual races will focus upon the wise investment of what strengths God has entrusted to us.

Follow Godly Counsel

Seventh, God leads His way through godly counsel, through the corporate wisdom of others—a spouse, a pastor, a friend, a mentor, a parent, a prayer partner.

The wisdom of Solomon says, "Where there is no guidance, the people fall, but in abundance of counselors there is victory" (Proverbs 11:14). *Guidance* is a nautical term that pictures the steering of a ship into a port. God steers my life into His will through the wise counsel of others.

Without such guidance, I will stray off course during the race. But with the collective wisdom of other believers, there is victory. Their counsel will help steer me correctly along God's track and toward God's victory.

DON'T GET OFF TRACK!

Let me give you one last strategy: Don't get off track! This may sound too negative, but it needs to be said.

Unfortunately, the potential exists to get off track during the race. I can misread the signs. I can veer off the course. I can overstep the boundaries and leave the track.

I do not mean to imply that we can lose our salvation in Jesus Christ. Such is impossible. The Bible clearly teaches the eternal security of the believer. Once I become a child of God through the new birth, I can never be unborn and put out of the family. Once saved, always saved.

By leaving the track, I mean that I can wander from His will. I can stray from the clearly marked track that God has laid before me. I do not lose my salvation, but I do lose my way. I lose my sense of direction and precious time.

So I must be careful to stay "on track."

When I leave the track to pursue my own path, I must reenter

God's track as soon as possible. Precious time is being wasted. If I stay off track too long, I might even become disqualified by God and lose a reward.

Clearly, obedience in the Christian life is very important. Every step of the way.

Some Christians, after starting on the right course, become diverted from the track on which God originally set them. They just veer over to the side. They sit down and rest in the grandstands. They become passive spectators rather than prize-winning champions. Some believers even get busy serving in the stands. Selling hot dogs. Taking up tickets. But they are not in the race. They are off track and out of God's will.

The Christian's race begins when a believer is born into God's Kingdom and ends when he enters God's presence. The interval between is the time he has to complete his spiritual course.

If he strays from his course, he loses valuable time. The only way to complete the course within the allotted time is to stay on course.

We have a limited time to finish our spiritual race. In a sense, we are running against the clock. So, make "the most of your time, because the days are evil" (Ephesians 5:16).

PUTTING IT ALL TOGETHER

This chapter has focused upon the four key strategies for running the race set before us. They will surely lead to victory at the finish line.

Do you remember what they were?

First, run your own race! We each run our own race. Don't run somebody else's race. Be who God uniquely created you to be.

Second, follow God's track! God has divinely prepared a track for you to run—His will. Simply discover and follow God's will for your life.

Third, read the signs! God's will is not hidden. You will find it by following God's Word, the Spirit's witness, "sanctified" common sense, your heart, open doors, your strengths, and godly counsel.

Fourth, don't get off track! Be careful not to veer off the track. Don't stay off course. Precious time and energy will be lost.

These four strategies are crucial for victory.

NOTES
1. Lloyd John Ogilvie, *Your Will God's Will* (Eugene, OR: Harvest House Publishers, 1989), page 34.

2. A. W. Tozer, as quoted by John Blanchard, *Gathered Gold* (Phillipsburg, NJ: Evangelical Press, 1985), page 203.
3. J. I. Packer, *Hot Tub Religion* (Wheaton, IL: Tyndale House, 1988), page 114.
4. R. C. Sproul, "God or Chance?" from the sermon series, Live from The Falls Church, Ligonier Ministries, 1986.

CHAPTER 9

IT'S ALWAYS TOO SOON TO QUIT!

★

"WINNERS NEVER QUIT. QUITTERS NEVER WIN."
I can still see that sign hanging in our locker room. Plain as day. It had been mounted there by my high school football coach to build character and instill courage within us. The letters were hand-painted onto a stained wooden plaque. But more importantly, that sign would become inscribed upon my heart. And indelibly etched upon my soul.

I can still see it. "WINNERS NEVER QUIT. QUITTERS NEVER WIN."

The message came through loud and clear. This was not rocket science. It would become the bedrock foundation of our every drill, our every practice, our every game.

A quitter? To this day, no word is so revolting or distasteful. The words "I quit" were not allowed in our vocabulary. Quit is a four-letter word. I would rather die than quit. Call me anything, just don't call me a quitter.

My coach spent three years building into us the virtue of endurance. Some call it perseverance. Others tough-mindedness. Whatever. It was drilled and instilled into us. You just never quit. No matter how impossible the odds. No matter how tough the opponent. No matter how dark the hour. You just *never* quit.

147

Never!

A champion *never* throws in the towel. He would rather eat the blasted towel than throw it in.

Endurance means never quitting, regardless of the score. You suck it up and go. If you are playing poorly, you hang tough until you can turn it around. When the chips are down, you buckle your chin strap. You just *never* quit.

What Makes a Winner?

The mark of a winner is his heart. The will to win. The resolve to never give up. The drive to always press on to the goal. When the going gets tough, the tough get going.

Call it heart. Perseverance. Character. Call it whatever you want. God calls it endurance.

Take, for example, a gifted athlete who is blessed with every advantage: size, height, speed, muscles, strength. He is the total package. A physical specimen. Inevitably, he is competing against a less-gifted athlete, who is smaller, slower, shorter, less muscular.

So often, the less-gifted athlete beats the swifter and more muscular one. Strange as that is, even Solomon recognized "that the race is not to the swift" (Ecclesiastes 9:11).

What makes the difference?

The edge lies deep within. The difference is the heart. The will to win. A winner has the willpower and staying power to endure in the heat of battle. He overcomes whatever is necessary to win. Whatever the opposition. Whatever the difficulty, be it mental fatigue or physical pain. Whatever. He endures all to win.

I can still see that sign: "WINNERS NEVER QUIT. QUITTERS NEVER WIN."

This truth is equally applicable in the Christian life. God's champions never quit. To win the incorruptible crown, we must run with endurance and press on to the finish. Quitters never win. Not in God's race.

The Heart of a Winner

The Bible says, "Let us *run with endurance* the race that is set before us" (Hebrews 12:1, emphasis added). The key here is endurance. Perseverance. Staying power.

This chapter is an anatomy of the heart of God's champion, of a man who is pursuing the ultimate prize. If we were to peel back the heart of God's champion one layer at a time, what would we discover? I believe we would feel the heartbeat of a deep commitment to run the race with endurance. To finish the race, come hell or high water.

Show me what it takes to stop you, and I will show you whether you are a champion or not. I am amazed at what little things eventually stop us in God's race. Petty things. Peripheral things. Hurt feelings. Misunderstandings. Trivial pursuits.

I must tell you that this chapter will be both comforting and convicting. It is a two-edged sword. It cuts both ways. It will be comforting to those of you who are undergoing a personal trial and testing. This chapter will encourage you to endure and press on because a crown awaits you. Hang in there, my friend.

James put it this way: "Blessed is a man who perseveres under trial; for once he has been approved, he will receive the crown of life" (James 1:12). The one who endures and perseveres through trials will win the crown.

Men, did you get that?

A crown awaits you if you will persevere through your fire.

But at the same time, this chapter will be most convicting if you are complaining about your problems and wanting to bail out. If you are whining your way through the Christian race, this chapter will be a swift kick to the backside. Maybe you have stopped running. Perhaps you have given in to the pain, the weariness, the exhaustion. Hey, get back in the race! Stop that incessant whining. Suck it up!

Remember, this is a book for men who win. Not men who whine! Get a grip!

Now, let's look at this factor of endurance and answer three simple questions: What is it? What does it look like? How can I live it?

WHAT IS ENDURANCE?

The Christian life is a long-distance marathon—not a one-hundred-yard sprint. Endurance is more important than sprinter's speed. The last one-hundred yards of the race are more important than the first one-hundred yards.

The Bible says, "Let us *run with endurance* the race that is set before us" (Hebrews 12:1, emphasis added). Endurance (the Greek work is *hupomone*) means a steady determination to keep going. The word combines the verb *to bear up* with the prefix *under*. It literally means "to bear up under," as bearing up under a heavy load. It means to bear up patiently while running under the constant stress and demand of a marathon.

We're talking about perseverance, steadfastness, and persistence. To keep running even when you want to stop. To never give up. To refuse to quit.

The Christian life is a protracted obedience in the same direction. It requires hanging tough through the daily grind. Day after day. It will push us to the very limit of what we can endure. Remember, this is a marathon—twenty-six-plus grueling miles—not a short sprint.

The First Marathon

Let's consider the origin and significance of the term *marathon*. The year was 490 BC. On the open plains near the small town of Marathon, the ancient Greeks met the invading Persian army in a strategic battle. If the Persians won, the Greek Empire would surely topple.

Against impossible odds, the Greeks charged into the Persian camp, catching their enemy by surprise, and defeated the Persians, thus saving the Greek Empire from sure defeat.

A Greek soldier—Pheidippedes—was then dispatched to run to headquarters in Athens, twenty-two miles away, with the good news of victory. With determination and resolve, Pheidippedes ran through the night all the way from Marathon to Athens.

Upon entering the city of Athens, he sprinted to his superiors. "Rejoice," Pheidippedes gasped, "we have conquered!" As he delivered the message, he fell to the ground. Dead.

Pheidippedes became a Greek hero. A symbol of endurance and determination. As a tribute to this faithful soldier who ran so bravely through the night, the "marathon" race was born. Runners in the Greek Empire would soon attempt to duplicate his courageous feat, calling up the same endurance.

How then did it become twenty-six-plus miles?

The precise distance of the marathon was not fixed until recently. The distance Pheidippedes ran from Marathon to Athens was slightly more than twenty-two miles. In 1908, the Olympics were held in London, and the marathon was extended to twenty-six miles, 385 yards. Why such an unusual distance? That year, the Olympic race would begin at Windsor Castle and end at the new White City Stadium because an English princess wanted to watch the start of the race from her castle window and then view the finish from her seat at the stadium. To meet the request of royalty, the length of the race would have to be extended. And it was.

This new distance, set to please Her Highness, was measured to be exactly twenty-six miles, 385 yards. Two miles longer than the previous marathon. This became the standard distance for all marathons, even to this day.

What is the significance of this background information? When we compare the Christian life to a marathon, we are talking about a long-distance race. The Christian life is a long-distance haul. It is no short sprint. We don't run a while and stop, then run again. A marathon race requires perseverance and sustained effort.

I fear there are too many "one-hundred-yard dash" Christians. They begin well, sprinting out of the starting blocks. They are at church every time the door is opened. They read their Bibles and their enthusiasm is obvious to all. But eventually, they burn out and drop by the wayside. They go up like a rocket. And come down like a rock. In the day-to-day grind of the race, they eventually weaken, waver, and lose heart.

Now, let's suppose *you* are running a marathon. For the first mile, you are leading the pack. At the halfway mark, you are further ahead than you have ever been. At twenty miles, you are way ahead. Everybody is behind you.

But at the twenty-five-mile mark, the "bear" jumps on your back. You're dying. You're wanting to quit. The blisters on your feet are killing you. Your lungs are gasping for air. Your knees are wobbling. You don't want to keep going any longer. Your body is screaming at you: "Stop! I can't take it any longer. There's got to be an easier way."

What do you do? Do you give in? Do you quit trying, quit running? Do you just pull over to the side and sit down? That would be the easy way out.

No, you choose to endure. You choose the hard way. Because you know in your heart, no matter how *fast* you have run, no matter how *far* you have run, no matter how *far ahead* you are, if you quit now, you will *lose* the prize.

Men, some of you are in danger of quitting.

Listen, it is *always* too soon to quit!

Some of you are in danger of quitting your marriage. Taking the easy way out. It matters little that you began your marriage well. What matters to God is that you *finish* well. Finish your race with your spouse still with you.

Others of you are weakening to the lure of the world. You are about to replace your passion for Christ with the lust of the world. Don't let it happen. Again, that's the easy route. Persevere in your love for Christ.

WHAT DOES ENDURANCE LOOK LIKE?

In order to run with endurance, we must have a realistic idea of what it involves. We have looked at a definition. Now, let's consider a description of endurance. There are four basic components.

A Long-Term Commitment

First, if I am to run God's race with endurance, I must have a long-haul commitment to Christ. I must see my commitment as lifelong, not a ninety-day option.

Walter Alston managed the Brooklyn and Los Angeles Dodgers for twenty-four consecutive years. At the beginning of each year, he would sign a one-year contract. He signed twenty-four one-year contracts. His commitment was for only one year at a time.

Some people live the Christian life this way. Just making short commitments each year, to be reconsidered and renegotiated annually.

Men, it can't be this way. We make one long-term commitment to Christ at the beginning of the race. It is not subject for renegotiation annually, to be renewed at our whim.

I began God's race with the commitment that I follow Him the rest of my life. Wherever He leads, I will go. Whatever He requires, I will give. I *will* run with endurance to the finish line. That is my front-end commitment. Jesus says, "No one, after putting his hand to the plow and looking back, is fit for the kingdom of God" (Luke 9:62).

Men, maybe some of you have never stopped to consider that this is not a one-hundred-yard dash, but a marathon. You were once running in a dead sprint, but now you're just dead tired. Because you soon discovered this is a marathon.

No runner would ever finish a marathon if he entered thinking he was running a one-hundred-yard dash. Never. He would never "just happen" to run twenty-six-plus miles. He could only finish if he knew on the front end that it was a marathon and had resolved, "I am going all the way to the end."

Running the Christian race with endurance requires making a lifelong commitment to go all the way with Christ. We must purpose and resolve to finish strong, no matter what. To live every day for Christ. For the rest of our lives.

Pain and Agony

Second, we must recognize that running a marathon involves pain and agony. This is not a Sunday stroll in the park. This is an agonizing marathon. It involves discomfort and suffering. Men who win have counted the cost and know that without pain there is no gain.

Jesus says, "In the world you have tribulation" (John 16:33). His race involved a cross. And so will ours: "Jesus said to His disciples, 'If anyone wishes to come after Me, let him deny himself, and take up his cross, and follow Me'" (Matthew 16:24).

The Greek word for race (*agon*) is the very word from which we get the English word *agony*. Literally, Hebrews 12:1 says, "Let us run with endurance the agony set before us." God's race is *agonizing*. Did you hear that? Agonizing. A blessed agony, yes. But agony, nevertheless—grueling, demanding, draining, stressful, taxing, tiring, torturing. Don't let anyone tell you otherwise.

We will experience the pain of self-denial and cross bearing and persecution and rejection and misunderstanding and Satanic attack and thorns in the flesh. We must undergo trials and mortification of the flesh and long hours and the storms of life and the squeeze of this world and even God's discipline. The agony of repentance and the deep conviction of our sin and mourning over our wrongs will assail us. This is all par for the course. It's all hard work and sacrifice. God's marathon is painful and agonizing.

Paul shares his spiritual diary in 2 Corinthians 4:8-10: "We are afflicted in every way, but not crushed; perplexed, but not despairing; persecuted, but not forsaken; struck down, but not destroyed; always carrying about in the body the dying of Jesus, that the life of Jesus also may be manifested in our body."

A Major Gut Check

The apostle says he ran with endurance "in afflictions, in hardships, in distresses, in beatings, in imprisonments, in tumults, in labors, in sleeplessness, in hunger" (2 Corinthians 6:4-5).

His marathon concluded, Paul then catalogs some of his trials, which included the following:

> Five times I received from the Jews thirty-nine lashes. Three
> times I was beaten with rods, once I was stoned, three times
> I was shipwrecked, a night and day I have spent in the deep. I
> have been on frequent journeys, in dangers from rivers, dangers

from robbers, dangers from my countrymen, dangers from the Gentiles, dangers in the city, dangers in the wilderness, dangers on the sea, dangers among false brethren; I have been in labor and hardship, through many sleepless nights, in hunger and thirst, often without food, in cold and exposure. (2 Corinthians 11:23-27)

The Christian life is a serious marathon to me. (I'm worn out just reading this.) It is one major gut check. It was for Paul. And it will be for you and me, too. We are exposed to much the same things that Paul was as we run God's race.

Too often, we seek the easy way out. But God's way involves pain and suffering.

I have men come to my office and whine, "Pastor, I want out of my marriage. I'm just not happy." They want to quit running. Quit their spouse. Quit their marriage. Quit their children. The easy way out.

I will say, "God wants you to remain faithful in your vow to your wife." Too often, I hear in response (and it breaks my heart), "But God wouldn't want me to be unhappy. I've met somebody else who really turns me on."

What I want to do is jerk them up by the lapels, pull them up close, and say, "Listen, suck it up! Gut it out, man! This is a marathon. If you are just trying to feel good, you're in the wrong race. Buck up!" Mind you, I don't say that. At least not in those exact words. But I want to.

However, I do say, "I want to help you honor your marriage vows. Run with endurance. Hey, it's *only* another forty years. That's nothing compared with eternity. You can endure another forty years."

Men, the Christian life is not the subtraction of problems from life, but the addition of power to endure them. What about you? Are you looking for the easy way out? There is no painless path. Not in God's marathon.

An Aggressive Effort

Third, running with endurance requires my aggressive effort. I must give an all-out effort.

When the Bible says, "Let us run with endurance" (Hebrews 12:2), it is calling us to action. I must assume the responsibility to endure. This is not something I just sit back and let God do.

Now, don't get me wrong. I believe God must give me the power to run. And I believe that He is at work within me (Philippians 2:13). But *I* must pick up one aching foot and put it before the other. I must keep running. I bear that responsibility.

When I hear a passive view of the Christian life like "let go and let God," I get the clear picture that I should shift into autopilot and stop running. It urges me to just let God take over, and He will do it. This mindset is dangerous because it paralyzes my aggressive effort. Yes, God will take over, but only as I assume my responsibility to run with endurance.

Men, I want to point out another danger to my aggressive effort—an overemphasis of God's sovereignty to the exclusion of pressing human responsibility. Now, I believe in God's sovereignty. Absolutely, totally, unequivocally. But a constant focus upon divine sovereignty to the neglect of my human responsibility is paralyzing. Our race demands endurance. And endurance demands our effort. I can't sit around and speculate, "I wonder if I am predestined to keep enduring." That's crazy. God says, "Run with endurance." Just do it!

I must step out by faith, trusting in His grace, and run with endurance. I am responsible before God to endure. He will enable me, but I must endure. I must pursue holiness. I must pursue obedience.

Paul writes, "I press on in order that I may lay hold of that for which also I was laid hold of by Christ Jesus. . . . One thing I do: forgetting what lies behind and reaching forward to what lies ahead, I press on toward the goal for the prize of the upward call of God in Christ Jesus" (Philippians 3:12-14).

This proclamation pictures a runner with aggressive, energetic endurance. He is straining every muscle to win. He is "reaching forward," giving his all to press to the finish line. So must we.

A Strong Finish
Fourth, I must finish strong if I am to run with endurance. The last one-hundred yards are more important than the first one-hundred yards. It is not enough to start strong. I must finish strong.

Maybe you are thinking, *I am retired. I am going to drop out for awhile. I've done my time. Now it's time for those younger people to get involved.*

The Devil told you that.

You may be retired from the office, but you are never retired from Jesus. All your retirement does is give you more time to serve God. Don't stop running!

I have some great prayer warriors in my church: Older folks who are world-class runners in God's race. They are not retired; they are refired. In fact, I think they are just now hitting their stride. Instead of slowing down, they are picking up their pace. The closer they draw to the finish line, the faster they are running. May their tribe increase.

Men, we must finish well. This requires endurance. There has never been an athlete who has ever won who did not endure.

Never, never, never quit.

It is always too soon to quit!

The Slowest Marathon, the Greatest Victory

In the 1986 New York City Marathon, almost twenty thousand runners entered this famous race. What is memorable about it is not who won, but who finished last. His name is Bob Wieland. He finished 19,413th. Dead last. Bob completed the New York Marathon in—are you ready for this?—four days, two hours, forty-eight minutes, seventeen seconds. Unquestionably the slowest marathon in history. Ever.

What makes Wieland's story so special?

Bob ran with his arms.

Seventeen years earlier, when he was a soldier serving in Vietnam, Bob's legs were blown off in battle. When he runs, Wieland sits on a fifteen-pound "saddle" and covers his fists with pads. He "runs" with his arms.

At his swiftest, Bob can run about a mile an hour, using his muscular arms to catapult his torso forward. One "step" at a time.

Bob Wieland finished four *days* after the start. What did it matter? Why bother to finish? Here's why: There is a victory to be experienced in just finishing the course. Bob Wieland ran with endurance. In my estimation, he won because he ran with the greatest endurance, overcoming the greatest adversity.

The Christian life is much like this. The Bible says, "Many who are first will be last; and the last, first" (Matthew 19:30; see also 20:16). It will take another world to determine who the real winners are down here on earth.

You may believe you are so far behind that it is no use to even try to finish. That is where you are wrong. Endure and finish the course. Leave the evaluation to God. Remember, it is the last one-hundred yards that really count.

Champions like Bob Wieland, who finished last down here, will be crowned winners up there.

The Apostle's Marathon

Paul finished well.

He ran God's marathon, beginning on a Damascus road and enduring all the way to his death just outside of Rome. He sprinted to the finish. Shortly before his death, Paul wrote, "I am already being poured out as a drink offering and the time of my departure has come. I have fought the good fight, I have finished the course, I have kept the faith" (2 Timothy 4:6-7).

As Paul approached the finish line, he did not slow down. With head held high and eyes on the goal, the apostle pushed to the tape. He widened his stride; he picked up his pace; he sprinted to the finish.

Jesus finished well.

He ran God's marathon for our life beginning in a stable in Bethlehem, and He endured all the way to the cross. He did not pull up short. The night before He was crucified, Jesus prayed to the Father, "I glorified Thee on the earth, having accomplished the work which Thou hast given me to do" (John 17:4). He finished the course!

When Jesus died on the cross, He cried out, "It is finished!" (John 19:30). He had finished the race God had set before Him. Redemption was accomplished! Jesus sprinted all the way to the finish line and burst the tape with His chest out and head erect.

I am reminded of a poster depicting a young football player, sitting dejected, battered, and beaten, with the caption "I quit." In the background is the shadow of the cross on Calvary with the caption ". . . but I didn't."

No, Jesus didn't quit. He finished the race.

Men, how will it be with you? Will you sprint to the finish? Are you running with endurance?

Winners never quit. Quitters never win.

HOW MUST I ENDURE?

We've defined it. We've described it. Now let's get intensely practical. I want to talk about some specific areas in which you and I must endure.

Certainly, I could say we must endure in every area of the Christian life, and I would be right. But time and space do not allow me to pursue *every* area. (Such a pursuit would be a marathon in and of itself.)

In the Bible, there are some specific areas mentioned in which we are encouraged to endure and not lose heart. It is on four of these areas that I want to focus our attention.

In each of these key areas, we have a natural tendency to quit. To stop running. I know I sure do. We need the prodding of the Holy Spirit to spur us to continue running—with patience and perseverance.

I am talking about areas like prayer and witnessing. Areas like love and good works. It is in these areas that we often grow weary and tired. And lose heart.

Let these next pages be an encouragement to pick up the pace, to widen your stride, and to sprint to the finish.

Relentless in Prayer

The first specific is prayer. I find it interesting that the only area in which Jesus instructs us not to lose heart is in the area of prayer. That tells me two things. One, we must have a real tendency to lose heart and grow weak in the area of prayer. Two, prayer must be especially important if Jesus singles it out.

When Jesus told the parable of the relentless widow, He taught His disciples that "they ought to pray and not to lose heart" (Luke 18:1). We must not lose heart in prayer. We must never give up in prayer.

Now, why would we so easily lose heart in prayer? Because when we pray, we do not usually receive the answer to our prayer immediately. So often, there is only silence. No response. No answer.

The illness remains. The needed job is still unoffered. The loved one is still lost. The injustice is not righted. Pray as you might, God has not yet answered.

So we lose heart and become discouraged. We live in an instant society, and when we do not get an instant answer we stop praying. We quit running in prayer. We get up from our knees and reason, *It is just not going to happen. God is not going to change it.* And endurance goes out the window.

Jesus knew we have this inherent weakness. So He told the following parable to encourage us to endure. To not give up in prayer. Jesus said,

> "There was in a certain city a judge who did not fear God, and did not respect man. And there was a widow in that city, and she kept coming to him, saying, 'Give me legal protection from my opponent.' And for a while he was unwilling; but afterward he said to himself, 'Even though I do not fear God nor respect man, yet because this widow bothers me, I will give her legal

protection, lest by continually coming she wear me out.'
. . . Hear what the unrighteous judge said; now shall not God
bring about justice for His elect, who cry to Him day and
night, and will He delay long over them? I tell you that He
will bring about justice for them speedily. However, when the
Son of Man comes, will He find faith on the earth?" (Luke
18:2-8)

Our Lord is teaching that we must endure in prayer. We must
continually come before God's throne with our requests. Even with
the same request over and over.

In another place, Jesus explained prayer this way: "Ask, and it shall
be given to you; seek, and you shall find; knock and it shall be opened to
you" (Matthew 7:7). Do you see the increasing intensity of this prayer
thrust? From asking to seeking to knocking. It pictures an aggressive
pursuit of God in prayer.

These verbs are in the present tense. They are most properly translated, "*Keep on* asking . . . *keep on* seeking . . . *keep on* knocking." In
other words, pray with endurance. Don't give up so easily in prayer. Be
relentless. Don't quit praying.

Men, have you slowed down in your prayer life? Have you stopped
altogether? Jesus says, "Pray and do not lose heart." You can start again,
right now.

Relentless in Evangelism
A second area in which we must endure is witnessing. I believe we have
a tendency to easily lose heart in our personal evangelism. Why is that?
Again, for two primary reasons. One, much like in prayer, when we do
not see immediate results, we lose heart and stop witnessing. Two, we
can receive persecution and ridicule when we witness, causing us to
lose heart.

Consider Paul's enduring example: "I suffer hardship even to
imprisonment as a criminal, but the word of God is not imprisoned. For
this reason I endure all things for the sake of those who are chosen, that
they also may obtain the salvation which is in Christ Jesus" (2 Timothy
2:9-10).

Paul wrote these words from a Roman prison cell shortly before
he was put to death. It would have been very easy for him to become
discouraged and to stop witnessing when he was put into jail.

Did Paul quit witnessing? Did he quit speaking Christ's name?

No, quite the contrary. Paul endured because he was confident of the sovereign working of God in the hearts of lost men. He knew that his witnessing would not be in vain because God has His people who will believe. So he endured in the face of great persecution knowing that the Word of God could not be imprisoned.

Men, we need to be reminded of this great truth. God has a chosen people who will surely come to faith in Christ. When men refuse our offer of the gospel, we need not lose heart because we know the sovereign purposes of God will still move forward. If one refuses Christ, another will receive Him. So, let us endure in our witnessing.

To whom have you witnessed and received a cold shoulder? A boss? A loved one? A neighbor? Do not quit witnessing. Run with endurance. Stay after them. God can overrule in their hearts. He can pry open even the hardest heart. Be encouraged.

Relentless in Love

Third, we must endure in loving others. Here is another area in which we can easily stop running with endurance. People can disappoint us, can't they? Hurt us. Even offend us. It can become very difficult to love some folks. Yet Paul says that love "bears all things, believes all things, hopes all things, endures all things" (1 Corinthians 13:7).

It is the nature of love to endure. Love refuses to quit reaching out, even in the face of rejection and opposition. It will not give up on someone, even when everyone else has given up.

Such enduring love is certainly the nature of God's love toward us. Despite our rejection of Him, He continued to reach out to us and to bring us to Himself. The story of the prodigal son verifies this. Really, it is the story of the forgiving father and his enduring love. It is found in Luke 15:11-24.

The son demanded his inheritance immediately, which is tantamount to telling his father, "I wish you were dead." A father's inheritance was not distributed until the time of the father's death.

Once he received it, the son crassly and coldly took the money and ran. He turned his back on his father and went to a far country. He just wanted to get as far away from his father as possible.

But he soon blew his money and then decided to come crawling back home. He came back on his hands and knees, begging to be received back.

How did the father respond? Did he fold his arms, furrow his brow, and give his son a lecture? No way! The father endured in love, despite

his son's rejection, and never ceased loving his boy.

When the father saw his son coming, his heart broke with love. He took off running down the road to meet his prodigal, embraced him, smothered him with kisses, and called for a feast.

He had never stopped loving that boy.

Men, that is precisely how we are to love others. Though others mistreat or belittle us, we are to endure in our love toward them. We must never quit loving them.

Toward whom have you grown cold in your love? Your wife? A once-close friend? An overbearing boss? An unkind family member?

Run with endurance. Love endures all things.

Relentless in Good Works

Let's consider one final area: good works. We must not grow weary in serving one another.

The Bible says, "Let us not lose heart in doing good, for in due time we shall reap if we do not grow weary. So then, while we have opportunity, let us do good to all men, and especially to those who are of the household of the faith" (Galatians 6:9-10).

As we run God's race, we can become so tired that we weaken in serving others. Losing heart and growing weary carries the idea of becoming exhausted and giving up in the race. We all face that danger while running the marathon.

You must exert energy to get energy.

STICK IT IN THE END ZONE!

Yes, it is still there. The sign. WINNERS NEVER QUIT. QUITTERS NEVER WIN. This slogan became my "creed" in my senior year in high school. It was only then that it came off the wall to grip my heart.

The scene was Jackson, Tennessee. Our opponent was the Jackson High Golden Bears. Undefeated. Ranked number three in the state. We, the White Station Spartans, were also undefeated and ranked in the top ten. The entire city was abuzz as two undefeated teams prepared to clash for western Tennessee bragging rights.

The game sure lived up to its advanced billing. It was a bone-crushing standoff from the kickoff to the final gun. With three minutes left in the game, the score was 7-6. The Golden Bears were clinging to a thin lead. We took the ball on our own thirteen-yard line. Eighty-seven yards to pay dirt. It looked like eighty-seven miles. I don't think we

even had eighty-seven yards total offense all night. This would be our last shot at winning. It was do or die. Now or never.

As quarterback, I huddled our team together and gave my best Knute Rockne speech: "I'm calling on each one of you to give everything you've got left within you. We've played together for the last five years. We've practiced together. Run together. Bled together. Sweated together. Now, let's win together.

"We will remember this drive for the rest of our lives. Forty years from now, when I see you at a class reunion, we will remember whether or not we stuck it in the end zone. Let's give it everything we've got and win this game."

With deep resolve, we broke the huddle as men on a mission: to stick it in the end zone. With every tick of the clock, every yard of advancement became more and more precious.

We moved the ball to midfield. I encouraged the guys, "Only fifty yards to go!" Two fourth-down situations left us no choice but to go for broke. This was no time to punt. Our backs were against the wall.

We converted both "suicide" fourth downs.

The clock continued to tick.

With each first down, we gained new confidence. Finally, we marched down to Jackson's five-yard line. With eighty-two yards behind us, we knew the last five would be the toughest. We *had* to score to win. The five-yard line is not sticking it in the end zone.

It was third down. Only fifteen seconds remained. We had two downs to score, but we wanted the touchdown on third down. If we didn't get it, we would be forced to kick a field goal, and that would spell big trouble. I was the placekicker. (That's why we were behind 7-6.)

One of our running backs brought the play in. "Power Sweep Right." The proverbial "Student Body Right." We lined up in strong formation right, which told the Golden Bears, "We're coming this way. Right at you." They answered with a stacked defense, ready for the challenge.

The line was drawn in the sand.

Both grandstands were on their feet screaming.

On the snap of the ball, I pivoted and pitched the ball to our fullback, sweeping right end.

Jackson High blitzed everyone. Everybody shot the gaps. I was immediately hit and driven face down into the turf, unable to see the outcome of the play. I just lay there waiting to hear which grandstands would explode.

Would it be theirs or ours? Then I heard it.

Our stands erupted! We had scored and won the game! We did it. Eighty-seven yards of glory. We had stuck it in the end zone. We had won.

You Can Stick It in the End Zone, Too!

Men, this is the kind of endurance we need in the Christian life. A deep resolve to run all the way to the finish line. A commitment to persevere, no matter what.

Some of you may be eighty-seven yards away in your marriage. You are wanting to throw in the towel. Don't. Hang tough.

Others of you may be fourth and five in your prayer life. Don't punt. Go for it. Reintensify your commitment in prayer.

Still others of you may be running out of time to reconcile a broken relationship. Don't settle for anything less than a complete restoration.

Endure. You can do it! With renewed resolve, you must determine to hang in there. Don't settle for anything less. Stick it in the end zone for the glory of God.

You say, "I want to do that. But how do I endure? I feel so weak. How can I hang in there?"

I have good news for you. In your weakness, God's strength is perfected. You are a prime candidate to experience the supernatural power of God to endure. I'm going to tell you how to endure in the next chapter. So stay tuned.

Let me simply conclude this chapter by saying it is always too soon to quit. Don't give up. You can do it, by God's help and strength. Don't lose heart.

Just do it!

CHAPTER 10

KEEP YOUR EYES ON THE PRIZE!

★

M en, in the last chapter we talked about how winners never quit and quitters never win. We must run with endurance. Now, let me encourage you to discover the strength to run God's race. To pursue the ultimate prize.

"Worst to First"

The 1991 World Series will long be remembered as one of the greatest ever played. Perhaps the greatest. It was a Cinderella story come true for the Atlanta Braves and the Minnesota Twins as both teams, in the span of one year, went from "worst to first" in their divisions to reach the World Series. There were five one-run games. Four were won on the game's final play, three went into extra innings. A true classic.

It all came down to the seventh and deciding game. For all the marbles. There would be no tomorrow. More than fifty-five thousand frenzied Twins fans were rocking Minnesota's Metrodome. Homer hankies were everywhere, urging the home team on.

The workhorse of the Twins' pitching staff, Jack Morris, was sent to the mound on a mission. There was one thing and one thing only on his mind—to win it all. The outcome of the game, the World Series, and the entire 1991 season all rested squarely on his broad shoulders.

Picture this: After eight pressure-packed innings, the score is still knotted 0-0. This is baseball's answer to the arms race, a real pitchers' duel. Mounting a serious rally, the Braves load the bases with only one out. Morris never blinks. He has waited a lifetime for this moment. Every ounce of concentration is riveted on the business at hand.

Jack Morris is focused.

The three Braves runners pose a serious threat to the Twins' place in history. One mistake from Morris and the score is 4-0, Atlanta. Sid Bream, the Braves' lefty batter, digs into the batter's box and begins waving a dangerous bat. A global television audience is glued to this epic moment in baseball history. Both dugouts are deathly still, except for the usual chewing and spitting. The deafening roar escalates from the partisan crowd. This is one of those moments you feel in the pit of your stomach. But Morris is numb to it. All he can see is the heart of Brian Harper's catcher's mitt.

Jack Morris is focused.

As Morris glares in for Harper's signal, he blocks out every distraction in this den of noise. His face is expressionless. Deadpan. His eyes bore a hole in his catcher's mitt, which is positioned low and inside in the strike zone. He toes the rubber, pauses after a slow stretch, glances at the runner on third, and then zeroes in on the catcher's mitt.

For one split second, Morris is absolutely frozen on the mound. He kicks his leg toward the plate and hurls a rocket low in the strike zone. Bream swings and makes contact. At the crack of the bat, all three Braves runners break. A sharp grounder bounces high off the synthetic turf to the Twins' first baseman, Kent Hrbek, who smothers the ball and fires a strike to home plate for out one. The catcher, standing on the plate, fires back to Hrbek at first for out two. A 3-2-3 double play! And the Twins are out of the inning. The bullet is dodged.

Jack Morris dances off the mound with a glazed stare, oblivious to the pandemonium that has just erupted around him.

Winners Block Out the Distractions

Winners must be able to focus. To block out all distractions. To zero in on the goal.

Jump with me from the diamond to the hardwood. Michael Jordan, the greatest basketball player on this planet, is at the free throw line shooting a one-and-one. The Detroit Pistons' defense has been clinging to this human highlight film like a cheap sweater. But nobody can shut him down. How do you contain the wind?

The Pistons' Dennis Rodman has been given the impossible task of stopping Jordan. Sure. In Jordan's face all night, Rodman still can't contain him. So Jordan is back on the line to shoot the one-and-one.

As Jordan eyes the basket, the Pistons' rowdy crowd rises to its feet to distract the Bulls' scoring machine. Behind the backboard, Detroit diehards are stomping their feet, waving their hands, shaking their programs. Anything to distract Jordan.

But Jordan doesn't even blink. His eyes are glued on the goal. Instinctively, he dribbles twice, sticks out his famous tongue, and with ice water in his veins, calmly converts both free throws.

Michael does not even see the intimidating crowd and their diversion tactics. He blocks out eighteen thousand screaming fans and goes about his business. (You know, men, just like we do all too often with our wives.) Just another day at the office.

Winners must block out distractions. Like Michael Jordan.

Winners Must Focus

Let's go back in time to the 1950s. Ted Williams was in the batting cage at Boston's Fenway Park taking his cuts. Unequivocally, the "Splendid Splinter" is one of the greatest hitters of all time. Arguably, the purest hitter in the game's history. Williams remains baseball's last .400 hitter, and when Ted called it quits, he retired with 521 lifetime home runs and a .344 career batting average.

What made Ted such a great hitter? Great eyesight? Perfect hand-eye coordination? Being a student of hitting? Yes, all of these things, but most of all, a rare ability to concentrate on the pitch. To block out all distractions. To focus.

As the story goes, his Red Sox teammates decided to test his notorious concentration skills by playing a prank on Williams. While Ted was hitting in the batting cage, his teammates quietly lit some firecrackers and tossed them at his feet.

Boom! Boom! Boom!

Guess what? Ted was so focused, he did not even blink. As the firecrackers went off at his feet, his eyes remained riveted on the pitch. He was so intense that he could block out every distraction. Even exploding firecrackers.

Winners must be focused. Like Ted Williams.

What do these three champions—Jack Morris, Michael Jordan, Ted Williams—have in common? Among many things, the ability to focus on a goal—whether a catcher's mitt, a basketball rim, or a pitched ball. The capacity to block out all other distractions and remain intent on the goal.

Champions compete as if wearing blinders. They are single-minded. Myopic. One-track-minded. Intent. Concentrated.

Do you think a major league pitcher could throw strikes if he were looking at the base runners? Do you think an NBA star could convert free throws if he were watching the antics of the crowd? No way. To win, one must be focused on the task at hand.

Winners must be focused. Like you and me.

The Bible says,

> Therefore, since we have so great a cloud of witnesses surrounding us . . . let us run with endurance the race that is set before us, *fixing our eyes on Jesus* the author and perfecter of faith, who for the joy set before Him endured the cross, despising the shame, and has sat down at the right hand of the throne of God. For consider Him who has endured such hostility by sinners against Himself, so that you may not grow weary and lose heart. (Hebrews 12:1-3, emphasis added)

Do you want to run with endurance and win the prize? Then fix your eyes on Jesus. This chapter is all about "fixing our eyes on Jesus." Running with eyes focused on Him. Being single-minded on Christ.

As we concluded the last chapter, I promised we would discover how to find the strength to run God's marathon with endurance. That will be our aim here. We will discover that fixing our eyes on Jesus produces the power we need to persevere. This chapter is critically important. Like the seventh game of the World Series. So read it carefully because here is how we find endurance to press on.

FIX YOUR EYES ON JESUS

What a runner focuses on during a race is critically important. As he comes down the straightaway, he must look straight ahead to the goal. To the prize before him. Not into the stands to see who is cheering. Not at the other runners. Not behind him. Such distractions would cause him to lose his balance, sacrifice his speed, or stray off track.

This principle holds true in the Christian life as well. What I focus my eyes on during the race will play a major factor in how I run the race. Therefore, we are not surprised that the Bible encourages us, "Let us run with endurance the race that is set before us, *fixing our eyes on Jesus*" (Hebrews 12:1-2, emphasis added). As I run God's race, I must be focused on Christ. I must be preoccupied with Him. My heart and mind must be fixed on Him.

Now, in order to understand what it means to be focused on Jesus, let's first determine what it does *not* mean. As I run God's race, I must not allow myself to become preoccupied with anything else, such as circumstances, self, Satan, other people, or even the Holy Spirit.

Not on Circumstances

First, our circumstances can become a dangerous distraction, stealing away the focus of our heart while we run. Too often, we allow our eyes to become fixed on our successes and failures, our good times and trials. Unfortunately, our circumstances are constantly changing—up and down, up and down. Therefore, our emotions and faith become like a roller coaster—up and down, up and down.

Whatever we focus upon controls our life. We come under the grip of our circumstances when we focus upon them.

Certainly, focusing on our circumstances is a very natural thing. But that is the problem. It is the natural thing to do, not the supernatural thing. The eyes of faith focus upon Christ, while the eyes of fear look at circumstances.

This was the Apostle Peter's problem. One night the twelve disciples were on the Sea of Galilee when a strong wind blew up. In the midst of the storm, Jesus came walking on the water toward their fishing boat (Matthew 14:22-33).

The disciples were terrified! They cried out in fear, "It is a ghost!"

Jesus spoke, "Take courage, it is I; do not be afraid."

Peter was overwhelmed at the sight of Christ walking on the water. In typical fashion, he wanted to come walking to Jesus. "Lord, if it is You, command me to come to You on the water," he said.

Jesus said, "Come!"

Peter hopped out of the boat and started walking on the water! First, one step. Then another. He was cruising.

Then something disastrous happened to Peter. He took his eyes off the Lord and began looking around at the crashing waves. Fear gripped his heart. And Peter started to sink.

"Lord, save me!" he cried.

Immediately, Jesus reached out His hand, lifted Peter up, and led him back into the boat.

Now, before we get too hard on Peter, remember that he at least had enough faith to get out of the boat.

What do we learn from Peter? As long as his eyes were fixed on Christ, he did the impossible and remained above his circumstances. But when he became distracted by the storm, he started to sink. And was soon under his circumstances.

The same principle is true as we run God's race. If we are to live above the circumstances, we must stay focused on Christ. As long as we do that, we can run on water. But the moment we lose sight of the Lord, we will surely sink. And get in over our heads.

Men, are you so focused on a problem that you have lost sight of the Lord? Maybe you are preoccupied with a career path now blocked. Or perhaps it's financial adversity. The greatest encouragement I can give you is to focus on the Lord.

We tend to sprint when things are going our way, but slow to a walk when things are not. That produces a "sprint, walk, sprint, walk" Christian life. Inconsistent. Erratic. Immature.

Not on Self

At other times, we are preoccupied with looking to ourselves. The result is the paralysis of analysis. We begin to overanalyze our motives. Or replay our past failures. We end up spending more energy questioning our motives than we do accomplishing the task. The Apostle Paul writes, "Forgetting what lies behind and reaching forward to what lies ahead, I press on toward the goal for the prize of the upward call of God in Christ Jesus" (Philippians 3:13-14). We are like a runner who is running with his head down, looking at his own feet or own arm motion, rather than looking straight ahead at the goal. No wonder we are slowed down and passed up by others.

Some of you may be victims of guilt. Satan is a grave digger, constantly shoveling up your past failures and faults. These are devilish distractions that impede the Christian's progress in pursuing the ultimate prize. Guilt should not be discounted. Often, it is a warning signal that something is wrong. But it should enhance our focus upon Christ all the more and require that we no longer dwell on our failures but on His grace and forgiveness.

Certainly, we must watch over our heart (Proverbs 4:23) and examine ourselves (2 Corinthians 13:5). But we must never allow ourselves to become preoccupied with ourselves.

Paul says, "If then you have been raised up with Christ, keep seeking the things above, where Christ is, seated at the right hand of God. Set your mind on the things above, not on the things that are on earth" (Colossians 3:1-2).

Not on Satan

Some Christians are, strange as it sounds, fixing their eyes on Satan. They have developed an unhealthy preoccupation with the Evil One. I sometimes think they fear Satan more than they fear God. Consequently, they see a demon behind every bush. They blame everything on the Devil.

But our eyes must not be focused on the opposition. We cannot win looking at the other team. If we do, doubts will arise and we will become defensive. Ultimately, we will lose.

Let me illustrate. I recently coached my twin boys' Little League baseball team. One of the first things I told the team was, "After you hit the ball, do not watch the other team field the ball. Just drop the bat and run to first base as fast as you can. But, do not—I repeat, do not—watch the other team!"

Guess what? My little sluggers would smack a line drive and then—you guessed it—just stand frozen in the batter's box and watch the other team field the ball. Only after watching them throw the ball to first base would they start to run. And all the while they were running to first base, they would be looking at the ball.

I would yell, "Run, run! Stop looking at the ball! Run!" Then they would run looking at me yelling at them.

Many a time they would be thrown out at first base by just a step. All because they watched the other team in the field rather than running focused upon the goal—first base.

There are a lot of Christians who live their lives just like that. They focus on the other team—Satan and his demonic host—rather than fixing their eyes on Christ. I agree we are not to be ignorant of Satan and his devices (Ephesians 6:10-17), but we must not be preoccupied with Satan. We must dwell on Christ, not the Devil.

Not on Other People

Some Christian runners are preoccupied with other people. They are looking at the other runners, or up into the stands to see if the crowd is approving. So much so that it causes them to stumble. Why? Because they have lost sight of the goal, Jesus Christ.

Men, we are headed for a fall if we are focused on others. Even our spiritual leaders may disappoint us. Maybe they didn't keep their word. They may not practice what they preach. If they fall into sin, it can cause us to stumble if we are riveted on them.

Let's face it. Our expectations of spiritual leaders are sometimes unrealistic. We put them on too high a pedestal. And when they fall, it can cause our whole Christian life to go into a tailspin if we focus on the man of God rather than the God of the man.

All this can lead to disappointment, disillusionment, and despair.

Let's consider again our race analogy. If we are way ahead of another runner, our tendency is to slow down. But remember, we do not compete against each other. God is measuring us against Christ, not the other runners. He may be expecting far more from us than from them.

Conversely, we may perceive that others are way ahead of us and become discouraged, lose heart, backslide, and come to a standstill. That would be tragic because God may be expecting far more from the front runners than He is from us.

I must confess to you the constant danger I face. I love to hear great preaching, just as I love to preach. Sometimes, the former is the enemy of the latter. For example, I love to listen to Billy Graham preach. Or Chuck Swindoll. Or Charles Stanley. But sometimes when I hear them preach, rather than encouraging me, it actually discourages me. Why? Because they are way ahead of me. In fact, their greatness can make me not even want to preach. Because no way do I measure up to them.

Instead, I must remain focused on Christ. Yes, I can benefit greatly from these godly men, but I must not look to them. I must only look to Christ. When I look to Him, I am always encouraged because I feel privileged to preach His Word.

Not on the Holy Spirit

I have purposefully saved this distraction—the Holy Spirit—for last. You may be saying, "Wait a minute! Time out! What is wrong with fixing my eyes on the Holy Spirit?"

Please notice that Hebrews 12:2 does not say "fixing our eyes on the Holy Spirit." Some Christian runners have a preoccupation with the third member of the Godhead—the Holy Spirit. But the Holy Spirit's preoccupation is making us preoccupied with Jesus.

Jesus says,

"But when He, the Spirit of truth, comes, He will guide you into all the truth; for He will not speak on His own initiative, but whatever He hears, He will speak; and He will disclose to you what is to come. He shall glorify Me; for He shall take of Mind, and shall disclose it to you. All things that the Father has are Mine; therefore I said that He takes of Mine, and will disclose it to you." (John 16:13-15)

The Holy Spirit's desire is that we be focused on Jesus Christ, not Himself. That *is* the Spirit's chief ministry. He is pointing us to Jesus. Bringing Christ more clearly into focus.

When the Holy Spirit becomes an end in Himself, then we have misunderstood His ministry. The Spirit's ministry is a means to an end—to focus on Christ.

Adrian Rogers has well said, "Whenever we see a parade with the Holy Spirit out in front, something is wrong. Jesus is always to be the One out front and the Holy Spirit is standing on the sidelines pointing us to Jesus."[1]

But on Jesus Christ

Okay, enough of the negative. Now, to the positive. On whom must we fix our eyes? Jesus Christ. We must be "fixing our eyes on Jesus the author and perfecter of faith" (Hebrews 12:2).

The word *fixing* (Greek word, *aphorao*) means "looking away to, focusing attention on, gazing intently upon." To fix our eyes on Jesus means to look with the eyes of faith to Christ. It means to be preoccupied with Christ. To trust Him. To love Him. To seek Him. To meditate upon Him. It is, quite simply, a Christ-centered life. Jesus only. Jesus always. No divided attention.

We are to run with eyes for nothing and no one except Jesus. Just as a runner concentrates on the finish line, so we must be singularly focused on Jesus Christ, the goal and object of our faith. Our eyes must be trained on Him without yielding to distractions.

Looking to Jesus is a life of faith. It is a looking with the heart that trusts Christ completely. As the dying Jews looked to the uplifted serpent in the wilderness and were healed, so we are to look to Jesus with a heart of faith (Numbers 21:4-9, John 3:14-16).

God says, "Turn to Me, and be saved, all the ends of the earth; for I am God, and there is no other" (Isaiah 45:22). There is no one else to look to for salvation and strength.

We must be *constantly* looking to Jesus. The same act of faith required for salvation must become a part of our daily lives. Paul instructs us, "As you therefore have received Christ Jesus the Lord, so walk in Him" (Colossians 2:6). More than an initial act of faith, we must maintain a life of faith. "Fixing," a present participle, could be translated "*always* fixing our eyes on Jesus." Throughout the entire race, the believer must be always looking to Jesus. Not just on Sundays. But every day, all day, never allowing distractions to steal the focus of our faith.

We must be *intently* looking to Jesus. Not in a daydream. But with alertness of mind. To be totally absorbed with Christ. Our gaze must be resolutely fixed on Him who is both our goal and the prize.

Too many Christians are running with their eyes fixed on the grandstands. They are much too concerned with what others in the stands are thinking. They are so preoccupied with the approval of others that they lose sight of Christ's approval. What do my parents think? Is my boss watching? Do my friends approve?

Where Is Your Camera Aimed?

I recently saw a television report from Texas A&M. (I promise, this is not an Aggie joke. But let me tell you one: How do you get an Aggie to laugh on Saturday? Tell him a joke on Wednesday.)

During spring training, the Aggie coaches mounted a small video camera on the helmet of their quarterback. They then put a special set of goggles on his face mask with an infrared light that followed the focus of his eyeballs. This caused the camera to videotape whatever the quarterback was focused on.

As the Aggies went through their passing offense, the coaches were able to monitor their quarterback's vision. The quarterback took the snap, set up in the pocket, looked downfield, and threw to his receiver. At the end of practice, the coaches sat down and watched the video. On the screen, they would see exactly where their quarterback was looking.

Was the quarterback distracted by the defensive linemen's rush? When did he visually pick up his primary receiver? Did he quickly read the free safety? When did he pick up his secondary receiver? When did he look for his safety valve? All of this is critically important to a quarterback.

A successful quarterback must focus on the right keys. His eyes must be fixed on the right object. At the right time. A successfully executed play would hinge on where the quarterback was fixing his eyes. Ultimately, the outcome of the game would hinge on the quarterback's eyes.

The same is true spiritually. We must fix our eyes on Jesus. And keep them there.

If God were to mount a camera on your eyes and heart, what would it record? If God were to video the focus of your heart today, what would it reveal?

CONSIDER JESUS' EXAMPLE

As we run with eyes fixed on Jesus, we must also "consider Him." Our minds must be engaged in a careful study of Jesus Christ. The Bible admonishes us, "Consider Him who has endured such hostility by sinners against Himself, so that you may not grow weary and lose heart" (Hebrews 12:3). As we run, we must consider Him.

The word *consider* (*analogizomai*) means "to reckon, compare, weigh, think over." It is a mathematical term signifying "to compute by comparing things together." It means to take a hard look, an analytical look, and come to a conclusive decision. Even so, we must take full note of Christ and run our race accordingly.

We must consider Jesus, who is "the author and perfecter of faith" (Hebrews 12:2). The word *author* (*archegon*) means leader, founder, pioneer. It portrays one who takes the lead, one who goes in and blazes the trail for those who follow. In running God's race, Jesus Christ is our Leader, the One meant to be followed. He set the course and we are to follow hard after Him.

Jesus is also the "finisher" (*teleioten*) of faith, the One who perfectly completed God's race which we run. He ran the race of faith to its triumphant finish.

Having now finished, Jesus shouts words of encouragement to us to follow His example and run with endurance. By His words and life, He shows us how to run victoriously.

Specifically, we consider three aspects from the life of Christ: His endurance, His focus, and His reward.

His Endurance

First, we should consider Christ's endurance as He ran God's marathon. What a champion Jesus is! As He came down the homestretch of His race, He endured the hostility of sinners and the cross. Jesus is the epitome of endurance, the ultimate Role Model, the perfect Example.

In the Garden of Gethsemane, Jesus sweated drops of blood as He agonized in prayer under the shadow of the cross and poured out his heart to God: "My soul is deeply grieved, to the point of death. . . . Father, if it is possible, let this cup pass from Me; yet not as I will, but as Thou wilt" (Matthew 26:38-39). There Jesus, engulfed in sorrow, turned Himself over to His betrayer and was arrested by the Roman cohort.

Yet, He endured.

Then Jesus suffered a mockery of justice and an attack on His personage. Through the night and early morning hours, He endured six trials—three Jewish, three Roman—where He was interrogated, falsely accused, ridiculed, mocked, and spit upon. Before Pilate, He was scourged with a whip, His back lacerated; He was crowned with spikelike thorns, His skull pierced; His dignity was attacked; He was robed in purple and beaten with a rod and His beard was plucked from His face, marring His appearance.

Yet, He endured.

He was presented to the mob scene outside the Praetorium. Pilate said, "Behold, the Man!" But the crowd—aroused by the sight of His blood like hungry sharks at feeding time—wanted more blood. They cried out, "Crucify, crucify!" (John 19:1-6).

Yet, He endured.

Sentenced to die as a degenerate criminal, Jesus was forced to carry His cross through the jeering streets of Jerusalem. A sign of condemnation, guilt, and shame. He staggered under the heavy load and a Cyrenian helped him carry this, His own torture chamber, to the execution sight.

Yet, He endured.

At Golgotha, the Roman soldiers stripped this blameless "criminal" and nailed Him to a wooden cross. A large spike was driven through each wrist. Another spike was sent through his crossed legs. With the victim now attached, the cross was hoisted up and sort of slam-dunked into the ground.

Jesus was suspended between Heaven and earth, suffering the cruelest death imaginable. Those passing by hurl abuse at Him. It is not enough that He be put to death. He must be abused and shamed as well. He struggled for every breath, pulling up with His weary arms to exhale.

Yet, He endured.

At high noon, the sky became mysteriously dark, as at midnight. The sins of the world were being laid upon His back. Even the Father forsook Him now. He was all alone. His holy body became the repository for all the filthy depravity of man. The wrath of God thundered as Jesus was engulfed by God's fierce judgment. Only the damned already in hell can faintly begin to know His agony.

Yet, He endured.

The finish line was now in sight. His blood has been shed, making the perfect atonement for sins. Redemption is secured! As His lungs gasped for air, He sprinted through the finish line. Victoriously, He cried, "It is finished!" The Victor bowed His head and gave up His spirit.

Never has anyone endured such hostility, such pain, such suffering. He died bearing the sins of the world. He died absorbing the hellish wrath of God. He died rejected by God and men. He endured faithfully to the end of His race—the Jerusalem Marathon.

Men, consider Him. Jesus is our Leader in God's race. By His life, He marked the course that each one of us will travel. It is a race that involves a cross, self-denial, and death. The Apostle Peter corroborates this: "For you have been called to this purpose, since Christ also suffered for you, leaving you an example for you to follow in His steps" (1 Peter 2:21). God's race involves a cross for each of us.

When is the last time you considered His sufferings? As we run with endurance, we must consider Him! If He endured His cross, so must we endure ours. Is a slave greater than his Master?

His Faith

Second, consider Jesus' faith. Throughout His marathon, Jesus kept entrusting Himself to God and looking to the promised joy set before Him. This is how Jesus received strength to endure. By faith. By trusting God. By fixing His eyes on the joy set before Him.

Jesus endured the cross because of His complete dependence upon God. During His earthly ministry, Jesus did not use His divine power for His personal needs. That was reserved for others. Jesus resisted Satan's temptation through faith in God—not by snapping His fingers.

Amidst the suffering of the cross, Jesus endured by looking to "the joy set before Him." Psalm 16, a messianic psalm, speaks about the "fullness of joy" Jesus would experience in the presence of the Father. Jesus knew God would keep His word. After His death, He would surely come out of the tomb alive, be exalted to Heaven, and ushered into the "fullness of joy" (Psalm 16:11). Just as God's Word said.

Jesus endured the cross by focusing on His future joy. He looked beyond the pain to the prize. He kept His eyes on the prize. And never blinked.

Men, have you considered Jesus' faith? This is exactly how we are to run with endurance. By faith. By looking to the joy set before us. By fixing our eyes on Jesus. By keeping our eyes on the prize.

No, you are not Jesus. But you do have access to the power of Jesus through His Spirit. Maybe you are focusing on circumstances that scream, "You are losing." Maybe you are listening to the world that ridicules, "You're a loser." Maybe you believe your pain that says, "You have lost. It's over. Just sit down and quit. What's the use?" But with the eyes of faith, you have a future of hope that says, "You are winning!"

By faith, Paul ran with endurance, fixing his eyes on future glory: "For I consider that the sufferings of this present time are not worthy to be compared with the glory that is to be revealed to us" (Romans 8:18).

We must consider what joy awaits us in glory. We must keep our eyes on the prize. We will see God. We shall behold Christ's glory. We shall fellowship with Him, serve Him, and glory with Him. We shall receive the prize, inherit the family legacy, and reign with Him forever. We shall enjoy everlasting light, the joy of the Lord, and eternal rest. We shall possess our treasure in Heaven, bear an eternal weight of glory, and drink from the stream of life.

His Reward

Third, consider Christ's reward. Because Jesus endured the cross, He "has sat down at the right hand of the throne of God" (Hebrews 12:2). After Jesus died for our sins, He was raised, He ascended, and He was seated at the right hand of God. God richly rewarded His endurance.

The right hand of God is the place of supreme sovereignty. Absolute authority. He sat down there, signifying that His work of salvation was finished. No more sacrifice for sins is needed. It is finished! Jesus is seated in glory, resting and reigning.

Because Jesus wore a crown of thorns, He was given a crown of glory.

The Bible says,

He humbled Himself by becoming obedient to the point of death, even death on a cross. Therefore also God highly exalted Him, and bestowed on Him the name which is above every name, that at the name of Jesus every knee should bow, of those who are in heaven, and on earth, and under the earth, and that every tongue should confess that Jesus Christ is Lord, to the glory of God the Father. (Philippians 2:8-11)

Men, consider Jesus' reward. Faith honors God and God honors faith. Jesus obeyed God by faith, and God rewarded Him with a crown. The same is true in our lives. We will wear a crown only after we have carried a cross. There is no coronation without a crucifixion. No exaltation without humiliation. No reward without reproach.

Consider Jesus. Consider His endurance, His faith, His reward. He is the Leader of God's race. He marked the course we run, and He endured faithfully to the end. He is the embodiment of endurance. If we will follow His steps, we will receive His prize.

HIS STRENGTH IS OUR STRENGTH

Let me relate one last truth. I need more than an Example—especially a perfect Example. I need God's power to run God's race. I need the strength to endure. And what I so desperately need, God provides.

Here is what I want you to grasp. As I fix my eyes on Christ, God strengthens my faith to endure. Looking to Jesus puts steel in my faith. It bolsters my weakening legs and enables me to keep running, "fixing [my] eyes on Jesus the author and perfecter of faith" (Hebrews 12:2). As I focus on Him, He perfects my faith.

So, not only is Jesus before me as my Example, He is also within me as my Enabler, strengthening my legs and lifting my heart to endure.

Jesus is "the author and perfecter of faith." Where did this faith to trust Christ originate? Certainly not within our depraved hearts, once dead in sin. A dead heart is lifeless and unable to do anything toward God. Faith comes from above; it is the gift of God (Ephesians 2:8). It is given to us to believe (Philippians 1:29). From within, no one can take a step of faith and come to Christ (John 6:44). So Jesus must be the Author of faith with dead hearts. I first believed in Him because He first drew me to Himself.

He Brings Faith to Completion
Now, the One who authored my faith is also the "perfecter of faith." As the Perfecter of faith, He brings my faith to completion. When I am most prone to falter and waver, He works within my heart to sustain my

faith. God is working within our hearts, maturing, strengthening, and deepening our faith to endure.

The further we go in God's race, the more intense the pain becomes. The temptations intensify. We begin to weaken, and the desire to quit begins to override the desire to endure. Just when we want to pull over to the side, God strengthens our weakening faith and enables us to endure to the end.

God gives us the faith to press on. We run in His strength. The Bible says, "Work out your salvation with fear and trembling; for it is God who is at work in you, both to will and work for His good pleasure" (Philippians 2:12-13).

Paul wrote, "I labor, striving according to His power, which mightily works within me" (Colossians 1:29). As Paul ran God's race, he overcame the pain and resisted the temptation to quit through God's power mightily working within him. So, too, should we be encouraged to endure.

You may be saying, "Time out. That's great for Paul, but I am so weak, I don't think I can run another step." Be encouraged! I have good news. It is only in our weakness that God's power works. God told Paul, "My grace is sufficient for you, for power is perfected in weakness." The apostle concluded, "Most gladly, therefore, I will rather boast about my weaknesses, that the power of Christ may dwell in me. Therefore I am well content with weaknesses, with insults, with distresses, with persecutions, with difficulties, for Christ's sake; for when I am weak, then I am strong" (2 Corinthians 12:9-10). It was only when Paul was the weakest that he experienced God's supernatural power.

Men, did you get that?

When I am weak, then I am strong. Only then does the power of Christ work within me. When I can't, He can. And He will. When the marathon is the most grueling, I most fully experience His power to endure. No wonder Paul bragged about his weakness. Because that is when Christ most strengthens our faith and releases His power.

Do you feel qualified to experience God's power? All you need to feel is your weakness and your need of Him. If you are feeling weak, just stare into His glorious face. Love Him. Trust Him. Abide in Him. Rely upon Him. Rest in Him. And He will strengthen you mightily.

The Marathon of Life
Let me illustrate how Jesus strengthens us.

At the finish line stands the Judge of the ancient Greek games.

This is a different Judge than you are accustomed to. He is not to be feared, but trusted. He has earned the right to officiate because He is the greatest champion these games have ever produced. He is calling for you and me to share in His victory. Strategically positioned at the finish line, He patiently waits looking for the approaching runners.

This Judge has positioned the customary ladder at the finish line upon which is placed the cherished victor's crown. He knows that the sight of this crown will inspire weary runners to endure. The winner will receive the honor of having this wreath bestowed on his head by this Judge, the greatest of all champions.

The long marathon of life now winds its way back to the stadium. As the first runner makes his dramatic entrance back into the stadium, the crowd is on its feet.

This runner is so tired he doubts he has the strength to finish. Every fiber of his being wants to stop. His legs are cramping. His feet are blistered. His lungs are gasping for air. His mouth is wide-open, desperately sucking oxygen like a drowning man does air. His arms are so heavy he cannot move them. He tries to convince his mind that he can live with the pain. But that argument is short-lived.

The Finish Line in Sight!
He scantily musters enough strength to look up. With blurred vision, he sees the most inspiring sight he has ever seen. There, just ahead, he can see the finish line. The victor's crown. And this esteemed Judge. He has dreamed about that crown for years. Now, here it is just one hundred yards away.

But as much as he wants to sprint to the finish, he can't. His heart screams, "Sprint!" But his legs are deaf.

He looks up in desperation to the Judge. His face tells it all. It tells the story of his heart. "I can't go any farther."

His coach yells at him, "Get up, you loser! I knew you'd never make it. On second thought, just stay down." His words cut deeply.

He gets up on his knees, but collapses back to the ground.

Then something extraordinary happens. It is unheard of in the long history of the games. Never before witnessed.

The Judge, standing at the finish line, strips off His coat, drops His clipboard, and sprints to the collapsed runner. What will the Judge do? Drag him off the track? Lecture him on overcoming fatigue? Disqualify him?

The Judge's Sudden Move

Never before seen, this Judge, Himself a championship runner who once won this very race, stoops down and, with arms still strong and muscular, lifts the fallen runner to his feet.

Unexpectedly, the Judge swings the runner's arm over His shoulder and bodily carries this runner—exhausted, defeated, drained—toward the finish line.

The crowd is stunned. And silent. Then a murmur of wonder ripples through the crowd; they have never seen such an unprecedented act.

Fifty yards. Forty. Thirty. Only twenty now. Ten. Together, they lunge across the finish line ahead of the other runners. But what will be the ruling? Will such aid be allowed? Will the victory count?

Without hesitating, the Judge victoriously holds up the arm of this runner. He emphatically declares him to be the winner. The bewildered crowd bursts into applause.

Back at His seat, the Judge places the winner's wreath on the head of this marathoner. The exhilarated runner looks into the face of the Judge. Never has he seen such compassion. Such strength. Such understanding.

Then, placing His hands on the runner's shoulders, the Judge affirms, "Well done, My good and faithful runner. I am so proud of you."

The crowd chants his name over and over. But what rings true in this champion's ears are the Judge's words: "Well done, My good and faithful runner."

The Victory Goes To . . .

Nevertheless, the runner knows the truth. So does everyone else present that day. He never could have won without the Judge's strength. His victory is *really* the Judge's victory. He would never have finished, much less won, without the Judge. In humility, he removes the crown from his head knowing it is really not his crown. He places it back at the feet of its true owner—this strong and compassionate Judge. For all the stadium to witness.

Men, this runner's story can be our story. This scene can be repeated at the end of our race—if we will look to Christ. Sure, we stumble and fall. Yes, we grow weary and tired during our race of faith. If we focus on our failures and shortcomings, we will never get up. Even if we want to.

But if we fix our eyes on Jesus, the One who marked the course and ran victoriously, we will be empowered to finish the race. His strength will become our strength. If we will look to Jesus, we will find the needed strength to endure and win the cherished crown. Then, in that day, we will cast our crown back at His feet. Because our victory is really His victory in our life.

One day, we can hear Him say, "Well done, My good and faithful runners." All our pain will be quickly forgotten when we feel the strong embrace of His arms.

Maybe you think you cannot get up and run any longer. You do not have the strength to go another step. Let me assure you, if you will look to Christ, He will carry you across the finish line. Victoriously.

If you are down, look up to Him. Keep your eyes on the prize. And Jesus will carry you in His strong arms. You can endure in His strength.

NOTE

1. Adrian Rogers, "How to Be Filled with the Holy Spirit," sermon preached at Bellevue Baptist Church, May 6, 1973.

CHAPTER 11

BENCHED, BOOTED, AND DISQUALIFIED

★

Like a bone-jarring fullback, some subjects are hard to tackle. This chapter is one of those subjects. Hard-hitting. Powerful. It could run you over. But it must be stopped—dead in its tracks.

I don't want to just tackle this subject. I want to play "smash mouth" and hit it so hard that it never scores another point in our lives again.

Honestly, I wish I did not have to write this chapter at all. I would much prefer to simply wrap up this book with a positive "fire-you-up" chapter. But I would be less than honest with you—and, most importantly, with the Word of God—if I failed to warn you about a potential danger that has overtaken many a runner.

So, I'm going to put it on the line. As we run God's race, the Bible warns us about the ever-lurking danger of disqualification. The danger of being put out of the race. The danger of being sent to the sidelines and benched. The danger of being stripped of the prize.

Men, this subject is as serious as a heart attack. Buckle your seat belts. This will jar you. It jolts me just to have to deal with it.

Disqualification.

An ever-present peril.

Come with me to the 1988 Olympic Games in Seoul, Korea, where the world's finest athletes were gathered to go head-to-head to determine the fastest human on the planet in the one-hundred-meter run. The race would become the most publicized race in Olympic history, and headlining the star-studded field were the two marquee names in sprinting—Ben Johnson, the Canadian speedster, and Carl Lewis, the great American hope.

The Race for Global Bragging Rights
For years, Johnson and Lewis had been battling head-to-head for global bragging rights. This race would officially settle the matter once and for all.

Before a crowd of seventy thousand in Olympic Stadium, and a global audience of two billion viewers via satellite hookup, Johnson and Lewis got ready for their long-awaited duel.

In the blocks, Johnson's expression was one of angry, vengeful determination. Lewis appeared loose, confident, nonthreatened.

As the field of finely honed athletes settled into the starting blocks, the rising of the starter's gun brought the crowd to its feet. At the crack of the pistol, the runners simultaneously ejected out of the starting blocks.

At thirty meters Johnson was a half-stride ahead of Lewis. No problem. Lewis was a known strong finisher, Johnson a fader.

"Then," as Johnson said after the race, "I blew it out."

His face a mask of ferocity, Johnson continued to propel into the lead. At fifty meters he had a full meter lead. By the eighty-meter mark, he had extended it to two meters. By this time, Lewis could not close the gap. It was over.

Two meters from the finish, Johnson knew he had won. He cruised through the finish tape, his right arm raised victoriously, glaring audaciously back at Lewis. In your face!

The World's Fastest Human?
The timekeepers were stunned. They could hardly believe their eyes—9.79 seconds. A world record! The Canadian had just eclipsed all previous standards, breaking his own world record.

Lewis finished a distant second at 9.92, still his personal best and the American record.

Carl Lewis walked over to Johnson, standing at the edge of the track, and shook his hand. He had been blown away in the fastest sprint in human history.

On the victory stand, Ben Johnson was presented the Olympic gold medal and was officially recognized as the world's fastest human. Ever. He alone stood atop the athletic world. No one faster. No one stronger. No one greater.

Behind the scenes, a mere formality was being undertaken by the Olympic Doping Control Laboratory. (All runners are routinely tested for banned substances.)

Four hours after the race, the urine samples were analyzed by Dr. Park Jong Sei. One sample showed an illegal anabolic steroid. Not knowing to whom the numbered sample belonged, Park tested it once more.

The same result. Positive.

Then Park and two Canadian officials tested it and again found stanozolol in the specimen. Wanting to be certain, Park tested this sample twice more.

Each time, the result was the same—positive.

A deceiver had been unmasked. Ben Johnson!

The sinister plot among Johnson and his sponsors to cheat the athletic world had been foiled. With news that would send shock waves around the world, the International Olympic Committee (IOC) was promptly notified that Ben Johnson—the newly crowned world's fastest human—had an anabolic steroid in his system. A drug designed to beef up the muscles. A drug that gives bursts of power.

The Agony of Disgrace

A long night of deliberation followed for the IOC Executive Board. Clearly, Johnson was guilty. Unquestionably, he had violated the rules against using performance-enhancing drugs. Left with no other alternative, the IOC declared Johnson's race null and void. He was stripped of his gold medal, and the next day it was awarded to its rightful owner, Carl Lewis. Johnson was suspended from all international meets for two full years. Jean Charest, sports minister of Canada, announced that Johnson would be banned from Canada's national team for life. Johnson had made history, all right. The wrong kind.

All this would cause Johnson to lose millions of dollars in appearance fees and endorsements. In two short days, he went from the pinnacle to the pits. The record that Johnson so brazenly predicted would last for over fifty years did not even stand for fifty hours. In an international tragedy, Ben Johnson was buried in a grave of disgrace.

Busted. Loser. Shame.

There is a poignant, powerful lesson to be learned from the Ben

Johnson tragedy. Painted in painful colors, we see illustrated before our eyes the truth of God's Word. The Apostle Paul writes, "I buffet my body and make it my slave, lest possibly, after I have preached to others, I myself should be disqualified" (1 Corinthians 9:27).

Disqualified. Ouch! Few words contain such finality, regret, futility.

Men, as we run God's race, we must guard against the constant threat of disqualification. No matter how successfully we have run in the past, one wrong step can affect the rest of our life. Our race can be so quickly jeopardized. Wiped out. Canceled. Disgraced. Benched. Booted. Disqualified.

In this chapter, I want to answer the following questions: What sin disqualifies? What does disqualification involve? How can I avoid it? May I reenter the race?

These are critical questions that deserve careful answers. Let's look into the Word of God and discover what God says. The truth we will learn must be heeded. Seriously.

THE DANGER OF SEXUAL SIN

Probably the greatest danger facing us men today, as we run God's race, is the danger of sexual sin. Immorality. Adultery. Lustful thoughts. Sexual addictions. And all kinds of sexual perversions. Whatever you want to call it, God calls it sin, and it disqualifies us from the race. This is the wrong kind of running buck naked.

Speaking like a world-class athlete, Paul says, "I buffet my body and make it my slave" (1 Corinthians 9:27). Mixing metaphors, Paul then moves from the track to the boxing ring. Literally, buffet (*hupopiazo*) means to land a knockout punch under someone's eye and give him a black eye.

The Greeks were most fond of boxing, and it became a part of the ancient games. Wearing no gloves, the participants wrapped their hands and arms with leather strips. Fighters were not matched according to weight. Nor did they have timed rounds or a confined boxing ring. They simply slugged it out until one participant could no longer stand.

If the match went too long, the judges would call a halt and instruct the bloody participants to really get serious! They would attach rigid leather thongs studded with metal—yesterday's version of brass knuckles—to the fighters' fists. Then these fighters would battle until the match ended in permanent injury or death. It was the Greek version of sudden death.

The picture is graphic—ancient boxers fighting one another with knuckles bound with leather thongs, leaving their opponents black and blue.

A Knockout Punch

Figuratively, Paul is saying he beats his own body black and blue, knocking it out, if necessary, to win the race. The apostle then says he makes it his "slave" (*doulagogeo*), bringing it into subjection, as a slave to his master—Jesus Christ. We must present our entire body to His lordship and obey His will.

The "body" refers to one's fleshly desires. The lusts of the flesh. While Paul could be referring to any number of sins, I believe that at the heart of his warning is sexual sin. Other sins may be worse, but no other sin quite so uniquely disqualifies as sexual sin.

Paul uses a word here for body—the Greek word *soma*—that means our physical body. Paul is saying he buffets his physical body, which is in danger of sinful activity, lest he be disqualified.

How has Paul been using the term *the body*? In 1 Corinthians 6:18, we discover that a sin against the body (*soma*) is sexual sin. Writing on this verse, John MacArthur comments, "In referring to the body, Paul obviously had sexual immorality in view. In 1 Corinthians 6:18, he describes it as a sin against one's own body. It was almost as if he put sexual sin in a category of its own. Certainly, it disqualifies a man from church leadership. 1 Timothy 3:1 demands that elders be a 'one-woman man.'"[1]

Let's look at 1 Corinthians 6:18 and see what it says. Earlier in 1 Corinthians, Paul had been teaching that sexual immorality is a sin against one's own body. The apostle writes, "Every other sin that a man commits is outside the body, but the immoral man sins against his own body" (1 Corinthians 6:18). The word *immoral* (*porneia*) refers to any sexual perversion—whether premarital sex (before marriage), adultery (during marriage), homosexuality, lesbianism, or bestiality.

Paul is putting sexual sin in a category all its own. All the sins in the world are put in one column. And sexual sin is put in another. All sins are outside the body except sexual infidelity, which alone is against one's own body.

Destruction Like No Other

While immorality is not necessarily the worst sin (unbelief and blasphemy against the Holy Spirit fit that bill), sexual sin is unique in its character. Like a malignant cancer to the body, immorality internally destroys the soul like no other sin. Why is this?

Because sexual intercourse is the most intimate uniting of two persons, it causes a man to become one with the other person. Physically. Mystically. Emotionally. Paul puts it this way: "Do you not know that the one who joins himself to a harlot is one body with her? For He says, 'The two will become one flesh'" (1 Corinthians 6:16). Consequently, its misuse corrupts on the deepest human level, far more destructive than worldliness, drugs, or alcohol.

A man's sexual drive arises from within the body bent on personal gratification. It drives like no other impulse. When unlawfully fulfilled, it internally destroys the soul like no other sin.

So, Paul says, we must master our sexual drive and make it our slave, bringing it into submission to Jesus Christ. When aroused toward anyone other than our spouse, it must be dealt with severely, beaten black and blue, not pampered or caressed.

Concerning the flames of illicit lust, Solomon says, "Can a man take a fire in his bosom, and his clothes not be burned?" (Proverbs 6:27). The warm heat of passion will destroy a life, like a man inflamed because his clothes are on fire. Engulfed. Burning. A prison of fire. Unable to escape.

In the Sermon on the Mount, Jesus Himself taught the necessity of a pure heart. He quotes the Sixth Commandment, saying, "You shall not commit adultery" (Matthew 5:27). But Jesus goes further. He continues, "But I say to you, that every one who looks on a woman to lust for her has committed adultery with her already in his heart." Jesus goes to the heart of the problem—the human heart. The inner person where actions find their root. "Do not lust after and mentally undress a woman," Jesus is saying. "Lust equals adultery."

Then Jesus tells us to buffet our body until it is black and blue. Here is the knockout punch: "And if your right eye makes you stumble, tear it out, and throw it from you; for it is better for you that one of the parts of your body perish, than for your whole body to be thrown into hell. And if your right hand makes you stumble, cut it off, and throw it from you; for it is better that one of the parts of your body perish, than for your whole body to go into hell" (Matthew 5:29-30).

Men, this is serious buffeting!

At first glance, it appears that Jesus is calling for a literal mutilation of our body. "If you lust, just desocket your eye. If you fondle, amputate your hand." Should we take what He is saying here literally? If so, this book would be the blind leading the blind.

Actually, Jesus is speaking figuratively, employing a figure of speech called hyperbole, which makes a point through an exaggerated statement (you remember what your mom said: "I've told you a billion times not to exaggerate"). The right eye represents our clearest vision; the right hand, our first advance. Our Lord is saying, "Deal radically with sexual passion. Take whatever drastic steps are necessary to keep your eyes, hands, and whatever else pure and under control. Go to extreme measures—anything short of plucking out your eyes or chopping off your hand—to mortify your fleshly impulses." Do not gaze! Do not fondle!

Simply put, it would be better to go to Heaven blind than to go to hell with 20/20 vision. When I preached on this passage in my church, I entitled the sermon "Sex and the One-Eyed Christian" or "The Spiritual Cyclops." (We *did* pack the sanctuary for that one.) Jesus calls us to take whatever steps are necessary to remain pure in heart and deed. We must control where we go, what we do, what we watch, and the company we keep.

THE DISQUALIFICATION OF SEXUAL SIN

Disqualification. The word has a sobering ring about it. It sends a chilling tingle up the spine. *Dis*qualification. Hear Paul again: "I buffet my body and make it my slave, lest possibly, after I have preached to others, I myself should be *disqualified*" (1 Corinthians 9:27, emphasis added). The apostle is warning us that there are serious consequences to sin. Especially sexual sin.

The word *disqualified* (*adokimos*) was very familiar to those who attended the ancient Isthmian Games. It meant to be put out of the games. To be stripped of one's prize. Before the race, a herald announced the rules of the contest and the names of the contestants. After the race, he announced the names and cities of the winners. Also, the names of any runners who were disqualified would be called out by this herald.

When Paul said, "I have preached to others," he saw himself as a herald, preaching God's truth and announcing the rules of the game. At the same time, Paul was also a runner who competed in the games. His deep concern was not to become so busy preaching to others that he himself ignored the rules and failed to buffet his own body. If he failed to do so, he would suffer the embarrassment of proclaiming the rules and then be disqualified by them.

What is disqualification? At first glance, you might think it is los-ing one's salvation. Falling from grace. But all the Bible—from Genesis through the maps—teaches that we are eternally secure in Christ. Once saved by God's grace, we are kept by His grace. The Good Shepherd loses not one of His sheep (John 10:27-29).

Actually, disqualification means a loss of reward at the end of the game. Once safely reaching Heaven, it means to be stripped of God's reward, not of God's saving grace. I will go one step further. Disqualification also may mean being put out of the race while it is still in progress. To be benched. Let's look now at both aspects.

ULTIMATELY—STRIPPED OF FUTURE REWARD

It is possible for a runner to come to the finish line, apparently win the race, only to be stripped of the reward. Just ask Ben Johnson. Disquali-fication means a loss of heavenly reward. A failure to buffet one's body will cause forfeit of God's reward at the end of the race.

Why do I say that? The historical background of the Isthmian Games supports my case. A disqualified Greek athlete did not lose his citizenship, only his right to the crown. The whole emphasis of this context is rewards. The preceding verses (1 Corinthians 9:24-25) call us to run the race to win the crown. If we fail to do so, we will forfeit the crown and lose the reward in the end.

Let's turn back a few pages in 1 Corinthians to chapter 3. Paul is discussing the *bema*—the judgment seat of Christ. This is the same word he uses in 2 Corinthians 5:10 to describe the judge's stand at the Olympic Games. Although the imagery shifts from the athletic field to the construction business, the spiritual truth remains the same: unfaithfulness brings disqualification.

Paul writes,

> According to the grace of God which was given to me, as a wise
> masterbuilder I laid a foundation, and another is building upon
> it. . . . For no man can lay a foundation other than the one which
> is laid, which is Jesus Christ. Now if any man builds upon the
> foundation with gold, silver, precious stones, wood, hay, straw,
> each man's work will become evident; for the day will show it,
> because it is to be revealed with fire; and the fire itself will test
> the quality of each man's work. If any man's work which he has
> built upon it remains, he shall receive a reward. If any man's

work is burned up, he shall suffer loss; but he himself shall be saved, yet so as through fire. (1 Corinthians 3:10-15)

The purpose of the Final Judgment for every believer will be to test his life to determine reward or loss of reward.

The fire of judgment will reveal eternal works—gold, silver, precious stones—and it will burn up temporal, worthless works—wood, hay, and straw. Believers who build with gold, silver, and precious stones will be rewarded. But those who build with wood, hay, and stubble will suffer loss. Not loss of salvation. Simply loss of reward.

To be "saved, yet so as through fire" pictures a person who runs through the flames, personally unharmed, but with the smell of smoke on him. He escapes the fire, but all his life's work goes up in smoke. Destroyed. Disqualified.

We must be careful how we run because there is the real danger of being disqualified. And losing our reward at the end.

The Bible teaches we can run well and merit a crown, only to later stumble and lose what reward would have been ours. The Apostle John writes, "Watch yourselves, that you might not lose what we have accomplished, but that you may receive a full reward" (2 John 8).

We must hold on to what reward we have earned. Jesus says, "I am coming quickly; hold fast what you have, in order that no one take your crown" (Revelation 3:11). Our Lord concurs that it is possible to have earned a crown through a strong start and then later lose it through unfaithfulness.

IMMEDIATELY—FORFEIT
YOUR SPIRITUAL INFLUENCE

We are all responsible for spiritual leadership in one form or another—either as a spouse, a parent, a church leader, a Bible teacher, a pastor, or a parachurch worker. As a result, we can all experience disqualification.

Disqualification brings a present loss. It puts a runner on the sidelines while the race is still in progress. After spotting the infraction, the judge signals, "You're out of the race!" He boots him out of the race and escorts him to the bench.

Picture a runner who, in the midst of the race, breaks in front of another runner, cutting him off illegally. Or, he unexpectedly hops in a car and is driven ahead of the other runners, and then steps out in the lead. All before the watchful eye of the judge. He will be put out of the race. Disqualified. The judge will blow his whistle. The runner will be told to sit down. Immediately. Stop, do not continue running.

A person's spiritual influence is directly related to the integrity of that person's life. If he wants followers, his life must be worthy of following. A spiritual leader cannot live however he desires. His walk must be consistent with his talk.

Sexual sin uniquely disqualifies a runner in God's race, whether as a pastor, a church leader, a parachurch worker, a Sunday-school teacher, a small-group Bible leader, a soloist, or a choir member.

Falling into sexual sin causes an immediate loss of leadership. The leader sacrifices the integrity of his life and ministry, forfeiting the right to lead. According to the biblical standard of leadership, one is no longer qualified (1 Timothy 3:1-11). No longer above reproach. No longer a one-woman man. No longer managing his household well. No longer possessing a good reputation outside the church. Once qualified, he is now no longer qualified to lead.

Disqualified.

As Chuck Swindoll says, "It takes only one pin to burst a balloon. Once purity and trust are sacrificed, the ability to lead is gone."[2]

Take the life of David. Although a man of God, King David fell into serious sexual sin with a bathing beauty named Bathsheba. He tried to cover up his sin through another sin—the sin of murder—as he put her husband to death.

David eventually was brought to confession before God through the convicting confrontation of Nathan the prophet. Nathan pointed a finger in David's face and said, "Thou art the man." David, a year after his adultery, finally confessed his sin to God. The result? David was forgiven, but forgotten. His service for God went downhill from there.

No longer spiritually qualified to sit on the throne, David was chased from his kingdom by his two sons.

Nearly every verse of Psalm 51 records the monstrous effects of sexual sin in a believer's life. As so painfully revealed in David's life, we see that immorality soils the soul (verses 1-2,7,10), saturates the mind (verse 3), stings the conscience (verses 4,9), shames the character (verses 5-6), saddens the heart (verses 8,12), sickens the body (verse 8), sours the spirit (verse 10), severs the fellowship (verse 11), steals the power (verse 11), stiffens the will (verse 12), and stifles the tongue (verses 13-15). Our entire Christian ministry suffers!

After David confessed his sin—a year after he committed it, and then only because he was caught and confronted with it—he was forgiven, but fallen. Yes, he was forgiven of all his sin. But, no, he was no longer fit for the throne of Israel. The disciplining hand of God drove David from the throne, and his immediate ministry went on a downhill slide from that point onward.

This discussion, though, must raise the question of forgiveness. Shouldn't we be eager to restore our fallen brethren? To fellowship, yes. But to leadership? No. At least, not for a long while. This does not mean we "shoot our own wounded." By all means, we should be forgiving, accepting, and loving. We must be. It is the character of Christ. Not only that, but we should help repair the broken pieces of those who have sinned.

But that does not mean such a man remains qualified for leadership. That right to lead is forfeited. True repentance, rebuilding of character (it can be done!), and a regained sense of trust in the Body of Christ must occur before any restoration to leadership can ever begin. It could be a long while, pal. Think about it.

Imagine building credibility for over twenty years only to squander it. Utterly. In a moment of passion.

Men, the same tragedy can wreck our lives. We can lose the influence of our spiritual leadership as well as forfeit God's power through infidelity.

The evangelical landscape is strewn with the wreckage of men who have fallen into sexual sin. Their lives have been ruined; their marriages destroyed; their ministries stripped. All because of sexual immorality. It has hit pastors and television evangelists hard, causing many to be disqualified. And it has also hit the man in the pew just as hard, knocking many out of the race and onto the sidelines.

Three Important Places You Are Sidelined

Such a benching affects three primary areas. First, one's public ministry is sidelined. A teacher of God's Word, whether in the pulpit, Sunday school, or a small Bible class, who falls into sexual sin must step down. James writes, "Let not many of you become teachers, my brethren, knowing that as such we shall incur a stricter judgment" (James 3:1). The same strict requirement is placed upon a church officer—an elder or deacon—or ministry leader outside the church. He should step down from his place of responsibility. Or be asked to step down.

Second, one's family life is sidelined. An enormous breach of trust occurs with the man's wife, who will suffer damaged emotions. In most cases, the hurt is never repaired. The sexual sin becomes a cause for divorce and the breakup of the home. Children are pulled back and forth. A loss of respect for Dad results.

Third, one's personal witness is, likewise, sidelined. I think the world enjoys seeing a Christian fall into sexual sin. It feeds Satan's lies in their heart. They say, "I knew those Christians were a bunch of hypocrites." In the process, our viable witness is thrown out the window.

A Greater Tragedy

Despite this tragedy, I think what causes me even *greater* alarm is the trend today that discounts immorality and actually *fails* to see this sin as grounds for disqualification. I believe this tolerant attitude is far more dangerous than the sexual sin itself.

Unless you have been living on another planet recently, you are painfully aware that many highly visible Christian leaders have fallen into—let me call it exactly what it is—gross sexual immorality. That is painful enough. But compounding insult to injury, many of these spiritual leaders continue preaching from the same pulpit. Some step down for a few token months. But that sounds more like a vacation to me.

The Bible says they are disqualified. Out of the race. Out of the ministry. Put on the shelf. Let me say it plainly and painfully: They are no longer qualified to lead. Their integrity is shot, and our trust is lost.

If you interviewed a gardener to take care of your lawn and then went past his house and saw that his yard was sloppy and overgrown, would you trust him with the care of your lawn? If you went to the dentist to get your teeth checked and sat down in the chair only to look up to see that the dentist had a mouthful of rotten teeth, would you trust him to work on your teeth? Of course not. It follows, then, that an unholy spiritual leader has lost the right to call for holiness in the lives of others. No matter how high his television ratings.

Personal purity is always the platform for personal ministry. When purity is chucked out the window, so is the platform for ministry. Even those with a less visible ministry will suffer a severe disqualification.

THE DEFENSE AGAINST SEXUAL SIN

Men, if sexual sin is this deadly, we had better learn to avoid it. Specifically, how can we buffet our bodily impulses? It is critically important that we know how to buffet our body, lest we be disqualified. How do we bring our sexual drives into submission to Christ's lordship? Since God Himself has given us our sexual drive, how do we keep it on track? I want to suggest several steps which all men who win must take. We must buffet our eyes, our hearts, our feet, and our flesh, as well as enjoy our own spouse.

Guard Your Eyes

First, we must *guard our eyes*. Men are attracted and aroused mostly by sight. Therefore, what we place before our eyes is critically important. It is through our eyes that our heart is so often stimulated. We must purpose to guard our eyes and choose not to gaze upon another woman in a way that would wrongly arouse us and lead us as a pig to the slaughter.

Job said, "I have made a covenant with my eyes; how then could I gaze at a virgin" (Job 31:1). Now, that's commitment! We must make a no-less-serious commitment between ourselves and God *not* to gaze upon another woman. The word *gaze* is the key here. It means to take a second, enticing look. Perhaps even a third or fourth look. It is a deliberate looking that involves fantasizing with the mind.

Men, we live in the real world. Here, many women package themselves in ways that would make most advertisers green with envy. So we cannot always avoid "seeing" an attractive woman. It is the "gazing" that must be controlled.

One wise sage once said, "You cannot keep the birds from flying over your head. But you can keep them from building a nest in your hair." It was allowing a nest to be built in his hair that Job resisted. And so must we.

May I get specific? This means we must not linger at the magazine rack. Nor watch films or rent videos that sensually enflame lust. For some of us men who travel, our biggest struggle is with the television set in our hotel room and the lewd movies that are accessible to us. When no one is watching. "Five minutes free," the sign says. It should read, "Five minutes to bondage."

For others of us, the magazines we "read" are our downfall. Even once-reputable publications are now filled with sleazy advertisements and voluptuous swimsuit issues.

Cliff Barrows is Billy Graham's much-respected music leader. I like what Cliff does when he checks into a hotel room. He first drapes a towel over the television and then places his Bible on top of the towel.

That way, he has to fight through the Holy Bible to get to the trash on the tube. May his tribe increase.

Let me tell you two things we do around our house.

First, whenever I watch television, I do so with a remote control always in my hand. By hitting one button, I can immediately change channels. Especially when I am watching a ballgame with my young boys, this is an absolute necessity. You cannot watch a major sports program these days without being bombarded with nudity, bedhopping, and adultery via the commercials. An escape valve called a channel changer is critically important.

Second, whenever my sports magazines are delivered to the house, my wife first "deprograms" them by tearing out all the pages that contain "smut." And that is no small assignment. One sports magazine that I have received weekly since 1960 touts an annual swimsuit issue and is totally ripped apart.

Men, what about you? Have you made such a covenant with your eyes? Will you guard what you allow to visually come into your heart? Men who win do.

Strengthen Your Heart

Second, we must *strengthen our hearts*. One of the best ways to buffet our bodies is to replace sensual thoughts with wholesome ones. To occupy our minds and fill our hearts with godly truths from God's Word. To defend our hearts against lustful thoughts by filling them with God's Word. To the extent that our hearts are spiritually strong, we can resist sexual temptation.

Only the Word of God, dwelling in our hearts through the power of the Holy Spirit, can give us the strength to resist temptation's fleshly desires. I am sure you have heard about the "Just Say No" campaign regarding drug abuse. While I wholeheartedly support a drug-free society, the fact is, we cannot say no to a temptation until we have first said yes to Jesus Christ. Only in God's supernatural power can carnal temptations be resisted. And His power is transmitted through His Word and His Spirit.

The Bible says, "How can a young man keep his way pure? By keeping it according to Thy word. . . . Thy word I have treasured in my heart, that I may not sin against Thee" (Psalm 119:9,11). The Word of God is the greatest restraining force in all the world to keep us morally pure. When Scripture is treasured in our hearts, it shouts to our consciences to resist temptation and then fortifies the will to say no.

Likewise, the Holy Spirit does the same within. To be filled with God's Word works the same as being filled with God's Holy Spirit. Just compare Colossians 3:16 with Ephesians 5:18. It is the power of the Holy Spirit that leads me to put to death the sinful deeds of my body.

Paul put it this way: "If you are living according to the flesh, you must die; but if by the Spirit you are putting to death the deeds of the body, you will live. For all who are being led by the Spirit of God, these are sons of God" (Romans 8:13-14).

Activate Your Feet

Third, we must *activate our feet*. There are certain situations in which we have no business finding ourselves. None whatsoever. An old saying goes, "He who would not fall down ought not to walk in slippery places." So, get out of slippery places if you desire not to fall.

God's Word says, "Flee immorality" (1 Corinthians 6:18). That does *not* mean, "Stay and fight it." Instead, wisdom says, "Get out of there. Make tracks. Don't fight it. Leave!" Here, it is godly to run like a coward. Only a fool would stay and fight courageously.

That was Joseph's strategy. Sold into slavery in Egypt, Joseph soon rose to success and served in the house of Potiphar, an officer of Pharaoh. Potiphar so trusted Joseph that he left everything in charge of his "handsome" servant (Genesis 39:5-18).

Potiphar's wife "looked with desire at Joseph." That means "she checked him out from stem to stern and had the hots for this tall, good-looking guy."

"Lie with me," she whispered seductively.

But Joseph said, "No!" He refused. He would sooner lie down in a den of vipers.

She would not take no for an answer. Like a hungry piranha, she wanted him. Bad. So, on another convenient day, she spun her web around her catch. "Lie with me," she smiled, as she ran her fingers through his clothing. No doubt, the temperature was getting hot.

Guess what Joseph did? Stay and fight it?

No. He bolted. He ran away so fast that Potiphar's wife was left clutching a handful of his clothes. He fled immorality. He didn't stay to give her a Bible lesson on body life and field any follow-up questions. He got out of Dodge, pronto.

Men, you and I will find ourselves in situations that call for a similar response. Quick feet keep a clean heart. You may need to take your coffee break in a different place. You may need to turn and walk another direction in your hotel lobby. You may need to drive another way to work to avoid that billboard. Whatever. Just flee immorality.

Enjoy Your Wife

Fourth, we must each *enjoy our own wife*. A fulfilling sexual relationship with our wife does marvels to keep our heart pure. When the home fires are burning brightly, wildfire on the prairie is not prone to be a problem.

Solomon, writing under the inspiration of the Holy Spirit, discreetly recorded this bit of wisdom: "Drink water from your own cistern, and fresh water from your own well. Should your springs be dispersed abroad, streams of water in the streets? Let them be yours alone and not for strangers with you. Let your fountain be blessed, and rejoice in the wife of your youth. As a loving hind and a graceful doe, let her breasts satisfy you at all times; be exhilarated always with her love" (Proverbs 5:15-19).

One's sexual capacity is pictured here as a cistern or well full of water. Refreshing, clean, enjoyable. Solomon says to draw water from your own wife's well and share your water with her alone. Not with a stranger who contaminates and poisons. The word *exhilarated* means to be drunk, to be under the influence. Victorian prudishness was never called for in marriage. "Be drunk with the exhilaration of her breasts," says Solomon. But with no one else.

I will never forget the story I once heard Chuck Swindoll tell about this. This world-known author was preaching away from home and was put up in a nice hotel. As he got on the elevator to go to his room, two attractive women got on with him. They were dressed to kill.

"Which floor?" Chuck asked courteously, offering to punch the elevator keyboard.

"I don't know. Which floor are *you* going to?" one said. The innuendo was clear. The offer made.

About that time, the elevator arrived at Swindoll's floor. The doors opened, releasing its prey. Chuck stepped out, turned around to them, and said, "No, thanks. I don't need that cheap stuff. I've got all I need at home."

He then confidently spun on his heels and walked out of the lion's den. Without a scratch.

See what I mean? Keeping the home fires burning brightly helps prevent forest fires.

Resist Your Flesh

Fifth, we must *resist our flesh*. Even in applying these first four principles, we will still be met with temptation. That is the nature of the beast within us. We can help subdue it, but it nevertheless is there, like a sleeping bear, and can instantly be aroused, awakened, and brought out of hibernation.

Our sexual drive, like a ticking time bomb that could go off in a weak moment, will haunt us until the day we die. Therefore, we must actively choose to resist this deadly temptation whenever it comes knocking. We must keep the dead bolt to our heart locked.

With directness and frankness, the Bible does not stutter when it says, "Therefore consider [literally, "put to death"] the members of your earthly body as dead to immorality, impurity, passion, evil desire" (Colossians 3:5). How do we handle sinful passion? Kill it! Put it to death. Bury it immediately. Crucify it. Do not tolerate it. Not for one second.

Men, this is a matter of our will. We must choose to resist the desires of our flesh. Putting to death immorality, passion, and evil desire is a constant choice that we must make. Paul presupposes here that we will all be faced with this decision. To make no decision is to make the wrong decision. When temptation comes knocking, just say no.

CAN I GET BACK IN THE RACE?

Maybe you are saying, "Steve, you're too late. I have already fallen into such sin. Is there any hope for me? Can I get back into the race?"

Yes, you can have a new start.

Failure is never final as long as there is the grace of God. Confess your sin. Repent. Turn from it. Humble yourself before God. Seek to do His will. And in time, you can get back into the race.

How long does it take to reenter the race? That varies with each individual situation. Here is a basic principle: The more visible your ministry, the longer it will take to reenter. When trust and credibility are lost through immorality, restoration to ministry is a long, patient process.

Just the mere confession of sin does not immediately restore one back into the place of ministry. Time must be given to regain damaged credibility and to reearn trust. In addition to time, the fallen brother needs the godly counsel of others to let him know if he has regained the needed trust for public ministry.

In the case of a pastor or minister, that restoration is a long, perhaps even impossible, process. For a deacon or elder, such restoration may take years. For a Bible teacher, even more time may be required. Even for a father, respect must be regained over a period of time.

Lost Speed and Effectiveness

Let me give you one more sobering thought. I mention this not to condemn those who have already fallen in sexual sin, but to warn those who have not fallen and to put the fear of God into their heart. My point is this: After being sidelined through disqualification, do not assume that when you step back into the race you will run with the same speed and efficiency.

Again, consider Ben Johnson. After a two-year banishment from competitive running, Johnson made his long-awaited return to the world of track at the Hamilton Spectator Games in Canada. A sellout crowd of 17,050 fought a blizzard to get there. A national television audience was tuned in.

The question on everyone's mind was: Can Ben Johnson still run with his explosive, dazzling speed? Johnson totally dominated his last race, crushing the field in the 1988 Olympics. The twenty-nine-year-old sprinter had announced his intention of returning to the top, but could he?

As Johnson peeled off his warmups, he was noticeably less muscled than he once had been. Johnson's explosive start, which had always been his greatest asset, no longer bolted him out of the starting blocks into the quick lead.

One of his competitors remarked, "Before with Ben, most times you stepped into the blocks it was, 'Who's going to get second?' Now, it's, 'Who's in shape, who's worked harder?'"

The Canada race revealed Johnson to be a mere mortal. After two false starts, the field got away evenly. But Johnson did not immediately grab the lead. He was left flatfooted, coming out of the blocks third. Trying to play catchup, Ben's form was ragged.

Johnson made a late charge, good enough to push past all of the field—except for the winner. Johnson finished second by two-tenths of a second. "I'm just not race-fit yet," he said, estimating that he needed seven or eight more races to be sharp.

Men, the same is true in our race of faith. There are definite consequences to our sin. If we are disqualified, sure, we can come back later. All by God's grace. But not without losing a few steps of speed.

Trust must be reearned with a spouse. Honor must be reestablished with children. And sometimes it never happens. Lost ground is always difficult to regain. Effective teaching must be reempowered with a life of integrity. The light of your witness must be rekindled. All of which takes precious time.

I say all this to warn you. Resist the sensual lusts of your body. Buffet it. Because disqualification brings serious consequences.

Benched, booted, disqualified.

Just like Ben Johnson.

THE TRAGEDY OF MAGIC JOHNSON

Even as I write this, the tragic story of another Johnson is breaking on the national news. The fall of Magic Johnson. As one national commentator reported, "Magic Johnson lived the life that everyone dreams of, only now to live the life everyone fears."

Before a major press conference, Magic Johnson told the world that he now has the HIV virus. If this virus runs its normal course, it will result in AIDS. A death sentence has been passed on him. Physically, the "Magic Man" has been immediately disqualified from playing the game of basketball. Ultimately, he may well be disqualified from life itself.

Dr. Peter Hawley, medical director of the Whitman Walker Aids treatment clinic in Washington, D.C., is quoted as saying, "The disease often takes a decade to progress from infection to the murderous illness that destroys the body's defenses and kills its victim."

Magic Johnson was basketball. He won five NBA world championships. He led his college team to the NCAA championship. Magic has been the most valuable player of the NBA season, the NBA All-Star Game, and the NBA World Championship Series.

Because Magic failed to buffet his body, his entire life has come crashing down. Our culture says his actions—in coming forward and vowing to face the disease and educate the public—were heroic. But is Magic a hero? Should we name our public monuments after him? God's Word says his actions were immoral, indecent, and self-gratifying. Hardly virtues of a hero.

His failure to maintain moral purity has cost him everything. Surely, he would trade his multimillion-dollar salary, all his championship rings, and his days of glory if he could retract those brief moments of pleasure.

Magic is out of the game.

Benched, booted, disqualified.

Though many will applaud his plans to preach "safe sex," God's Word remains the same. Outside of marriage, there is no safe sex. Whatever we sow, we will reap. If we sow to the flesh—if we fail to buffet our bodies—we will reap to the flesh (Galatians 6:7-8).

Sounds like losing to me.

In an open letter to the *Los Angeles Times*, Pamela McGee, a basketball player herself, shared her insight into Magic Johnson. Pam played on two University of Southern California national championship teams. She was named an all-American and also played on the gold-medal U.S. Olympic team in 1984. She writes,

> As Magic Johnson stood at the podium, the world's superhero still stood 6-feet, 9-inches tall. And he is still standing head and shoulders above the world, having made the hardest announcement he has ever made in his life.
>
> At first, I thought it was a cruel joke. Tears overcame me. He used words such as 'HIV Positive' and 'the AIDS virus,' words that were foreign to my existence, because I am neither gay nor an IV drug user. Magic, the superhero—it would only happen to him.
>
> It hurt even more because Magic is a dear friend. It was Magic who showed me around L.A. the first week I entered USC. I was a then-frightened 17-year-old, a long way from home. Magic made me feel at home. He would pick my sister and me up on weekends and we would all party to the early hours in the morning.
>
> I guess it didn't surprise me that Magic has the disease. Knowing his flamboyant life-style, it was bound to happen sooner or later. Magic's closest friends always knew him as a major player and womanizer. He has had one-night stands with what he calls "freaks" across America.
>
> He was always being hounded by women who merely wanted to sleep with the "Magic Man." The reason he probably made it public is to warn the thousands of women he has slept with. So it didn't surprise me that he had the insidious disease called HIV.
>
> Two short months after his marriage to his longtime love Cookie, it just seemed that Magic had matured and was starting

over. It appeared that Magic was committed to one woman finally. It appeared he had his whole life in front of him.

My heart goes out to Magic. I have been on my knees praying constantly for him. The superhero is still my superhero, and a good friend.

Maybe it will take a Magic Johnson to wake us all up.[3]

Magic Johnson is now learning the hardball reality of the Apostle Paul's words. Because he failed to buffet his body, he is out of the game. Unable to finish his career. Unable to play for the gold medal in basketball in the 1992 Olympics.

Men, if there is one ounce of godly wisdom rattling around in our brain, we will take seriously Paul's admonition to buffet our body. Can we not learn from Magic Johnson's sin? Play with fire and you will get burned. Lay down with dogs and you will wake up with fleas. Magic's tragedy brings home to us the sobering realization that, apart from God's grace, any of us can be benched, booted, and disqualified.

As men who win—flee immorality!

Even magic won't make these consequences disappear!

NOTES
1. John MacArthur, *Shepherdology* (Chicago, IL: Moody Press, 1989), page 224.
2. Chuck Swindoll, as quoted by MacArthur, page 224.
3. Pamela McGee, letter in *Los Angeles Times*, November 9, 1991, section C, page 6.

CHAPTER 12

FOR GOD'S SAKE, GET IN THE RACE!

★

T he Comeback.

We all love to see a comeback. There is something about an against-all-odds, totally impossible comeback that inspires us and gives us hope. Something within us loves to see an athlete or team come from behind and snatch victory from the sure clutches of defeat.

We all have our favorite comeback stories. Roger Staubach used to rally the Cowboys Sunday after Sunday to a last-ditch victory. Arnold Palmer would come charging back from nowhere to beat the field. Battling back with no timeouts, Joe Montana has raised the two-minute offense to an art form and put the 49ers in the end zone countless times—with only seconds remaining. We all love to see a dramatic comeback.

These all make for good stories, but for me, there is one comeback indelibly etched in my memory. When you are talking comeback, you are talking the 1986 Masters. In the most improbable comeback in the much-storied history of the Masters, a forty-six-year-old "Golden Bear" named Jack Nicklaus came out of hibernation to beat a pack of flat-bellied young cubs.

Augusta National Golf Club was the stage for this high-drama miniseries whose script even Hollywood would not have dared to write. It was just too fairy-tale. If it were fiction, no one would have believed it.

As a major sporting championship, the Masters is special. In a class by itself. Fuzzy Zoeller so aptly put it, "I've never been to heaven and, as I think back on my life, I probably won't get to go. I guess the Masters is as close as I'm going to get to heaven." (Personally, I have often felt if I died at Augusta National, I'd go from glory to glory.)

Augusta National is steeped in rich tradition. Bobby Jones. The Amen Corner. The green jacket. Gene Sarazan's double eagle. Blooming azaleas. Budding dogwoods. Lightning fast greens. Towering pines. The winners—Hogan, Sneed, Nelson, Palmer, Nicklaus, Player, Watson—read like a who's who of golfing greats. Not to mention an international field of players who annually make their pilgrimage across the ocean to golf's mecca. Giants like Norman, Ballesteros, Faldo, and Olazabal.

Coming into the final round of the 1986 Masters, Jack Nicklaus was a distant four strokes behind the leader. The final day hardly got off to an auspicious start, as the Golden Bear missed makable putts of twenty, eighteen, five, twenty-two, and ten feet. By the time he reached the ninth green, Jack was running out of real estate.

As Nicklaus strained to read his ten-foot birdie putt on nine, he asked Jackie, his caddie son, "What do you see?"

"*Left* edge," said the eagle-eyed, younger cub.

"How about an inch out to the *right*?" replied the now nearsighted Bear.

They both laughed.

"I figured he saw something I was missing," said Jack, "so we split the difference." Nicklaus just putted it dead straight. And drained the birdie putt.

"That got me started."

Started? That's an understatement. Sinking that putt was the spark he needed. The competitive fires were suddenly rekindled in Nicklaus' heart. There was still life in the old Bear.

As Jack teed off on ten, Ken Venturi, the CBS analyst, uttered his now prophetic words, "The Masters starts on the number ten tee on Sunday afternoon." His words never rang truer than on this Sunday.

As a global television audience watched, the golfing world was about to witness the greatest comeback in Masters' history. With only nine holes left and still an insurmountable lead to overcome, Jack mounted his comeback.

First, a birdie at the difficult tenth. Then, entering Amen Corner—

the apex of challenge at this cathedral in the pines—Nicklaus birdied eleven. An eerie hush began to spread across the course.

"Jack's back" could be heard whispered across the landscape. Distant galleries began to peel off their favorites to follow Jack and become an eyewitness of history. Everyone wanted to view the ensuing spectacle.

But just as momentum was building, the iron door of opportunity seemed to slam shut at the twelfth hole. Nicklaus bogied the formidable twelfth, a testy par three over Rae's Creek. Gut-check time! This is where you separate the men from the boys. The Bear from the cubs.

Men who win rally. They find a way to win.

With his back pinned against the wall—and with no tomorrow— Nicklaus reached down deep inside and refused to quit. This momentary adversity only served to force his normally conservative hand into an all-out assault of the course. Jack would have to go all out now, firing at every pen.

The Bear rallied back with a birdie at thirteen. Followed by a par at fourteen. But par's not good enough when you are playing to win. Standing in the fairway on fifteen—a par five requiring a long second shot over a pond—the pensive Bear set aim on the distant green. Turning to his son, Jackie, he asked, "What do you think an eagle three would do here?" They both smiled.

With the deadly accuracy of an assassin, Jack pulled the trigger. Bull's-eye! He nailed it stiff on the pin. Twelve feet away from an eagle three.

The comeback was happening!

With nerves of steel and the delicate touch of a surgeon, the charging Bear hovered over this eagle putt. The gallery was so quiet, you could hear a pine needle drop on the pristine fairway. As the world anxiously watched, Jack stroked the eagle putt. Yes! An eagle three.

The Bear was back in the hunt.

The carnage of the course continued on sixteen, a par three over another pond. Jack struck a perfect iron, narrowly missing a hole in one by mere inches. Three feet away, Nicklaus sank another birdie putt. The explosion of noise, escalating in the natural amphitheater, was broadcast loudly to the other leaders around the course—the great Spaniard, Severiano Ballesteros; the steely-eyed Texan, Tom Kite; the "Great White Shark," Australian Greg Norman.

It had been six long years since his last victory in a major championship. But Nicklaus wouldn't pitch tent. Victory was within his grasp. The Bear smelled his wounded prey.

After pulling his tee shot short on seventeen, a par four requiring a precision tee shot carefully negotiated around the famous Eisenhower Tree, Nicklaus nailed a dead-eye short iron to within fifteen feet of the flag. Perplexed, Jack confessed, "This putt is impossible to read." So what did he do? He squinted and just banged it dead center. The putt wiggled left, bent back right, then dropped in the center cut of the cup. Birdie! And a tie for the lead!

All that remained was the eighteenth, an uphill par four back to the clubhouse. Jack barely missed a long birdie putt. Amid the bedlam of the gallery, Jack tapped in his par and embraced his son. The pair strode arm-in-arm off the eighteenth green. Triumphantly.

There was a new leader in the clubhouse!

Tom Kite, Seve Ballesteros, and Greg Norman all withered under the oppressive heat of the late rally staged by Nicklaus. Seve shanked a four iron into a watery grave on fifteen. Kite and Norman both missed makable putts on eighteen. And the green jacket was back on Jack.

Jack Nicklaus epitomized the essence of never giving up. A never-say-die attitude. Coming out of nowhere. Battling against impossible odds. Pushing down the backstretch. The Golden Bear wouldn't quit. Even when everyone else had counted him out, he staged one of the greatest comebacks ever. No, make that *the* greatest.

It is simply The Comeback.

You Can Make a Comeback!

Men, this scene can be replayed in your Christian life. *You* can come back. Some of you may feel so far behind in the Christian race, you think it is impossible to win. You feel so defeated, there is no need to sprint to the finish. Maybe you are looking back at wasted years and want to throw in the towel. Perhaps you are ready to concede, "What's the use trying?"

Well, I have good news. No matter where you are, you can still stage a comeback. Your Christian life can become one of the greatest comeback stories ever witnessed. Why do I say that? Because failure is never final as long as the grace of God is operative. You can come back.

By God's grace, we can overcome impossible odds to win God's crown. God's Hall of Fame is filled with many a comeback story, people who looked like life had them down, only to rally and bounce back to win.

As long as there is time in the race, as long as there is God's grace, as long as there is the will to win, there is the hope of victory.

This book is all about winning—winning God's race. It has called you to be a winner where it really counts—with God. As I close this book, I want to call you, one last time, to be a winner. Where it really counts. With God. No matter how far back in the pack you are.

I assume most of you reading this book are already Christians. You are already running God's race. But perhaps you have slowed down to a jog. Or a complacent walk. Maybe your spiritual fire and passion are gone. I want you to know—you *can* still come back!

In this closing chapter, I want to lead you in the necessary steps to reenter God's race. I want to help you return to championship form. I want to point you to refocus your eyes on the prize.

The passage we will look at is 1 Corinthians 9:24-26. Writing as one intimately familiar with the athletic arena, the Apostle Paul writes, "Do you not know that those who run in a race all run, but only one receives the prize? Run in such a way that you may win. And everyone who competes in the games exercises self-control in all things. They then do it to receive a perishable wreath, but we an imperishable. Therefore I run in such a way, as not without aim; I box in such a way, as not beating the air."

Here is how to reenter the race.

RECOMMIT TO WIN GOD'S RACE

First, make a recommitment to win God's race. Make winning the race your sole passion. Maybe it once was, but now you have grown cold. Well, recommit to winning the race.

Paul writes, "Do you not know that those who run in a race all run, but only one receives the prize? Run in such a way that you may win" (1 Corinthians 9:24).

As long as you are in the race, run to win. Not just to finish. But to win. No one just happens to make a comeback to win. Not when he is far behind. Only by believing it can happen, and with a renewed resolve to win, is a comeback accomplished.

If you find yourself far behind in the race, don't give up. Keep on running. You can still win. Don't quit.

Personally, I find it hard to redouble my effort to finish anything I do not think I can win. Right? Why bother if I cannot win? Listen, the truth about God's race is that you can still win. So, recommit to winning. I don't care how far behind you think you are, you can still come back and win. God would never say to *every* believer, "Run to win," if every believer did not have a chance to win.

When Paul says, "Run," he uses an imperative—a command. His words come with binding force upon our lives. This is not an apostolic "suggestion." Nor a divine "option." It is God speaking directly to us. He is saying, *"Run!* Don't walk. Don't stop. Don't sit down. *Run* because you can *still* win!"

When the hope of winning is extinguished, so is the competitive drive to excel. Consider Ben Hogan, a long-time sports hero of mine. As a young boy in Fort Worth, Texas, struggling to hit a one iron, I idolized my hometown hero, the "Texas Hawk." To this day, I hit Hogan Apex irons and woods. Even my young boys play with Hogan junior sets (complete with Hogan bags that match Dad's).

Regarded as the greatest pure striker of the ball, Hogan's sweet swing was known to make grown men cry. With a few tears of my own, it was my privilege to walk every hole of Hogan's last competitive round on the PGA Tour.

Upon retirement, Hogan felt his game was no longer suitable for public display. Not even lucrative offers and the emergence of the Senior Tour could lure him to play competitively. Sure, Hogan hits practice balls at his Shady Oaks club every afternoon. But no competitive golf. Why is that?

"There is no use in playing," replied Hogan poignantly, "if you cannot win."

In other words, good exercise is not a strong enough motive to get back into competition. Neither is the thrill of the crowd. Nor the enticement of money.

Only one thing could get Hogan back out on the links. That was the possibility of winning. If that prospect is gone, then so is the drive to compete. Winning—and only winning—is a strong enough drive to compete.

It is that drive to win that so many Christians need to recapture. The drive to excel. The reason so many Christians have stopped running is because they do not think they can still win. They think, *Why bother? I'm so far behind, I could never win God's crown.*

But you can still win.

Let's consider someone in the Bible, someone who fell behind in the race, but made a comeback. Let's look at Simon Peter, the disciple who suffered from "foot-in-mouth" disease.

During the days of Jesus' earthly ministry, Peter was sprinting along in God's race. He was the unquestioned leader of the Twelve. So quick to forsake all for Christ. So ready to defend Christ. So committed to the race!

Then—boom!—Simon Peter tripped and stumbled. On the night of our Lord's arrest, he fell head first, flat on his face. A belly flop. Peter out-and-out denied the Lord Jesus before—are you believing this?—a little slave girl. He flat-out denied Christ.

When she asked Peter if he was one of Jesus' disciples, he abruptly chided, "I am not" (John 18:17).

Three times, Peter denied the Lord. Finally, he began to curse and swear, "I do not know this fellow you are talking about!" (Mark 14:71). Folks, this is about as off track as you can get.

Talk about falling behind in the race. Peter had crashed and burned. He was like a race-car driver with a flat tire in the Indy 500. He was being lapped so quickly, he was getting dizzy. It was so bad for Peter that he left the Lord's work and went back to his fishing business.

If anyone looked helplessly behind in God's race, it was Peter. But guess what? Peter staged a comeback. He made a recommitment to get back in the race and win. To go all out to the finish line. And I believe he won.

Jesus confronted Peter, who had gone back into the fishing business, and gently probed into the heart of this burly fisherman. Jesus asked, "Simon, son of John, do you love Me more than these?" (John 21:15).

"Yes, Lord; You know that I love You," Peter replied (using a word with lesser strength for "love").

Three times, Jesus asked Peter this searching question. Perhaps once for each denial. And three times, Peter confessed that his love for Christ, weak as it was, was still there. Three times, Jesus recommissioned Peter, "Tend My lambs. . . . Shepherd My sheep. . . . Tend My sheep." In other words, "Get back in the race and run to win. You can do it."

Now cloaked with humility, Peter made a recommitment to win God's crown. He drove down a stake and purposed from this point forward, "I am going to run to win again." Did God honor this recommitment? You bet He did! Peter became the great preacher of Pentecost. The pillar of the early Church. The author of two New Testament books. I would say that's quite a comeback. He went from small to great. From a loser to a winner.

Despite his past failure, a future hope burned brightly in Peter's heart. All the way to the finish line. Toward the end of his race, Peter wrote, "And when the Chief Shepherd appears, you will receive the unfading crown of glory" (1 Peter 5:4). His heart was still set on the crown.

Men, if Peter can make a comeback after denying Christ, so can you and I. As long as there is the grace of God, we are not out of it. There is still enough time on the scoreboard to pull out a victory. But it must begin here, with making a definite recommitment to get back in the race and win.

As you read these words, where are you in your spiritual life? Have you lost your spiritual passion? Has your life gotten off track? Have you not been walking with the Lord? I want to urge you to repent—that is, turn things around—and get back in the race to win.

You can do it! You can still win!

RELINQUISH CONTROL TO GOD

Second, relinquish the control of your life to God. This is the second step of making a comeback. If we are to win, it takes more than a choice of the will to win again. We must exercise self-control and discipline.

Paul writes, "Everyone who competes in the games exercises self-control in all things" (1 Corinthians 9:25). Self-control is the key here. A disciplined life. Strict training. Rigorous self-denial. These are the marks of any champion.

What is self-control? The word (*enkrateia*) means restraining one's fleshly lusts. Resisting one's sinful appetites. It is a self-mastery. A curbing of one's sinful impulses. It is an ability to keep one's self in check.

Self-control is a fruit of the Spirit (Galatians 5:23). That means only the Holy Spirit can produce self-control within us. So we must relinquish the control of our life to Christ. We must submit to the Holy Spirit and trust Him to bear self-control within us.

With every step of the race, we must make a conscious decision to run by the Spirit, not by the flesh (Galatians 5:16). Our natural tendency is to run according to the flesh. This means to run yielded to self. Focused on self. Empowered by self. But God's Word says we must run according to the Holy Spirit. This means yielded to the Spirit. Empowered by the Spirit. Controlled by the Spirit.

The self-control we exercise is a resistance to the carnal impulses listed as the deeds of the flesh—"immorality impurity, sensuality, idolatry, sorcery, enmities, strife, jealousy, outbursts of anger, disputes, dissensions, factions, envyings, drunkenness, carousings" (Galatians 5:19-21). This is what our self-control must be against.

Here is the paradox of self-control: Self-control comes as the result of surrendering self-control. As I relinquish it, I gain it. As I relinquish the control of my life to God, He gives me the control over these vices. I can experience self-control when I give Him control.

We surrender when we present ourselves to God, like an animal sacrifice placed on the altar to God. Paul writes, "I urge you therefore, brethren, by the mercies of God, to present your bodies a living and holy sacrifice, acceptable to God, which is your spiritual service of worship" (Romans 12:1). Just as the animal was to be presented wholly and without blemish (that is, not blind, lame, or diseased), so we must present out lives to God. Wholly. Holy. A living sacrifice to God. Ready to love God, serve God, and glory in God.

General William Booth, founder of the Salvation Army, was asked the secret of his amazing Christian life. Booth answered, "I told the Lord that He could have all that there is of William Booth."

That is what we need to give God. All that there is of us. It doesn't take much to be winners. Just all there is of us.

In so doing, we must recognize the difference between involvement and commitment. It is more than just going through the motions. Lou Holtz, head football coach of Notre Dame, has pointed out the difference: "The Kamikaze pilot who was able to fly more missions was involved—but not committed."

Men, in what areas—or what one area—do you still wrestle with giving Christ the control? Recognize there is a spiritual battle going on there for territorial rights in your life. You need to surrender it to the Lord. Relinquish the control to Him.

REFOCUS ON THE ETERNAL CROWN

Third, refocus on the crown. This is the third step for staging a comeback. Athletes who lose sight of the crown slowly fade to the rear of the pack. If you have, refocus on the crown. You will feel a sudden burst of energy to move up in the pack. To win.

Knowing the powerful motivation of reward, Paul writes, "They then do it to receive a perishable wreath, but we an imperishable" (1 Corinthians 9:25). In this verse, the apostle contrasts two crowns— one temporal, one eternal—to show the infinitely superior motivation that we Christians have to run God's race. If the Olympic athlete strictly trains and sacrificially runs, all to win a temporal crown and brief acclaim, how much more ought we to be motivated to win the incorruptible crown.

Reward has always been a powerful form of motivation, especially in athletics. Today, professional athletes have "incentive clauses" written into their contracts to help elevate the level of their performance. Added cash bonuses will be theirs if they can reach certain levels of excellence. Like making the all-star team, leading the league in a particular category, or winning the most valuable player award.

The hope of winning God's crown was ever before Paul. This powerful motivation enabled the apostle to remain faithful, even to the end. From a Roman prison Paul wrote, "I have fought the good fight, I have finished the course, I have kept the faith; in the future there is laid up for me the crown of righteousness, which the Lord, the righteous Judge, will award to me on that day; and not only to me, but also to all who have loved His appearing" (2 Timothy 4:7-8).

Like an athlete looking beyond the agonizing race to the prize, Paul looked to receive his crown from Christ Himself. This crown, prepared by God for those who endure to the end, was to be Paul's reward. While in prison, Paul looked beyond the pain to the prize. He remained focused on the eternal crown.

R. C. Slocum, head football coach of Texas A&M, knows the power of focusing on the goal. Recently, his fighting Texas Aggies were in Fort Worth, Texas, preparing to play the TCU Horned Frogs in a key Southwest Conference clash. While A&M was in the midst of their afternoon workout the day before the game, Slocum unexpectedly called the team together at midfield. He announced that they were going to load the bus now and ride somewhere special.

Unknowingly, the Texas A&M team was driven an hour away to Dallas to see their season-long goal: the Cotton Bowl. Each New Year's Day the winner of the Southwest Conference is annually invited to play before a capacity crowd and a national television audience in the historic Cotton Bowl game. At the beginning of the season, it had been clearly stated that playing in the Cotton Bowl was the team's mission.

But it occurred to Slocum that many of his younger players had never even seen the Cotton Bowl. So, to heighten their motivation, the coach wanted his team to see the goal personally. If they could visualize it, it would greatly help them achieve it.

As the team bus arrived, the Aggies got out and walked across the storied turf of the Cotton Bowl. The "House That Doak Walker Built." A stage where Joe Montana, Earl Campbell, Roger Staubach, Bo Jackson, and Jim Brown had starred in Cotton Bowls past.

As Slocum gathered the A&M team around him, he peered into the future and said, "Look around, men. This is our goal. Come January first, this is our destiny." Young Aggie eyes were star-struck as they beheld the attainable goal before them.

Inspired to new heights, the Aggies exploded on an unsuspecting TCU team the next day, destroying them 44-7. What brought the best out of them? Most insiders will tell you refocusing on the goal raised them to a higher level of play.

Men, it is much the same in the Christian life. We must never lose sight of the crown. Keeping our eyes on the prize will elevate the quality of our Christian life. It will cause us to devastate our opponents and win the race.

Where is the focus of your life? Be honest. Where is it? Too often, we live focused on temporal goals and earthly records. No wonder we live so spiritually unmotivated at times.

Perhaps reading this book is a "fork-in-the-road" time for you to refocus on winning the incorruptible crown. It is time for you to take your eyes off this world's riches and become intent on winning Heaven's crown.

Her name was Florence Chadwick. She was synonymous with women's championship swimming in the 1950s. Florence was the first woman to swim the English Channel both ways. Her time of thirteen hours and twenty minutes from Cape Gris-Nez, France, to Dover, England, established a single-crossing speed record for women. She conquered the route from England to France three times—each time against the tide.

But one of her distance swims was not so successful. She failed to reach her goal. All because she lost sight of her goal.

The California coast was shrouded in fog the morning of July 4, 1952. On Santa Catalina Island, Florence Chadwick, age thirty-four, waded into the water and began swimming toward the California mainland twenty-one miles away.

The water was numbing cold that morning. The fog was so thick that Chadwick could hardly see the boats in her envoy, which were to scare the sharks away.

As the hours ticked off, she swam on. Fatigue was never a serious problem. It was the bone-chilling coldness of the icy water that was threatening.

More than fifteen hours later, numbed by the cold, Florence asked to be taken out of the water. She could not go on. Her mother, in a boat alongside her, urged her to go on. So did her trainer. They both knew the mainland had to be very close. Yet Florence quit. She got into the boat. And fell short of her goal.

The boat traveled only a very short distance until—sadly—the coastline could be seen. It was right there, so close! Florence had stopped only a half-mile short of the shore.

"If I could have seen the shore," she blurted out, "I would have made it."

Florence Chadwick was not defeated by the cold, nor by fatigue, but by the fog. The fog had obscured her goal. It blinded her eyes. So she quit.

Men, we must be careful never to allow ourselves to be blinded of our goal. If we are defeated, it will not be because of trials or fatigue. But because of the fog of limited vision. And our failure to see the Lord Jesus Christ and His incorruptible crown.

I urge you, do not allow anything to blind you. If you have lost sight of the goal, refocus on the incorruptible crown. It is essential to a successful comeback.

REALIGN LIFE'S PRIORITIES

Finally, realign your life's priorities. This is the fourth step to a successful comeback. We must bring everything in our lives into alignment with God and His Kingdom. Everything we do must be done with singleness of purpose—to win.

Paul writes, "Therefore I run in such a way, as not without aim; I box in such a way, as not beating the air" (1 Corinthians 9:26). In this verse, the apostle uses two metaphors. One from the world of running, one from boxing. These two athletic pictures are parallel and make the same point. They both call for singleness of purpose. Run with clear direction, not wandering around on the track. Box by throwing punches that hit their target; do not wear yourself out shadowboxing, nor by throwing wild punches that fail to connect.

Picture a championship boxer competing for the crown against a formidable foe. The bell sounds; the fight begins. As they meet in the center of the ring, this boxer becomes a windmill of punches, jabbing wildly in the air. But he never connects. His opponent keeps his guard up, but he never suffers a hit.

Soon, this first boxer begins to wear out. All this wasted motion! The more he boxes, the more he tires. Until he can no longer hold his gloves up. His arms are numb. He is now a sitting duck. Helpless. Defenseless. Totally vulnerable. At the mercy of the other boxer, who moves in for the easy kill.

What was the problem? It was certainly no lack of zeal or enthusiasm. Just a lack of direction. Wasted motion. There was no economy of effort. He failed to make his shots count.

Men, does this picture your life? No sense of direction. Like the cowboy who jumped on his horse and rode off in every direction at once. Too much wasted effort. Sure, the zeal and enthusiasm are there. But we are never striking a blow. Never connecting with a knockout punch.

A concert violinist playing in New York's Carnegie Hall was asked how she became so skillful. She replied, "Planned neglect." She planned to neglect everything that was not related to her goal. What do you need to plan to neglect?

All our activities must be directed with Spirit-given purpose. Our efforts must be on target. Wasted motion must be trimmed back.

What in your life needs to be brought into alignment with God's Kingdom? The expenditure of your time? The use of your money? The competitive drive to excel? Are you involved in too many projects? Too many ministries?

Too often, we frantically run from one Bible study to the next conference, trying to find what is missing in our Christian life. Too often, we take on more rather than concentrating our few punches on the target. Like a boxer with his shirt pulled up over his eyes, we frantically start throwing more punches, but none of them land.

What most of us really need is to better prioritize our time—with the Lord, with family, at the office, in our recreation. Too often, we prioritize our schedule when we ought to schedule our priorities.

So, here is how to make a comeback: Recommit to win God's race. Relinquish control to God. Refocus on the eternal crown. Realign life's priorities. You can still make a comeback with God. And win.

GET INTO THE RACE!

For some of you reading this book, a comeback is not what you need. You need to come to God for the first time. Some of you have never initially entered God's race. You do not need a comeback. You need a conversion.

Perhaps you need to enter God's race for the very first time. If that is the case, I can tell you how to do so. It is so simple, even a little child can do it. You simply must surrender your life to Christ and receive the free gift of eternal life.

I will never forget the Sunday a young businessman named Neal Winstead showed up in our church. Neal had it all going for him—successful, strikingly handsome, single, likable, winsome. He had everything going for him. Except God.

I had met Neal once years earlier in a wedding I performed. He had no time for God then. But something was different this time. Unexpectedly, Neal came to church and plopped down in the front pew, weary of the rat race and wanting out. As I preached God's Word, God was working in Neal's heart that Sunday.

A few days later, Neal called. "Pastor, could I take you to lunch?" he asked. It was obvious he was searching. He was restless. Weary. I said, "Sure."

As we sat down to eat lunch, I asked, "Tell me, where are you in your spiritual life with God?"

The emptiness in Neal's voice revealed he was a ripe blade of grain ready to be harvested.

I said, "Salvation is like passing through a narrow gate. Jesus Himself is that narrow gate. He alone is the door that leads to salvation. You enter God's Kingdom by taking a simple step of faith. Neal, have you ever come through that gate?"

A mist fogged his eyes.

I continued, "A lot of people respect this gate. They have admired the beauty of this gate. They have even acknowledged the gate's existence. They have even seen others go through the gate. They have heard others talk about their experience. But they have never personally entered the gate. Some people even walk up to the gate, ready to go through, and then back off. They just keep putting their foot up to that gate, but never go through.

"Neal, where are you? Inside or outside the gate?" I asked.

He choked out, "Steve, I keep putting my foot right up to that gate . . . and then I back off. I will step right back up to the gate again. But I always back off. I'm on the outside."

"Wouldn't you like to come through that gate today?" I pressed. "That gate is open today, and your toes are pushed right up against it. Why don't you take that step of faith and come on through?"

"Yes," he replied. "That's exactly what I want to do. Right now."

Neal and I returned to the church to pray. My office soon became a delivery room for the birth of a new spiritual babe. As the two of us got on our knees, my friend prayed and invited Christ into his heart. Neal Winstead came through the narrow gate into God's Kingdom.

He stepped out of the rat race . . . and into the right race.

He was born again.

Men, just as Neal did, so you, too, can step into the right race.

Our lives are filled with many decisions. What to wear. What to eat. Where to go. What to do. What to buy. Who to marry. Where to work. Many decisions are trivial; others are essential. But the one, single, most important decision you will ever make is the decision to enter the narrow gate. And run God's race.

Perhaps you are standing at the crossroads. Will it be the world, or Christ? Won't you take a step of faith today and come to Christ?

Nobody wants you to win more than God does.

AUTHOR

★

Dr. Steven J. Lawson is the Senior Pastor of The Bible Church of Little Rock, Arkansas. He has a B.B.A. from Texas Tech University, a Th.M. from Dallas Theological Seminary, and a D.Min. from Reformed Theological Seminary. A former sportswriter for the Texas Rangers and the Dallas Cowboys, he is also a featured speaker for the Billy Graham Evangelistic Association. Steve and his wife, Anne, have four children.